BADER'S
BIG WING
CONTROVERSY

BADER'S BIG WING CONTROVERSY

DUXFORD 1940

DILIP SARKAR
MBE FRHistS

AIR WORLD

AIR WORLD

BADER'S BIG WING CONTROVERSY
Duxford 1940

First published in Great Britain in 2021 by
Air World
An imprint of
Pen & Sword Books Ltd
Yorkshire – Philadelphia

ISBN 978 1 39901 715 2

Typeset by SJmagic DESIGN SERVICES, India.

Printed and bound in the UK by CPI Group (UK) Ltd.

Pen & Sword Books Limited incorporates the imprints of Atlas, Archaeology,
Aviation, Discovery, Family History, Fiction, History, Maritime, Military, Military
Classics, Politics, Select, Transport, True Crime, Air World, Frontline Publishing, Leo
Cooper, Remember When, Seaforth Publishing, The Praetorian Press, Wharncliffe
Local History, Wharncliffe Transport, Wharncliffe True Crime and White Owl.

For a complete list of Pen & Sword titles please contact

PEN & SWORD BOOKS LIMITED
47 Church Street, Barnsley, South Yorkshire, S70 2AS, England
E-mail: enquiries@pen-and-sword.co.uk
Website: www.pen-and-sword.co.uk

Or
PEN AND SWORD BOOKS
1950 Lawrence Rd, Havertown, PA 19083, USA
E-mail: Uspen-and-sword@casematepublishers.com
Website: www.penandswordbooks.com

MIX
Paper from
responsible sources
FSC
www.fsc.org
FSC® C013604

Contents

Author's Note & Glossary

The aviation-minded reader will notice that I have referred to German Messerschmitt fighters by the abbreviation 'Me' (not 'Bf', which is more technically correct), or simply by their numeric designation, such as '109' or '110'. This not only reads better but is authentic: during the Battle of Britain, Keith Lawrence, a New Zealander, flew Spitfires and once said to me 'To us they were just "Me's", "109s" or "110s", simple, never "Bf".'

In another attempt to preserve accuracy, I have also used the original German, wherever possible, regarding terms associated with the Luftwaffe, such as:

Adlerangriff	'Attack of the Eagles'
Adlertag	'Eagle Day'
Eichenlaub	The Oak Leaves, essentially being a bar to the Ritterkreuz.
Erprobungsgruppe	Experimental group, in the case of Erprobungsgruppe 210 a skilled precision bombing unit.
Experte	A fighter 'ace'. Ace status, on both sides, was achieved by destroying five enemy aircraft.
Freie hunt	A fighter sweep.
Gefechstand	Operations headquarters.
Geschwader	The whole group, usually of three gruppen.
Geschwaderkommodore	The group leader.
Gruppe	A wing, usually of three squadrons.
Gruppenkeil	A wedge formation of bombers, usually made up of vics of three.
Gruppenkommandeur	The wing commander.
Jagdbomber ('Jabo')	Fighter-bomber.
Jagdflieger	Fighter pilot.

Jagdgeschwader	Fighter group, abbreviated JG.
Jagdwaffe	The fighter force.
Jäger	Hunter, in this context a fighter pilot or aircraft.
Kampffleiger	Bomber aircrew.
Kampfgeschwader	Bomber group, abbreviated KG.
Kanal	English Channel.
Katchmarek	Wingman.
Lehrgeschwader	Literally a training group, but actually a precision bombing unit, abbreviated LG.
Luftflotte	Air Fleet.
Oberkannone	Literally the 'Top Gun', or leading fighter ace.
Oberkommando der Wehrmacht (OKW)	The German armed forces high command.
Ritterkreuz	The Knight's Cross of the Iron Cross.
Rotte	A pair of fighters, comprising leader and wingman, into which the Schwarm broke once battle was joined.
Rottenführer	Leader of a fighting pair.
Schwarm	A section of four fighters.
Schwarmführer	Section leader.
Seelöwe	Sealion, the codename for Hitler's proposed seaborne invasion of England.
Stab	Staff.
Stabschwarm	Staff flight.
Staffel	A squadron.
Staffelkapitän	The squadron leader.
Störflug	Harrassing attacks, usually by lone Ju 88s.
Stuka	The Ju 87 dive-bomber.
Sturkampfgeschwader	Dive-bomber group, abbreviated StG.
Vermisst	Missing.
Zerstörer	Literally 'destroyer', the term used for the Me 110.
Zerstörergeschwader	Destroyer group, abbreviated ZG.

Each geschwader generally comprised three gruppen, each of three staffeln. Each gruppe is designated by Roman numerals, i.e. III/JG 26 refers to the third gruppe of Fighter Group (abbreviated 'JG') 26. Staffeln are identified by numbers, so 7/JG 26 is the 7th staffel and belongs to III/JG 26.

Rank comparisons may also be useful:-

Gefreiter	Private 1st Class
Unteroffizier	Corporal, no aircrew equivalent in Fighter Command.
Feldwebel	Sergeant
Oberfeldwebel	Flight Sergeant
Leutnant	Pilot Officer
Oberleutnant	Flight Lieutenant
Hauptmann	Squadron Leader
Major	Wing Commander
Oberst	Group Captain

RAF Abbreviations:-

AAF	Auxiliary Air Force
AASF	Advance Air Striking Force
A&AEE	Aeroplane & Armament Experimental Establishment
AFC	Air Force Cross
AFDU	Air Fighting Development Unit
AI	Airborne Interception radar
AOC	Air Officer Commanding
AOC-in-C	Air Officer Commanding-in-Chief
ATA	Air Transport Auxiliary
ATS	Armament Training School
BEF	British Expeditionary Force
CAS	Chief of the Air Staff
CFS	Central Flying School
CGS	Central Gunnery School
CO	Commanding Officer
DCAS	Deputy CAS
DES	Direct Entry Scheme
DFC	Distinguished Flying Cross
DFM	Distinguished Flying Medal
DSO	Distinguished Service Order
E/A	Enemy Aircraft
EFTS	Elementary Flying Training School
FAA	Fleet Air Arm
FIU	Fighter Interception Unit
FTS	Flying Training School

AUTHOR'S NOTE & GLOSSARY

ITW	Initial Training
LAC	Leading Aircraftman
MRAF	Marshal of the Royal Air Force
MSFU	Merchant Ship Fighter Unit
NCO	Non-Commissioned Officer
ORB	Operations Record Book
OTC	Officer Training Corps
OTU	Operational Training Unit
PDC	Personnel Distribution Centre
RAFVR	Royal Air Force Volunteer Reserve
RFS	Reserve Flying School
RN	Royal Navy
RNAS	Royal Navy Air Service
SASO	Senior Air Staff Officer
SEAC	South East Asia Command
SOO	Senior Operations Officer
SSC	Short Service Commission
UAS	University Air Squadron
U/S	Unserviceable

Introduction

Group Captain Sir Douglas Bader was made a household name during the Second World War and in 1956, upon publication of Paul Brickhill's globally best-selling but romanticised Bader biography, *Reach for the Sky*, and Daniel Angel's film of the same name, starring Kenneth More, which hit the silver screen a year later. The swashbuckling, legless, Douglas Bader arguably remains the most famous RAF pilot of the war. Indeed, the world over he is held in a very special esteem and affection by the public, an inspiration and example on many levels, not least to the amputee disabled community.

This book, however, is not a romanticised tale. It is based upon factual evidence – which often departs substantially from the popular narrative – and investigates a distasteful thread of the Battle of Britain story. While Bader was not personally intending disloyalty, as such, to his Air Officer Commander-in-Chief, Air Chief Marshal Sir Hugh Dowding, he was, as Lord Dowding later commented, 'the cause of a lot of the trouble'. In his burning desire to propel 242 Squadron and himself, their leader, into the forefront of the action, the newsworthy but naïve acting squadron leader found himself used by darker forces, men with axes to grind and personal ambitions to further.

This is that story, one that must be told.

Dilip Sarkar MBE FRHistS

Chapter One

High Command: The Scene is Set

To understand the obsession of certain RAF high commanders with mass fighter formations during the Battle of Britain, and later consequences of these 'Big Wings', we must first examine their antecedents. Indeed, these personalities and relationships underpin the whole saga, so are essential to our appreciation of these still vexing events.

Our story begins with the man at the top: Air Chief Marshal H.C.T. Dowding, Commander-in-Chief of Fighter Command, 1936–1940.

Hugh Caswell Tremenheere Dowding was born at Moffat, some fifty miles south of Edinburgh, of English school-teacher parents, on 24 April 1882. Hugh's father, Arthur, had actually founded St Ninian's, a preparatory school in Moffat, in 1879, marrying Maud Tremenheere a year later. Hugh was the eldest of their four children, a daughter and three sons, all brought up in a dutiful middle-class family with Christian, Victorian, values. Educated at St Ninian's and Winchester, in 1899, the eldest Dowding entered the Royal Military Academy at Woolwich, receiving a commission as a 2nd Lieutenant in the Garrison Artillery. In 1912, by which time Lieutenant Dowding had served in Ceylon, Hong Kong and India, he attended the Military Staff College at Camberley. In an exercise there, Dowding found himself commanding

Hugh C.T. Dowding pictured shortly after being commissioned into the RAF. It was when serving as a fighter pilot in the First World War that he made an enemy of Trenchard, later the first Chief of the Air Staff.

1

six imaginary aeroplanes which he despatched together, on a flight of fancy from Camberley, to establish whether the Lincolnshire town of Grantham was in enemy hands. The instructor queried this decision, inquiring as to how the pilots would find their way. Dowding's response was simple: they would follow the railway lines, which to him appeared common sense. This the instructor also disputed, arguing that the pilots would collide. Dowding knew little or nothing about aviation at this time but could not accept this. Consequently, to expand his experience, having recognised that aviation would play a significant part in future conflicts, Dowding learned to fly, privately, at Brooklands. This was typical of the man.

Dowding once recalled that as a child he had 'never accepted ideas because they were orthodox, and consequently I have frequently found myself in opposition to generally accepted views... perhaps in retrospect this has not been altogether a bad thing'. In his thirties he had acquired the nickname 'Stuffy', on account of his Victorian primness. Described by contemporary Air Chief Marshal Sir Philip Joubert de la Ferté as 'an extremely entertaining companion out of office hours', this sense of fun 'did not, as a rule, extend to his work, and he could be extremely exacting and tiresome to his subordinates. He had, however, a great sense of justice which earned him the respect of all who worked with him.' Dowding's opposition to conventional opinion, however, underpins many of his clashes with authority. He was an individual, unorthodox, a free-thinker, and would advance his own opinions unflinchingly. Indeed, Dowding's biographer, that superb historian Vincent Orange, writes of Dowding's difficulty in accepting the need to persuade others that he was right about something, and compromise was not in his dictionary. To a degree, later in his career, this was understandable: as the RAF's most senior serving officer, he objected to criticism or resistance to his ideas and decisions from Air Ministry staff – all very much junior to him in age, rank and length of service.

Having gained his private pilot's licence, Dowding was able to take a three-month course provided by the Royal Flying Corps (RFC) at the Central Flying School (CFS), at Upavon in Wiltshire. Passing the course on 29 April 1914, Dowding received his coveted service pilot's flying brevet, or 'wings', then returned to soldiering. At the CFS, however, his instructor was one John Salmond, who would serve as Chief of the Air Staff (CAS) 1930–33; at Upavon, Dowding also met Hugh 'Boom' Trenchard, soon to become 'Father of the Royal Air Force'. In future, both these highly influential and well-connected men would become, according to Orange, 'bitter, secret and devious critics of Dowding's'. When the First World War broke out, as a trained pilot Major Hugh Dowding was required to serve in France with the RFC, and appointed to command 16 Squadron at Merville, engaged in artillery observation work. Major General Trenchard was by then General Officer Commanding (GOC) the RFC, to whom Dowding complained that his Squadron had received a batch of wrong-sized propellers. Trenchard objected to Dowding's 'pernickety primness' and ordered him to fit the aircrews as delivered. Dowding did as he was ordered, making the first, disastrous, test flight himself – and was nearly killed in the process. To Trenchard, the incident emphasised Dowding's 'self-righteous stubbornness'. Dowding considered it an outcome of 'Trenchard's technical stupidity'. Worse followed.

On 18 June 1916, Lieutenant Colonel Dowding was given command of No 9 (HQ), comprising four squadrons, at Fienvillers, near Doullens, ready for the infamous Battle of the Somme, which began on 1 July. From August 1915 until early 1916, the RFC suffered heavy losses due to the 'Fokker scourge', caused by the superiority of the German Fokker *Eindecker* monoplane fighter. Trenchard, however, insisted that the offensive be maintained – and, incredibly, forbade his aircrews to wear parachutes in the bizarre belief that the life-saving silk canopies were 'bad for morale'. The heavy casualties deeply troubled Dowding, who, after further differences with the GOC, was sent home on New Year's Day 1917. It would only later become significant that Dowding's replacement in France was Temporary Lieutenant Colonel Cyril Newall. By the Armistice, both Dowding and Newall were Temporary Brigadier Generals – but the latter was Trenchard's deputy and therefore in a position of great influence. On 1 April 1918, the RAF was born, Major General Trenchard the first CAS. The RAF College at Cranwell trained the service's officers, all permanently commissioned career professionals, while the RAF Staff College groomed future senior officers. Dowding, however, was not given a Permanent Commission, as a group captain, in Trenchard's junior service until 1 August 1919, possibly because of antipathy between the two in France.

Nevertheless, after various appointments, on 1 September 1930, Dowding was appointed Air Member for Supply and Research. Arguably, it was from that point onwards that 'Stuffy' Dowding began preparing for the Battle of Britain. The air power doctrine of the day, though, was almost exclusively focused upon bombing. Between 1926 and 1931, Air Commodore Newall, Trenchard's protégé, had served as both Director of

Operations and Deputy CAS (DCAS). Both Newall and Trenchard were confirmed 'Bomber Barons'. In 1921, Trenchard explained that:-

> It is not necessary for an air force, in order to defeat the enemy nation, to defeat its armed forces first. Air power can dispense with that immediate step, can pass over the enemy navies and armies, and penetrate the air defences and attack direct the centre of production, transportation and communication from which the enemy war effort is maintained. It is on the destruction of enemy industries and, above all, in the lowering of morale of enemy nationals caused by bombing that the ultimate victory lies.

Trenchard also said that, 'The aeroplane is the most offensive weapon that has ever been invented. It is a shockingly bad weapon for defence', considering fighters only 'necessary to keep up the morale of your own people'.

In 1932, the British Prime Minister, Stanley Baldwin, told the House of Commons:-

> I think it is as well for the man in the street to realise that there is no power on earth that can protect him from being bombed. Whatever people may tell him, the bomber will always get through. The only defence is offence, which means that you have to kill more women and children more quickly than the enemy if you want to save yourselves. I just mention that … so that people may realise what is waiting for them when the time comes.

After the First World War, disarmament held sway, with what little spending there was on defence reduced further still after the 1929 Wall Street Crash. Given the strategic thinking of the time, naturally investment was mainly in bombers. Inevitably, and fortunately as things turned out, Air Commodore Dowding disagreed with this conventional view of the bomber's invincibility. Although in agreement that the fighter force should not be expanded at the bomber force's expense, Dowding argued that a powerful bomber force would prove useless unless the fighter force was strong enough to ensure that its commander did not lose a decisive battle before the bomber force had time to deliver the 'knockout blow'. According to Dowding, Trenchard had 'forgotten that "security of base" is an essential prerequisite'.

HIGH COMMAND: THE SCENE IS SET

In 1933, Adolf Hitler and the Nazis came to power in Germany. Hitler soon denounced the Versailles Peace Treaty of 1919, which had severely restricted the size of Germany's armed forces, prohibiting an air force, and set about rearming, at first secretly then in open defiance of the hated Diktat. As time went on it became increasingly clear that the Führer was actually on course to restore Germany as a dominant military power. In October 1935, production of Professor Willy Messerschmitt's new single-engine monoplane fighter, the Me 109, was ordered. This fast and highly manoeuvrable little aircraft completely outclassed the wood and fabric biplanes then in service with the world's air forces, setting a new benchmark in military aircraft performance.

Back in 1930, the Air Ministry had issued a specification for a new monoplane fighter to replace the now obsolete biplanes with which its squadrons were equipped. This new design had to be capable of being both a day and night-fighter, which could be flown by the average pilot. The requirement was also for a greater speed, an enclosed cockpit and eight machine-guns. Among the British designers working on this project was Supermarine's Reginald Joseph Mitchell, whose sleek, bullet-like, racing seaplanes had already won the coveted Schneider Trophy, a matter of intense national pride. Hawker's Sydney Camm also produced a design, which, like Supermarine's submission was built around the Rolls-Royce Merlin engine, called the Hurricane; it first flew in November 1935, and was immediately ordered by the Air Ministry. The Hurricane reached the squadrons in January 1938, the Spitfire eight months later. Dowding, as Air Member for Research & Development, had much to do with commissioning the new designs, and his technical mind was concurrently considering a truly new-fangled science: Radio Direction Finding (RDF), more commonly known as radar. In the event, radar would prove nearly as crucial as fighter aircraft.

The RAF air exercises in August 1934 had shown the weakness of the existing 'early warning system', which depended largely upon the Observer Corps' reports, meaning that enemy aircraft could only be detected if they ventured within sight and earshot. Even when practising with the ancient Vickers Virginia, which plodded through the sky at just 80 mph at 7,000 ft, the warning provided was inadequate. Acoustic locators had proved of little use, and the Chandler-Adcock system of radio-direction, which allowed aircraft to be plotted and controlled from the ground, relied upon the 'target' aircraft sending regular transmissions – hostile aircraft, however, were unlikely to be so obliging. A more general means of detection was therefore required, but had yet to be discovered, and this became of increasing concern:

Mr A.P. Rowe, the Air Ministry's Assistant Director of Scientific Research, reported to his chief, Harry Wimperis, that 'unless science finds a new method of assisting air defence, any war within ten years will be lost.' In 1932, work by the Post Office indicated that aircraft reflected radio signals, prompting further research by Robert Watson-Watt who, in 1935, submitted his report on the subject. This inspired memorandum identified three areas of research: the re-radiation of aircraft waves (to detect aircraft), radio-telephone communications between fighters and ground controller, and a means of transmitting coded signals from aircraft (so as to identify friend from foe). Immediately recognising the significance of this detailed study, Wimperis requested £10,000 for further experimental work. Dowding advised caution and requested a practical demonstration: 'Let us first see if the system works,' he said. A month later the scientists sufficiently impressed Dowding and the research went ahead, in great secrecy, on the Suffolk coast. This new technology, together with the new eight-gun monoplane fighters, would soon form the cornerstone of the Radar-Based System of Early Warning, Interception & Control. This was one crucial respect in which Britain was far ahead of Germany's scientists. Radar, in fact, brought to an end any chance whatsoever that the 'bomber will always get through'. A new chapter in aerial warfare had quietly begun, in which Dowding was playing a key part and was best-placed to learn about, and understand, the various technical and scientific developments involved. This knowledge would prove invaluable.

For more than a decade, all functions of air defence had been overseen by the Air Defence of Great Britain (ADGB), although the Commander-in-Chief of which was responsible for both fighter and bomber forces, a matter which Dowding felt 'ponderous'. With Germany clearly rearming, the British Expansion Programme of 1936 saw the creation of five separate commands: Fighter, Bomber, Coastal, Training and Maintenance. Dowding's personal first-hand experience as a fighter pilot during the First World War, together with his involvement in commissioning the Spitfire and Hurricane, and knowledge of radar, marked him as the perfect choice for RAF Fighter Command's first Air Officer Commander-in-Chief (AOC-in-C). Now he could really get to grips with his vision to ensure 'security of base'. Air Marshal Dowding was fifty-four when he took up his new appointment on 14 July 1936. The new Fighter Command's headquarters was located at Bentley Priory, a large country house situated to the north of London, at Stanmore. There the new AOC-in-C discovered some 'lamentable deficiencies to be made good', his immediate task being to create the 'ideal Air Defence System', and his experience to date uniquely equipped him to do so. Dowding's belief that ensuring security of the home base 'overrides all considerations' now rose to the fore, his unshakeable belief in this leading to an obstinate insistence that his demands for improvements and resources be met. Consequently, Dowding would find himself from hereon in almost constant dispute with the Air Staff, where, he later wrote, his name 'stank'. When he became AOC-in-C of Fighter Command, Dowding's aspirations were to ultimately succeed Marshal of the RAF (MRAF) Sir Edward Ellington as CAS, unaware that Air Vice-Marshal Newall was already being groomed to take over the top job. Newall, who had taken Dowding's place in France twenty years before and was junior to him in rank and service, was the preferred choice of Lord Swinton, the Secretary of State for Air, and became CAS in 1937. Dowding was cut to the quick – but had he left Fighter Command at that juncture, arguably the outcome for Britain, just three years later, would have been disastrous.

Upon formation in 1936, Fighter Command consisted of just one group, No 11, and for administrative purposes, both 22 Army Cooperation Group and the civilian Observer Corps. From the outset, the primary function of 11 Group, was the defence of London and the south-east, which remained the case when 12 Group was added in May 1937, with responsibility for the protection of eastern England. It is vitally important to understand that at this time any air attacks made by Germany were expected to approach from the east, across the North Sea and, due to the range involved, such raids were assumed not to involve a fighter escort. At that time, therefore, 12 Group, defending the industrial Midlands and the North, represented a crucial responsibility. Nonetheless, 11 Group, as it included the capital, was always seen as the primary area. On New Year's Day 1937, Dowding was promoted to Air Chief Marshal, and entrusted the prestigious 11 Group to Air Marshal Leslie Gossage. On 14 December 1937, Air Commodore Trafford Leigh-Mallory became AOC 12 Group – which would have far-reaching consequences for Dowding and, ultimately, Fighter Command.

Trafford Leigh-Mallory was born on 11 July 1892 at Mobberley, Cheshire, his father, Herbert, being rector of the Anglican church there. The younger brother of George Leigh-Mallory, the celebrated mountaineer, Trafford Leigh-Mallory was educated at Haileybury, winning an Exhibition Scholarship to Cambridge's prestigious Magdalene College in 1926. It was while a member of the Literary Club there, in fact, that he first became acquainted with one Arthur Tedder – later MRAF, Deputy Supreme Allied Commander for Operation OVERLORD, and CAS 1946–1950. Having achieved a law degree, Leigh-Mallory applied to the Inner Temple to

Air Vice-Marshal Sir Trafford Leigh-Mallory commanded Fighter Command's 12 Group under Air Chief Marshal Dowding's overall command. He would clash with Dowding in the Second World War, vowing to effect his replacement.

become a barrister, but was thwarted in his ambition when the First World War broke out in 1914. Commissioned into the King's Liverpool Regiment, Lieutenant Leigh-Mallory served in France, suffering a leg wound in June 1915. While recuperating, Leigh-Mallory volunteered for the RFC and was soon flying BE2d observation aircraft with 5 Squadron at Droglandt. At this time, the RFC's role was largely to act as scouts for the army, providing information regarding German troop movements and spotting for the artillery. On 10 May 1917, Temporary Major Leigh-Mallory became OC (Officer Commanding) of 15 Squadron, and six months later took over 8 Squadron, continuing to fly army cooperation sorties. Leigh-Mallory was an unpopular squadron commander, being aloof and snobbish, and more concerned with logistics than men's lives. With 8 Squadron, Leigh-Mallory increased his experience of army cooperation, his unit carrying out the first air-to-tank liaison. For his wartime service, Leigh-Mallory was appointed to the DSO, his leadership of 8 Squadron and extensive experience of army cooperation laying the foundation of his subsequent RAF career.

Unlike Hugh Dowding, Leigh-Mallory's name appeared in the first 200 Permanent Commissions for the peacetime RAF, published on 1 August

1919. After training and staff appointments, in 1933 Group Captain Leigh-Mallory began a year-long course at the Imperial Defence College – the most senior of all service staff colleges. In 1937, Air Commodore Leigh-Mallory became AOC 12 (Fighter) Group, setting up home with his wife, Doris, at Woodborough Hall, Hucknall, Nottinghamshire. So it was that an army cooperation expert, with significant experience of training and administration – but one of fighters – became entrusted with the aerial defence of the industrial Midlands and the North.

In 1938, another key player enters our stage: Air Vice-Marshal Sholto Douglas. Born at Headington on 23 December 1893, Douglas was the son of an academic, and educated at Emanuel and Tonbridge Schools before going up to Lincoln College, Oxford, reading 'Greats'. Commissioned into the Royal Field Artillery in 1914, the following year Douglas transferred to the RFC, becoming an observer in 2 Squadron at Merville, before training as a pilot. Three months later, Lieutenant Douglas returned to France, flying the two-seater Bristol BE2c Fighter during the 'Fokker Scourge'. Awarded the MC, Douglas went on to command 43 Squadron, flying Sopwith 1½ Strutters, then 84 Squadron, operating single-seater SE5s on the Western Front, winning a DFC. After the First World War, however, Douglas left the service to fly as a commercial pilot, but was persuaded by none other than Trenchard himself to rejoin the RAF in 1920. Having attended the IDC and commanded RAF North Weald, Douglas instructed at the IDC before becoming Director of Staff Duties at the Air Ministry on New Year's Day 1936. Two years later, he was promoted to air vice-marshal and became the Assistant CAS (ACAS). It was now that this Trenchard favourite clashed with Dowding.

Air Vice-Marshal Sholto Douglas, the Deputy Chief of the Air Staff, was a personal friend of Leigh-Mallory's and also entertained enmity toward Dowding, although years later attempted to distance himself from this.

In June 1938, Douglas informed Dowding that he must form nine squadrons of Boulton-Paul Defiants for day-fighting. The Defiant was a two-seater, its armament provided by a turret-mounted battery of four

9

.303 Browning machine-guns, fired by an air gunner. While the turret, it was true, could rotate forward, the guns were fired electronically by the pilot but were not synchronised to fire through the propeller arc and so could only fire at an angle of 20°. The Defiant possessed no wing-mounted, or other, fixed forward-firing armament. The turret and gunner, of course, added weight, the aircraft's powerplant being the same Rolls-Royce Merlin engine powering the lighter Spitfire and Hurricane. Whereas, for example, the Spitfire Mk IA's top speed was 367 mph, and the Me 109E-3 348 mph, the Defiant lagged behind at 304 mph. The problem, though, was that the lack of practical pilot-fired forward-firing armament meant the Defiant lacked the instant eye-to-hand coordination required in modern day-fighting. The ACAS was clearly basing his support of the Defiant upon his own experience of flying the two-seater Bristol Fighter – the Air Ministry ordering some 450 Defiants in the mistaken belief that the BE2c's success would be emulated. While Douglas argued that 'for work over enemy territory a two-seater fighter is best', the point missed was that the BE2c's success was in no small part due to its pilot-fired forward-facing armament. Dowding instantly appreciated this and was angry that such an important decision had been made without his consultation. Douglas, however, ever the politician, was supported by both Air Vice-Marshals Sir Edgar Ludlow-Hewitt, the AOC-in-C of Bomber Command, and Donald Stevenson, the Deputy Director of Home Operations. It was originally intended, in fact, to have fifteen Defiant squadrons, this being reduced to nine when Stevenson began having doubts about the type. Dowding continued opposing the Defiant, which was commissioned at the expense of more Spitfires and Hurricanes, but his plea that the turret fighter be confined to training was rejected. Fortunately, in the event, only two Defiant squadrons were raised – but it was tragic indeed that in 1940 Dowding would be proved right only through the virtual annihilation of these gallant squadrons, which saw the aircraft relegated to a stop-gap night-fighting role. Here, though, was another example of antipathy between Dowding and another high commander, and that Dowding, the chief of Fighter Command, was not consulted regarding the Defiant prior to it being ordered, and others making decisions concerning his command is evidence of the Air Ministry's attitude toward him long before the Battle of Britain.

In July 1938, however, help was at hand for Dowding when his new Senior Air Staff Officer (SASO) arrived at Bentley Priory: Air Commodore Keith Park. In this loyal and tough fighter ace from New Zealand, Dowding was to find the perfect right-hand man.

HIGH COMMAND: THE SCENE IS SET

Originally Dowding's Senior Air Staff Officer at Fighter Command HQ, Keith Park, a tough, no-nonsense fighter ace from New Zealand was promoted to Air Vice-Marshal and given command of the prestigious 11 Group, defending London and south-east England. Having expected elevation to this position, as the more senior man, this only served to exacerbate Leigh-Mallory's 'curious enmity' towards Dowding.

Keith Rodney Park was born in Thames, Auckland, on 15 June 1892. In 1914, he answered the call and joined the artillery as a lance-bombardier, seeing action on Gallipoli with the ANZAC big guns, where he was commissioned. In August 1915, Park became a regular officer in the British army, continuing to serve in the Dardenelles until Allied forces were evacuated in 1916. That year, Park fought in the Battle of the Somme, until a shell exploded beneath his horse, killing the animal and wounding the man. Invalided back to 'Blighty', Park was declared 'unfit to ride a horse' owing to his wounds – but was accepted for flying training by the RFC. Having successfully gained his 'wings', by the time Park was posted to 48 Squadron at La Bellevue in 1917, flying the BE2c, his log book recorded 135 flying hours, this experience preparing him well for aerial combat. By now, Park was already a battle-hardened officer who understood the ground situation from a soldier's perspective and knew what was expected of him in the air. An exacting professional, Park even took personal care of his aircraft's armament and sights, in addition to taking a keen interest in the technical aspects of both airframe and engine.

Following a series of successful combats with Albatross scouts, Lieutenant Park and his observer were both awarded the MC on 19 August 1917, for 'dash and tenacity'. Over the next twenty-six days, Park and his observers destroyed a further seven enemy aircraft, damaging seven more. Recommended for a DSO by his commanding officer, Major-General Trenchard decreed that a Bar to the MC was sufficient. Park had earned respect and learned important lessons regarding the conduct of fighter warfare. In 1922, reflecting upon his Western Front experiences, Park maintained that in future wars, squadrons should be widely dispersed on the ground; ground strafing would be best undertaken by

11

small, fast, agile scouts with forward-firing armament; close escorts would be ineffective when opposition was encountered, and, finally, tactics must be studied well in advance, rather than 'on the spot'. Here, then, was clearly a forward-thinker and decorated fighter ace of great skill and experience.

Upon return from France, Park received two training commands before attending a course at 2 School of Navigation and Bomb Dropping, where voluntary long-distance flights were encouraged – leading to Captains Park and Stewart flying a 1,880 circuit of the British Isles. Only the second time such a journey had been achieved, the flight attracted much media attention. In June 1919, Park was awarded the DFC, ostensibly for this intrepid flight – in reality, the decoration was intended to compensate him for a catalogue of bureaucratic errors preventing well-deserved promotion. The episode infuriated Park, now a married man who had decided on a long-term career in the service, and embittered him towards the Air Ministry, the incompetence of which meant that in the promotion stakes he had been left behind by certain contemporaries. On 1 August 1919, Park was given a Permanent Commission and became a flight lieutenant, commanding a reserve of surplus aircraft at Hawkinge – where a certain Squadron Leader Sholto Douglas re-enters our story.

When preparing for the 1920 Hendon Air Pageant, Douglas suggested a daring low-level flypast by three Handley Page V/1500 bombers, a type included in Park's reserve. Douglas arranged with Park that they would each fly one, another colleague the third. The display was expected to be the Hendon highlight, but Trenchard, the CAS, was less impressed and rebuked Douglas, as the senior officer involved, for the low-level stunt – described in the *Aeroplane* as 'a terrifying sensation'. Trenchard's disapproval also reached Park, already concerned about his lack of promotion, leading to Park and Douglas distancing themselves from each other. Indeed, this distance never reduced, and may have been significant twenty years later, as we will see. Park then served in Egypt until June 1926, when appointed by Air Marshal Sir John Salmond, Commander-in-Chief of Fighter Command's predecessor, ADGB, to command 'Operations, Intelligence Mobilisation and Combined Training', based at Uxbridge. As ADGB was then only a year old, Squadron Leader Park was involved with preparing Britain's modern aerial defences almost from the outset.

In November 1927, Park was given command of 111 Squadron, flying Armstrong Whitworth Siskin biplane fighters at Duxford. On New Year's Day 1929, he was promoted to wing commander and left 'Treble One' that

March, returning to Uxbridge and undertaking a staff role at HQ Fighting Area. Not for the first time, Park drove himself so hard that he became ill; a medical board in 1930 sent him on leave for a month, insisting on a complete break from work – echoed by Fighting Area's commander, Air Vice-Marshal Hugh Dowding. The association between these two officers, therefore, began over a decade before the Battle of Britain.

The period January 1931 – August 1932 saw Wing Commander Park commanding RAF Northolt, concluding six years' experience in front-line home defence. The next five years, however, were spent in appointments away from fighters, as Chief Instructor at the Oxford University Air Squadron, and then, in 1934, when a 43-year-old group captain, he became the British Air Attaché in South America. Three years later, in December 1937, Group Captain Park returned to fighters, at last, when he became Station Commander at Tangmere, that famous fighter station on the South coast, near Chichester. There he enjoyed a last fling flying Hawker Furies, before promotion to air commodore on 1 July 1938 – and appointed Dowding's SASO at Fighter Command. Unsurprisingly, given his experience, Air Commodore Park immediately grasped the concept of the System of Air Defence – and would help improve it. Fortunately for Britain, these two men, Dowding and Park, knew as much about fighters as anyone else in the world outside of Germany at that time. In this, the Germans had the edge, though, given that Hitler's support of the fascist General Franco during the Spanish Civil War of the mid-thirties had provided a unique opportunity to test and prove weapons and tactics. The performance of Germany's Legion Kondor in Spain also indicated just how dangerous the Luftwaffe was, which, coupled with Hitler's aggressive foreign policy and military expansion, emphasised the urgency of the hour for those working on Britain's aerial defences.

As SASO at Bentley Priory, Air Commodore Park was largely concerned with fighter tactics, the first clash with the Air Ministry arising over the Defiant issue. After the Munich Crisis of September 1938, Park reported upon deficiencies in Britain's preparedness to meet an aerial threat from Germany. Fighter Command, Park stated, was ten squadrons short of the minimum number required for Britain's defence, and only 25 per cent of existing units were equipped with new monoplane fighters; the Sector Control System required expansion in Scotland and south-west England, more airfields were needed, with improvements required to those in use, and there were insufficient RDF stations and manpower. The report was accurate but not well-received at Whitehall.

A report in October 1938 from Air Vice-Marshal Leigh-Mallory, AOC 12 Group, was even less well-received at Bentley Priory. In this memorandum, concerning the air defences North of London, no mention was made of monoplanes, the emphasis being upon local, as opposed to area, defence. No appreciation was apparent of certain aspects of the System, including numbers of searchlights and communications. For this plan, however, Leigh-Mallory requested twenty-nine of Fighter Command's forty-one squadrons, thus leaving just a dozen for the rest of the country, including the defence of London. Dowding and Park were horrified at what amounted to a complete misunderstanding of the basic principles of fighter defence.

At this juncture it is vital that we explore and understand the System of Air Defence...

Chapter Two

The System

In 1943, the Air Ministry published a pamphlet outlining the 'System'.

Fighter Command

At the time of the Battle of Britain, Fighter Command was organised into four Fighter Groups. Each group was, for purposes of tactical control, subdivided geographically into a number of sectors. A sector consisted of a main fighter station and airfield, sector headquarters and operations room, also one or more satellite or forward airfields upon which were based a number of squadrons varying in accordance with the situation and the need for good dispersal.

No. 11 Group's area covered South-East England and, consequently, it was this group which bore the brunt of the fighting, although other groups extensively reinforced the air battle from time to time and, in addition, fed into No. 11 Group a regular supply of fresh squadrons to relieve those worn down by intensive air fighting.

Operations Rooms

The heart of each headquarters at command, groups, and sectors, was its operations room. This varied somewhat in size and complexity depending upon the scope and function of the headquarters and upon the amount of detail regarding our own squadrons that it was necessary for the commander to have before him; but the ultimate object of all operations rooms remained the same: to ensure the utmost rapidity in the issue of orders. For time was the essence of the problem; with machines of war moving at the rate of 5 miles a minute, the issue of written orders was out of the question and the

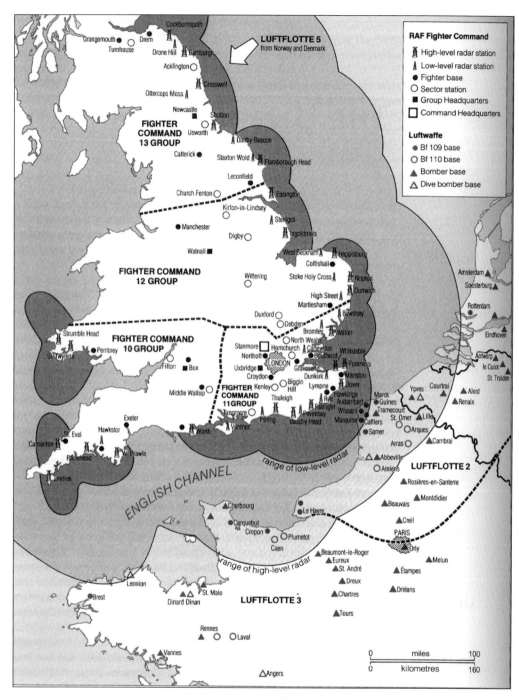

Fighter Command's group boundaries and radar coverage.

only possible course was to cut the length of orders to a minimum and to use direct telephone, whether landline or radio. To effect this, the operations room had, first, to portray physically the movements of enemy aircraft and, where necessary, of our own fighters, over the whole country and the sea approaches thereto (or such part as was appropriate to the headquarters concerned); second, to show how soon and in what strength our own squadrons could leave the ground; and third, to provide an adequate and reasonably secure network of communications both by landline and radio telephony.

Air Raid Intelligence

The essential basis of any air defence system is, of course, a good air-raid intelligence system. In this country, during the Battle of Britain, as now, such a system comprised a chain of radio location stations sited around our coasts. The function of these stations was the detection of all aircraft approaching this country over the sea. This early warning was vital since the German Air Force was in occupation of airfields just the other side of the Straits of Dover, which could be crossed in four or five minutes. It was supplemented over the land by the Observer Corps, whose function was to take over and 'tell on' the tracks of all aircraft as they crossed our coasts and proceeded inland to their targets.

During the Battle of Britain, information received by radio location was transmitted to Fighter Command headquarters and after passing through a 'filter room', was telephoned direct to one of the plotters in the Command operations room and simultaneously to those at the group and sectors affected. Information received from the Observer Corps followed the reverse course, being passed through observer centres to fighter groups and sectors and repeated by the group tellers to Fighter Command and adjacent groups.

Display of Information

In all Fighter Command operation rooms was a large table map upon which this air-raid intelligence could be accurately plotted as tracks, after such tracks had been identified as hostile, friendly or doubtful. Seated round the table map were a number of plotters, each one connected by a landline to the appropriate reporting centre. From these centres the plotters received minute-to-minute information of the progress of enemy aircraft towards and over this country, together with their numbers and height. The plotter displayed on the table map suitable symbols indicating the identity, numbers, height and track of the aircraft concerned. Thus each RAF commander, from the Commander-in-Chief in his operations room at Fighter Command down to the sector commander in his operations room at a fighter station or airfield, had continually before him the same moving picture of the enemy as the situation continually changed at the speed of modern flight. Naturally, the area that had to be covered by the picture presented to a sector commander was much smaller than the area required for the command or group operations room, but insofar as their responsibilities were severally affected, it was the same picture.

During the heavy attacks in September it was found that in No. 11 Group Headquarters operations room the table got too congested, so all detail regarding enemy raids and the fighter squadrons detailed to intercept was transferred to a slotted blackboard on the wall known as the Totalisator, leaving the map clear except for the raid numbers and symbols for our squadrons in the air.

Each operations room contained an elevated dais which might extend much of the way round the room; a gallery was sometimes added between the dais and the floor of the room. On the wall was shown complete meteorological information including wind and clouds and, at groups and sectors, the strength and degree of readiness of our own squadrons. In sector operations rooms arrangements existed whereby the minute-to-minute position of our own fighters was also plotted on the table map.

Transmission of Information and Orders

In the centre of the dais sat the controller with his assistants responsible for the issue of orders. In the gallery or on the dais sat the tellers, who passed on the information appearing on the table map to plotters in other operations rooms. Accommodation on the dais was provided for representatives of the Observer Corps, AA guns and searchlights and the Ministry of Home Security. Very complete intercommunication was provided; for instance, the controller in a group operations room could, by moving a switch, speak directly to any of his sectors, and the controller in a sector operations room could speak through R/T with any of his squadrons in the air or at their dispersal points on the ground.

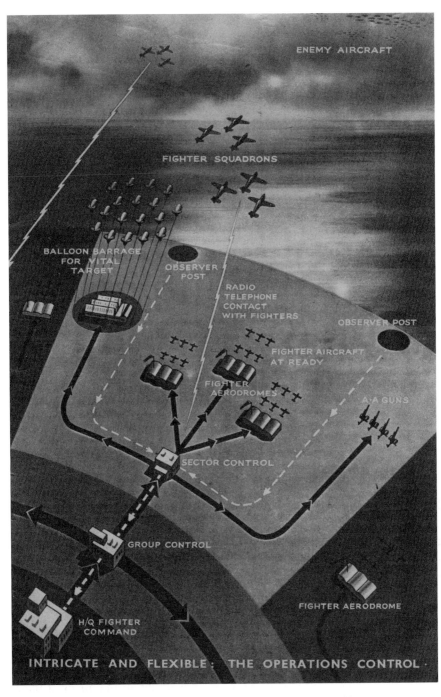

The System of Fighter Control, as explained in a wartime pamphlet.

At Fighter Command headquarters was the main operations room. In addition to the Commander-in-Chief Fighter Command and his staff, it contained the Commander-in-Chief AA Defences and the Observer Corps Commandant, or their representatives, liaison officers from the Admiralty, Bomber and Coastal Commands, as well as a Home Security official. It fulfilled many functions. Information from the various sources was coordinated and analysed and the reported formation identified as friendly or hostile and, if the latter, was allotted a number. Where any doubt existed as to the responsibility, raids were allotted to groups. The air raid warning system was operated through certain trunk exchanges in direct telephone communication. The Commander-in-Chief Fighter Command exercised general control over the opening of AA gunfire and the exposure of searchlights, through the Commander-in-Chief, AA Command. He also controlled the balloon barrage through his group commanders. Group commanders decided which sector should meet any specified raid and the strength of the fighter force to be employed. Sector commanders detailed the fighter units.

Responsibility of Commanders

This system enabled RAF commanders at each different level immediately to dispose their 'air forces to meet any situation as it could be seen threatening or developing before his eyes on the table map'. It enabled the Commander-in-Chief to reinforce groups with fighters from an adjacent group as and when he saw where the weight of the enemy's attack was likely to fall. It enabled a group commander to organise his squadrons in the various sectors at the appropriate states of preparedness to leave the ground, and to order his readiness squadrons off the ground at a moment's notice. It enabled a sector commander to carry out interceptions with incoming raids, since he could see on his table map the minute-to-minute position, course and height both of the incoming enemy formation, and of his own outgoing intercepting fighters. He could thus, by R/T, issue orders to his formation leaders in the air, giving the compass course to steer and height at which to fly so as to ensure the best chance of interception.

When once visual contact in the air with the enemy raid had been made, the executive control of the fighters passed automatically from the sector commander in the operations room to the man on the spot, the leader of the fighters, who in turn issued to his pilots by radio telephony his executive orders for the conduct of the ensuing air battle. Interception depended finally on being able to see the enemy, so although the system worked well by day, it was not sufficiently accurate to effect interception at night against raiders not illuminated by searchlights.

When the battle was joined, it was the function of the sector commander or his representative in his operations room to 'listen-in' and observe radio silence during the fighting, unless it appeared that other enemy fighters or bombers were approaching the area, when the formation leaders were duly informed. Immediately the battle was over, it became the function again of the sector commander to take control and assist his pilots to regain their home base or nearest airfield if necessary, particularly when, as often happened, squadrons became much split up during a dog-fight or when bad weather intervened and petrol was low.

Group, and to a lesser degree, sector commanders had many factors to keep in mind: the necessity for holding some squadrons in reserve to meet further attacks that might develop at short notice; recalling squadrons at the right moment to land for refuelling and rearming; petrol endurance; probable expenditure of ammunition. All these had constantly to be weighed up and decisions made very rapidly.

The whole technique of operating fighters in defence of Great Britain and the facilities provided in Fighter Command operations rooms were the result of a steady process of development over many years. Arrangements are never static. Improvements in methods, in layout and in equipment of operations rooms, are constantly being introduced. However, the existing arrangements today are, in their essentials, the same as they were in the days of the Battle of Britain.

AA Guns

The anti-aircraft guns, under the command of General Sir Frederick Pile, took no small toll of enemy aircraft, and during the heavy attacks on London, rendered great service in turning them back, both by day and night, through the weight of their barrage. On some nights as many as 60 per cent, of the enemy aircraft approaching London from the south dropped their bombs in open country or on the fringe of the barrage, and then went home. They also rendered direct service to our fighter aircraft, first by breaking up enemy formations, thus rendering them more vulnerable to fighter attacks, and secondly by indicating to our pilots in the air the position of enemy aircraft by shell bursts. On the dais were the tellers, passing on plots as they appeared on the centre table to fighter group and sector operations rooms and adjacent observer centres.

Where conditions permitted, posts re spaced so that all aircraft flying over the country e within sight or sound of at least one post and continuous tracks ere therefore obtained at the centres. Each track was given a separate symbol to maintain its identity, and when 'seen', the height and number of aircraft re reported and 'told' forward. The Observer Corps organisation was the sole method of tracking enemy aircraft overland during the battle, and its efficiency enabled many successful interceptions to be made and this contributed in no small degree to the result. It was also essential for the air raid warning systems.

In addition to the work in connection with Air Defence, the organisation was of great value in enabling our own aircraft, lost in thick weather or at night, to be grounded. Any aircraft thought to be in difficulty owing to its erratic course, the sound of its engines or distress signals was specially tracked and told forward. In some cases, RAF airfields were asked by centres to light their landing lights and fire pyrotechnics to help the aircraft down.

The Operations Room at Duxford, in 12 Group.

THE SYSTEM

The organisation was a very democratic one, members being drawn from all classes of society, but all were animated by the knowledge that their work was of vital importance to the country and to the Royal Air Force. Their skill at recognition reached an astonishingly high standard. During the severest winter known for half a century, every post and every centre was continuously manned day and night by these civilian volunteers, many of them over sixty years of age. Their motto is 'Forewarned is Forearmed'.

The foregoing perfectly explains the 'System' – and is an essential reference to which the reader may perhaps return for clarification on certain points as our tale progresses.

Chapter Three

'... this curious enmity of Leigh-Mallory's'

While Air Vice-Marshal Leigh-Mallory's memorandum had reflected a failure to comprehend the System, in January 1939 Air Commodore Park, with a full grip on the subject, wrote to the Air Ministry openly criticising the fighter tactics being promoted at the time.

The approved methods for attacking enemy aircraft, including types of formations likely to achieve the most concentrated firepower, were the domain of the Air Fighting Committee at Whitehall. The problem was that modern monoplane fighters had only been in service a few months, and the RAF had yet to go to war in them. Consequently, the tactics decided were a matter of conjecture and results of experiments by the Air Fighting Development Establishment (AFDE). This led to the 'vic' of three fighters, in a V formation and tightly grouped, becoming the standard section formation. A fighter squadron comprised twelve operational aircraft, equally divided into two flights, 'A' and 'B', each of which were sub-divided into two sections of three, Red and Yellow for 'A' Flight, Green and Blue for 'B', with each pilot given a number, hence Red One, Blue Two etc. The idea was that a squadron would fly in vics line astern, each vic attacking, in their neat formations, before breaking away and being replaced by the next section in line. In this way, it was perceived that a section of three could bring to bear twenty-four machine-guns, instead of a single fighter's eight. During the Spanish Civil War, however, the Germans had discovered that such formations were useless in practice, pilots concentrating more on formation flying that searching for the enemy, and quickly appreciated that fast, modern, monoplane combat required space and flexibility. The Luftwaffe, therefore, came up with the Schwarm, a section of four fighters in line abreast, stepped up, each protecting the other, with some 200 metres between each machine, removing the need for precise formation flying. In battle, the section broke into the Rotte, the fighting pair of leader, whose job it was to take the shot, and wingman, there to watch his leader's back. This sub-section was entirely flexible, responding to tactical situations accordingly. The Fighter Command Manual of Air Tactics, however, stipulated that a fighter must only attack from directly below or astern. Air Commodore Park understood the impracticality of this, writing that 'latitude' was required. Far-sightedly, Park added that 'The possibility of bombers having fighter escorts even in attacks on London should not be overlooked.'

In February 1939, Park issued new instructions: 'Fighter Command Attacks 1939'. Although these still concentrated upon attacks against ponderous bombers, and assumed that combined firepower was advantageous, it was wisely emphasised that these instructions were not a drill to be blindly followed, because formation leaders, having been guided to the interception by ground control, were encouraged to use their own initiative and act accordingly. While how best to use formations was carefully considered, so too was the intercepting formation's size. On 3 April 1939,

A flight of Hurricanes in two sections of three, the standard Fighter Command formation envisioned before the war.

A squadron of Spitfires in the standard 'vics' of three in line astern. It is not widely appreciated that before the Battle of Britain, most training revolved around the flight, not squadron flying as a cohesive unit, and in the air pilots could speak to their own squadron and controller, but not other airborne units. This meant that airborne control of large formations was impossible.

'... THIS CURIOUS ENMITY OF LEIGH-MALLORY'S'

Air Vice-Marshal Gossage, AOC 11 Group, sent a memorandum on this subject to his sectors and squadrons:

> The Air Officer Commanding-in-Chief Fighter Command has stated that his policy in regard to the engagement of enemy bomber formations is to match a fighter against each bomber of the enemy formation so far as this is a practical proposition.
>
> In Fighter Command Attacks 1939, it will be noted that this policy does not find its fullest expression in that the largest number of bombers which are simultaneously engaged by fighters is six. This limitation is at present occasioned by the following considerations:
>
> i) Some squadrons have not had their monoplane fighters long enough to be able to employ them efficiently in formations greater than sections or flights.
>
> ii) In Air Exercises the best and most economical use has to be made of the target aircraft which can be obtained for interception practice. For instance, if sixty bombers are available they are best used in flights or sections in order to give the maximum practice to as many fighter flights as possible, as opposed to operating the bombers in two masses of thirty, or five formations of twelve aircraft.
>
> iii) It is desirable, from the point of view of training junior leaders, that interception exercises shall be carried out by flights or sections, so that the maximum amount of practice, initiative and experience can be obtained.
>
> Thus it will be seen that training in the tactical handling of the formations of squadron strength has not been pursued as it might have been.
>
> The AOC-in-C holds the view that the squadron is likely to be the largest tactical unit employed by the simultaneous attack of a large enemy formation, and that if two or more squadrons have to be despatched to engage such a raid, squadrons would attack in succession, as individual units, acting upon the initiative of the squadron commanders when interception has been made.

Gossage's memorandum is of interest because it clearly outlines Dowding's thoughts regarding the size of intercepting formations, particularly that it was considered perfectly permissible for two or more squadrons to intercept concurrently, if the size of the enemy formation made this necessary. Clearly, then, Dowding's was not an inflexible insistence that small formations must always be used. It is noteworthy, too, that Gossage writes that multiple squadron formations would not attack as a cohesive whole, but in succession as individual units. There was one very good reason for this, which also applied during the forthcoming Battle of Britain: the limitations of radio telephony. The radio sets fitted to RAF fighters enabled the pilots of a particular squadron to talk to each other and the ground controller – but not to other airborne squadrons. Until this restriction was overcome, therefore, it was impossible for squadrons to instantly communicate during an interception – something not widely appreciated, even today. The memorandum also emphasises that because monoplane fighters were so new, with squadrons still converting to, and becoming familiar with, their operation, not all squadrons had actually flown as a single unit, but in flights or sections. That there was more experience and interception training to be provided to the flight formation, it also followed that this would be the obvious and preferred tactical formation.

In July 1939, 11 Group conducted a simulated defence of southern England against an 'attack' by Bomber Command, A week later, 12 Group did likewise in response to a similar 'raid' on northern England. A de-brief at Bentley Priory noted that 11 Group's interception success rate was a reasonable 60 per cent. 12 Group's was less, but sheeted home to Leigh-Mallory's fighters having begun practising the new interception techniques later than Gossage's, and 12 Group's RDF was found to be less reliable than 11's. The exercises were unrealistic, however, owing to the small number of bombers provided by the AOC-in-C Bomber Command, Air Chief Marshal Sir Edgar Ludlow-Hewitt. The following month, though, another exercise went ahead involving a larger number of bombers, the results of which were rather embarrassing for Air Vice-Marshal Leigh-Mallory. A low-level 'raid' had surprised certain of 12 Group's sectors, forcing the AOC to thereafter mount resource-hungry standing patrols. Indeed, Dowding and Park considered this an overreaction. Moreover, too many 12 Group fighters had been diverted from the primary function of intercepting bombers attacking vital targets, and were instead defending their own bases. Furthermore, during a night 'attack', the all-important 12 Group Operations Room was evacuated for ten crucial minutes. Dowding consequently directed Leigh-Mallory that in future neither group nor sector operations rooms were to be evacuated unless dictated by damage. These were, of course, the very nerve-centre of the System, without which the whole process broke down. Suffice it to say, the 12 Group AOC's performance in this exercise bode not well.

On 9 August 1939, the Air Ministry wrote to Air Chief Marshal Dowding on the subject of 'Tactics v Massed Bomber Formations':

> On the one hand it is said that the air fighting problem does not really extend beyond the tactical situation involved in combats between units of squadron size, because a massed attack of the type envisaged will, in fact, take the form of a number of squadron formations in quick succession, possibly some hundreds of yards apart. Furthermore, to meet such an attack it is unlikely that a fighter formation exceeding squadron strength will be mustered and operated as one tactical unit before interception, and the chances of more than one fighter squadron attacking at the same moment are very small. The air fighting problem, therefore, is covered adequately by the investigations of the AFDE by formations of squadron strength.

Wing Commander G.M. Lawson, an officer of Park's Operations staff, provided the following information to inform the AOC-in-C's reply:

> It is considered that a fighter tactical unit consisting of more than one squadron would not be able to carry out the role of interception and attack as efficiently as a squadron formation. It would take longer to climb to the height of the enemy formation, and it could not manoeuvre as quickly into position for the attack. In all probability, unless the enemy was intercepted at very close range, the wing fighter formation would have to split up in order to close quickly with the enemy bombers. It would probably be necessary in any case for the wing fighter formation to split up into squadrons or flights in order to bring effective fire against the greatest number of bombers at the same time. Attacks in wing formation would be impractical in conditions of heavy cloud, bad visibility or at low height.
>
> The school of thought which is in favour of large formations suggests that the aim should be to concentrate in strength before attacking.

It is considered that time is the important factor in interception and attack. The aim should be to attack the enemy as soon as possible, and not to wait until we have concentrated in strength before attacking.

The Memorandum gives particulars of the area covered by a large bomber formation. It is improbable that this represents a true war picture. It ignores the probability of dispersion after a long flight over the sea, after heavy AA fire, and after attacks by our fighters. The enemy bomber formation would almost certainly be dispersed over a larger area, and in groups which would be unable to support each other by rear gunfire when the fighters attacked. These dispersed groups of bombers could be dealt with more effectively by fighters operating in flight or squadron strength.

Apart from the operational objections referred to above, it is suggested that peace training must be egulated to war conditions. It might be possible to train our regular fighter squadrons in wing tactics in peace, but it is doubtful whether it would be possible to maintain that high standard in war.

On 19 August 1939, Dowding replied to the Air Ministry:

It is only a year ago since there existed a considerable body of opinion to the effect that high-speed monoplane fighters would not be able to deploy and deliver a simultaneous attack against an enemy formation owing to the danger of collision or shooting one another.

2. These fears, although not groundless, are proving to be exaggerated, and sections and flights are now habitually deployed for attack and we are working toward the habitual deployment of complete squadrons.
3. The training required for these tactics, however, is by no means inconsiderable and, although I am glad to say that no collision has yet occurred in aircraft deployed for straightforward attack following a direct approach, I have observed several instances in which one fighter has flown into the cone of fire of another when the target aircraft have adopted a rotating method of avoiding action.

4. While, therefore, I do not discount the possibility of mass deployment at some future time, I can say without hesitation that even tentative and experimental work in this connection would be premature at present.

5. My own opinion (which I do not want to over stress at the moment) is that the squadron will always be the largest tactical unit which it will be practically expedient to employ.

6. The main object of simultaneous and combined attack is to secure superiority of fire, and each individual fighter has at present so great a superiority of fire against its 'opposite number' that the situation may be considered satisfactory, and we ought not to sacrifice the speed, flexibility and safety of our deployment for theoretical advantages which are likely to be illusory in practice.

7. I agree that, on the evidence available, the Geschwader of twenty-seven or thirty aircraft is the most likely formation in which the Germans would deliver their attacks, but I should propose to operate against such formations at the present moment by flights in succession, and later by squadrons.

8. A further point is that under our present organisation, squadrons use different wavelengths, even when they are in the same sector, and cohesion of attack would be difficult to ensure unless all aircraft were on the same wavelength.

9. I should make it clear that the above remarks apply to the fixed-gun single-seater fighter. If, and when, multi-seater fighters are adopted in the Service, the problem must be reconsidered on its merits.

Clearly, Dowding was receptive to 'mass deployment' in future, if appropriate. In order to ensure a rapid, effective and safe reaction to any threat, however, the AOC-in-C emphasised that the flight, or in time squadron, was the 'largest tactical unit which it will be practically expedient to employ'. One of the main reasons for this, as explained, was that tactical training on the new monoplane fighters revolved around the flight of six aircraft, not, as yet, the whole squadron of twelve operating cohesively. With squadrons only beginning to learn how to operate as one, there was no question of a multi-squadron wing at this time, purely for practical purposes, taking aside any tactical considerations. Moreover, Dowding confirmed that the limitations of communications made command and control of a large fighter formation impossible. The correspondence, however, sharply evidences the great consideration that had been given to formation size by Dowding, and the very good reasons for his views.

In September 1939, the same month in which Britain and France declared war on Nazi Germany, following Hitler's invasion of Poland, Air Vice-Marshal Leigh-Mallory caused further concern at Fighter Command HQ. Dowding had expressly ordered his group commanders not to issue their own local instructions regarding the movement of squadrons, because this was dealt with by Fighter Command battle orders. Local arrangements, therefore, only served to confuse the issue. Dowding, of course, was conscious of the bigger picture, appreciating that in response to a changing military scenario, squadrons may need to move freely about the Command. Despite having been told to cancel his local orders of 5 September 1939, on 26 September Leigh-Mallory wrote further to both his sectors and Dowding:

> In view of the small number of squadrons in any one sector, and taking into consideration the fact that the Germans may deliver large scale raids on such important places as Birmingham, Derby and Sheffield, it is highly desirable that it should be possible to concentrate aircraft from as many other sectors as possible onto the front of the threatened target.

On 1 October 1939, Dowding responded:

Dear Leigh-Mallory

I have been reading your 12G/S.1292 dated 26 September 1939, on the subject of lateral reinforcement.

2. I find your paragraph 2 very difficult to understand. I take it you mean that in some circumstances Digby would require reinforcements, and in other circumstances Wittering.
3. In the former case you would have five squadrons at Digby, and in the latter no less than seven squadrons at Wittering.
4. Now I have delegated tactical control almost completely to groups and sectors, but I have not delegated strategical control, and the threat to the line must be regarded as a whole and not parochially. The units at Debden and Duxford

may be urgently required at short notice for the defence of London and, although they have been put under you to balance the number of stations in groups, this function of theirs must not be overlooked. (You will remember there is an emergency order 'Concentrate on London', which involved action by these two stations.)

5. Then again, I do not wish normally to operate more than three squadrons from one aerodrome, or four squadrons under one sector commander. Aerodromes must not become too crowded, and our organisation allows only four wavelengths to each sector. This of course does not prevent formations flying and fighting in another sector, so long as they are operated by their own sector controller.

6. I note that you have made arrangements to operate a fifth wavelength in a sector by means of the R/T Tender, but this was not the purpose for which R/T Tenders were provided.

7. The last part of your letter is difficult to understand. I imagine that the crystals referred to are for ground sets only.

8. Please do not think that I am criticising you in this letter. I admire the energy and foresight which you are bringing to your task. I would only ask you to remember that Fighter Command has to operate as a whole, and reinforcements and readjustments may have to be made between groups and not only within them. We require a simple and flexible system which can be put into effect at short notice and with the minimum of preliminary arrangement. My idea is that I shall never put more than four squadrons into a sector, that crystal and control arrangements exist for this to be done in such a way that any squadron, and not only a previously selected squadron, can be moved, and that if more than four squadrons have to intercept and fight in any one sector they will do so under the control of neighbouring sector commanders.

Air Chief Marshal Dowding had provided clarity, were any required, to the 12 Group commander regarding Fighter Command's strategy. Significantly, Dowding indicated that there was every intention of using 12 Group squadrons to reinforce 11 Group's over London if necessary (Debden was in 12 Group until August 1940, when absorbed by 11 Group). On 3 October 1939, Air Vice-Marshal Leigh-Mallory replied, acknowledging that his previous letter 'concerning lateral reinforcement cannot have been a very good memorandum as it misled your regarding my intentions', going on to say that:

2. This matter has been frequently discussed by me with my sector commanders, and this type of reinforcement has been practised during some of my Group exercises, so that my sector commanders are fully conversant with my ideas. This is why the whole scheme was not more comprehensively explained in my memorandum.

3. What I have in mind is a German mass attack of say 300–400 aircraft being delivered against one of the important objectives in the Midlands. In any one sector I have only twenty-four aircraft for day operations, and consequently if such an attack develops, I must be able to bring aircraft from adjoining sectors to counter it.

4. I can assure you that there is no intention on my part to upset the strategic situation in the Command, but only to make the greatest tactical use of the units in my Group. This scheme provides purely for air reinforcement, and it is not intended that any aircraft should land at an aerodrome other than their own, so that the times during which squadrons would be away from their parent aerodromes would vary between about forty minutes, in the case of Digby reinforcing Wittering, and Wittering reinforcing Digby, and about an hour and a half for Duxford reinforcing Digby.

5. As it is purely an air reinforcement, the Duxford squadrons would be in R/T touch with either their own ground station or with one working their wavelength at Digby, by which it would be possible to recall them in the event of a threat developing further South.

6. You will see from the above remarks that I have no intention of departing from what you say in paragraph 5.

7. In regard to paragraph 6 of your letter, if you remember, last autumn when it was laid down how the R/T Tenders should be allotted, they were sited so that sectors could operate on the front of adjoining sectors. With this end in view, the R/T tenders in the Wittering Sector, for instance, were sited at:

Wainfleet All Saints, from which aircraft from Wittering could fly up as far as Dona Nook, and

West Raynham, from which it is possible to operate as far as Great Yarmouth and Honington into the Duxford Sector.

8. To take a concentrated attack on Rolls-Royce at Derby, as an example, as how I was proposing to carry out this type of reinforcement. Digby would carry out the first interception about Skegness. Wittering then intercept about Horncastle, working with their R/T Tender at Wainfleet All Saints. Digby would carry out a third interception in the neighbourhood of Digby; the Duxford squadrons, as they have furthest to come, would intercept in the area Newark, Bottesford. The Germans might very easily direct a mass attack of 300–400 aircraft against Derby, and even with this method of reinforcing I would only bring sixty fighters into action against them.

9. With regard to paragraph 7 of your letter, the crystals referred to are for ground sets only, as with this type of reinforcement there would not be time for aircraft to land and change crystals as the opportunity would be lost.

10. I can assure you that in any operations of this nature I shall always be watching the situation to the South of me most carefully, as I realise the reinforcement of London may, in certain circumstances, become my primary task. With this end in view I have arranged not only to concentrate the Duxford or Debden squadrons for that purpose but for Debden to hold a crystal for No 213 Squadron, which they could operate on their fourth R/T set, and 213 Squadron could thus be utilised to operate in the vicinity of Harlow.

Leigh-Mallory's letter certainly helps us appreciate the limitations of airborne communications in use at the time. The letter appears to have reassured Dowding, who replied a week later, acknowledging that he had 'misunderstood' Leigh-Mallory's original letter, adding that:

> ... if one sector controller does not try to handle more than four squadrons, the plan ought to work all right.

> The chief difficulty might be from jambing [*sic*] between wave-lengths of units in adjoining sectors, but I see that you intend to operate units one after the other and not simultaneously. In the example you give in paragraph 8, do not overlook the possibility of some of the earlier squadrons being able to land and rearm quickly so as to be able to have a second go on the return journey.

At the time, however, Dowding had more pressing matters at hand, not least grave concerns regarding Fighter Command's overall strength, which was eighteen squadrons below the fifty-two considered necessary to defend Britain. Indeed, Dowding was steadfastly resisting the Air Ministry's efforts to send more fighter squadrons to France and reduce his strength to a mere twenty-six squadrons. In a letter to the Under-Secretary of State for Air on 16 September 1939, Dowding rightly described this as 'a grim prospect – the number is exactly half that laid down by the Air Council as necessary for the defence of the country'. The letter was both detailed and lengthy, concluding that his concerns were,

> written as much from the offensive as the defensive aspect. Presumably the time will come sooner or later when we will wish to take offensive action with our bomber striking force. When that time comes it will be necessary to be strong at Home, so that we may not be diverted from our aim by fear of reprisals.

Time and time again, Dowding's was the voice of both experience and reason resisting foolhardy decisions by the Air Ministry. It would not, however, win him many friends at Whitehall.

Leigh-Mallory was concerned about the strength of 12 Group, and wrote to Dowding on 24 October 1939:

> I feel most uneasy about the number of squadrons at present in 12 Group. I have, up to the present, lost three squadrons to the Field Force; No 616 permanently to 13 Group, and now No 19 sent North to reinforce 13 Group.
>
> In the last Command Battle Order, no less than four of the squadrons shown under No 12 Group are non-effective as far as I am concerned. They are:

19 Squadron – attached to 13 Group.
616 Squadron – now belonging to 13 Group.
229 and 222 Squadrons – neither of which has any aircraft.

In addition, 46 Squadron is standing by to go out to France.

2. We have recently been faced with a phase in which the Germans have been attacking coastal objectives. It seems to me from watching the international situation that we may be approaching very near the time when Hitler resorts to entirely different methods and begins to bomb military objectives in Great Britain itself, such as Rolls-Royce at Derby and various shadow factories and aero-engine factories in the Birmingham, Wolverhampton and Coventry areas. If such an attack develops, my position is a most precarious one.

3. I only have seven day-fighter squadrons at the present moment. Of those, 610 and 611 cannot be regarded as more than 50 per cent efficient when compared to the regular squadrons. They are a very different proposition to 602, 603 and 607 Squadrons, which were all in a very much more advanced state of training. That leaves me five reasonably well-trained squadrons with which to meet a really intensive attack on the Midlands. If one counts 610 and 611 together as one squadron, it gives me a total of six.

4. With the big area I have to defend and the weight of attack which may be delivered against me, I wish to place on record that I think this inadequate.

Leigh-Mallory's letter would not have told Dowding anything he did not already know, and hence why his horns were currently locked with the Air Ministry over the issue of Fighter Command's overall strength. Moreover, paragraph 4 was clearly an unashamed back-covering proviso. Air Commodore Park, Dowding's SASO, noted, though, that the AOC 12 Group's report was inaccurate: both 264 and 266 squadrons were at Sutton Bridge, and the Gladiator biplane-equipped 141 Squadron was in the process of converting to Blenheims. Also, 19 Squadron was actually returning to Duxford, its home station, after a brief deployment to Catterick. In March 1940, Dowding gave Leigh-Mallory an interview at Bentley

Priory, after which the latter stopped off at Park's office before leaving. The loyal SASO was later to recall that 'Leigh-Mallory was very angry and said that he would move heaven and earth to get Dowding sacked.' Park himself was consequently 'greatly annoyed', recalling that as a result of this incident his 'peacetime friendship for Leigh-Mallory drained very rapidly'. It is not known what the interview between Dowding and Leigh-Malory was about, but the timing of it suggests that it may have had a significant outcome.

In February 1940, Air Marshal Sir William Welsh had succeeded Air Marshal Sir Leslie Gossage as AOC 11 Group. As explained, although at this time German air attacks were expected to be incoming over the east coast, making 12 Group Britain's aerial frontline, as 11 Group included London, it was still considered the primary group command. That being so, with the experience of having commanded 12 Group since December 1937 behind him, Leigh-Mallory might have naturally expected to be next in line to command 11 Group, as and when the job became available. On 13 April 1940, however, Park was informed of his promotion to air vice-marshal and appointment to succeed Welsh in command of the prestigious 11 Group. In view of Leigh-Mallory's performance to date, however, it is hardly surprising that Dowding passed him over for this primary command, instead appointing his able former SASO. Dowding was not, though, personally aware of Leigh-Mallory's hostility towards him, this only being revealed by Park in 1968, during the making of the 1969 film *Battle of Britain*. Had Dowding been aware, he would have sought Leigh-Mallory's replacement immediately. Long after the war, Dowding told Robert Wright, his one-time personal assistant, that he should have been much 'stricter with Leigh-Mallory' who 'was not prepared to follow my orders, and I should have got rid of him'. As AOC 11 Group, Air Vice-Marshal Park would also soon have to 'endure', wrote Wright, 'this curious enmity of Leigh-Mallory's'.

For all of Leigh-Mallory's 'curious enmity', the fact remains that Keith Park, a warrior born and bred, was the perfect choice for the key command. Having spent two years working closely with Dowding as his SASO, Park fully understood the System and the overall strategy. Dowding's delegation of local tactical control to group commanders, however, meant that the role and importance of group AOCs was a vital one. Park was able to think in terms of handling 11 Group tactically inline with the overall Fighter Command strategy, which was essentially preserving limited resources while executing the greatest possible damage to the enemy. It would soon be largely Park's responsibility to fight the forthcoming tactical battle – against the known enemy at least.

Chapter Four

'That's exactly
what I've been warning you about!'

The 'knockout blow' for which Britain was braced when the Second World War broke out on 3 September 1939, never came. Unable to physically assist Poland, owing to the geography involved, in anticipation of an attack on the West, the British Expeditionary Force (BEF) and Advanced Air Striking Force (AASF) went to France, hunkering down along the Franco-Belgian border throughout that fateful autumn, and into the winter. For the first three months of 1940, little happened. The Soviets finally overwhelmed the Finns, and U-Boats continued attacking Britain's North Atlantic shipping, but elsewhere the 'Phoney War' persisted. With the exception of the Czechoslovaks and Poles, few people had unduly suffered from the conflict thus far. In early April 1940, Hitler invaded Denmark and Norway, drawing Anglo-French forces into a hopeless campaign in Norway's inhospitable terrain. Abruptly, on 10 May 1940, the great and long-awaited storm finally broke: Hitler invaded the Netherlands, Belgium, Luxembourg and France.

Two days later Liege fell, and panzers crossed the Meuse at Dinant and Sedan. Hitherto, in the naïve hope of remaining neutral, the Belgians had refused Lord Gort's BEF permission to fortify their border with Germany. Now the Belgian king called for help, the BEF pivoting forward from its prepared defences on the Belgian-French border. The British advanced for sixty miles over unfamiliar ground expecting to meet the German Schwerpunkt – point of main effort – which was expected to follow the same route as in the First World War. It did not. The Netherlands was certainly attacked – the Dutch Air Force being wiped out on the first day – but the main enemy thrust was cleverly disguised. As Allied eyes were firmly focused on the Belgian-Dutch border, Panzergruppe von Kleist achieved the supposedly impossible and successfully negotiated the Ardennes, much further south. German armour poured out of the forest, by-passing the Maginot Line, rendering its concrete forts useless. The panzers then punched upwards, towards the Channel coast – ten days later the Germans had reached Laon, Cambrai, Arras, Amiens and even Abbeville. Indeed, Erwin Rommel's 7th Panzer covered ground so quickly that it became known as the 'Ghost Division'. The effect on the Allies was virtual paralysis, so shocking was the assault, unprecedented in speed and fury. Civilians in Britain were equally shocked – not least after the bombing of Rotterdam on 14 May 1940, reportedly caused 30,000 civilian fatalities (although post-war estimates put the death toll at nearer 3,000). Hard on the heels of Guernica and Warsaw, Rotterdam's fate was terrifying news indeed.

The British Advanced Air Striking Force (AASF) had flown to France on 2 September 1939. Fairey Battle light-bombers went first, followed by Blenheims and Hurricanes – but no Spitfires. And Dowding only spared Hurricanes for two reasons: first, due to political pressure, he had no choice but to support the French by providing a certain amount of his precious fighters; second, that being so, he wisely decided only to send Hurricanes, which he knew were inferior to the Spitfire. Moreover, there were precious few Spitfires available in any case – certainly insufficient to send to France, thereby weakening Britain's defences for – as Dowding would later see it – for no good purpose. On 10 May 1940, though, there were six squadrons of Hurricanes in France. One week later the equivalent of six more squadrons had crossed the Channel, and another four were operating from bases on the south-east coast of England, hopping over the Channel on a daily basis but returning to England – if they could – at the end of each day. Losses in France rapidly stacked up. The Air Ministry acted as though these casualties were a complete surprise. Dowding's sharp riposte was 'What do you expect? When you get into a war you have to lose things, including precious aircraft. That's exactly what I've been warning you about!' His fears regarding the wastage of fighters were now being realised. The crux of the problem was that the more fighters Dowding was forced to send to France, the further he weakened Britain's defences. Although Churchill later wrote that Dowding agreed with him the figure of twenty-five squadrons to defend Britain, the latter dismissed this statement as 'absurd'. With the French constantly clamouring for more fighters, and putting Churchill's War Cabinet under increasing pressure, things came to a head on 15 May 1940.

On that day, Dowding joined Newall, the CAS, at a Cabinet meeting. Both men spoke out against sending more fighters across the Channel. These could not, however, be entirely denied, as elements of the BEF were poised to attack enemy communications near Brussels. Dowding was dissatisfied and later commented that,

> There had already been serious casualties in France, and they
> alone had been worrying me a very great deal. I had to know
> how much longer the drain was going on, and I had to ask for
> a figure at which they would shut the stable door and say no
> more squadrons would be sent to France.

Unable to request an interview with the Cabinet every time a new demand
for fighters was received, on 16 May Dowding sat and composed the
strongest case he could to prevent further fighters being drained away in a
battle already lost. The following is extracted from that letter, which Robert
Wright described as 'one of the most important documents of the early part
of the Second World War':

> I must therefore request that as a matter of paramount urgency
> the Air Ministry will consider and decide what level of
> strength is to be left to the Fighter Command for the defence
> of this country, and will assure me that when this level has
> been reached not one fighter will be sent across the Channel
> however urgent and insistent appeals for help may be.
>
> I believe that, if an adequate fighter force is kept in this
> country, if the fleets remain in being, and if the Home Forces are
> suitably organised to resist invasion, we should be able to carry
> on the war single-handed for some time, if not indefinitely. But,
> if the Home Defence force is drained away in desperate attempts
> to remedy the situation in France, defeat in France will involve
> the final, complete and irremediable defeat of this country.

The CAS endorsed Dowding's view, and no further Hurricane squadrons
were sent across the Channel. Most importantly, squadrons of the superior
Spitfire were being preserved for Home Defence. By 19 May, the situation
on the Continent had deteriorated further still. On that day the War Office and
Admiralty began facing the possibility of evacuating the BEF from France.
Churchill finally saw sense: the Prime Minister's decision was recorded in a
minute: 'No more squadrons of fighters will leave the country whatever the
need of France.' By the following day, only three of Dowding's squadrons
remained on the Continent. He considered that this 'converted a desperate
into a serious situation', or, as Wright put it, he was now 'able to mend some
fences'. The importance of this change in policy cannot be overlooked: yet
again, the defence of Britain had occasion to thank 'Stuffy' Dowding.

While Dowding was fighting the political battle to preserve fighters and especially retain Spitfires for the defence of Britain itself, Leigh-Mallory was trying to get 12 Group into the war. Operating from Martlesham Heath on the east coast, shortly after first light on Easter Monday, 13 May 1940, six Defiants of 264 Squadron took off, escorted by six Spitfires of 66 Squadron's 'A' Flight, bound for the Dutch coast. While patrolling off The Hague, a formation of 12/LG 1 Stukas dive-bombing a railroad was attacked. Unfortunately, the Ju 87s had fighter escort: Me 109s of 5/JG 26. In the subsequent action *five* of the six Defiants were destroyed by the German fighters, and a Spitfire was also despatched, the pilot of which crash-landed and returned home safely. This was a pointless sortie, however, which cost the lives of good men. It was also contrary to Dowding's policy of preserving fighters for Home Defence. This appears to be an early indication of just how wrong Leigh-Mallory could be in his determination to get 12 Group involved. On 18 May 1940, as Dowding agonised over the Battle for France bleeding away his precious fighters, Leigh-Mallory, incredibly, visited 19 Squadron at Duxford, arranging for the Squadron's proposed move to France. Again, this is an early indicator of Leigh-Mallory's inability to think beyond his own interests. Fortunately, there was no repetition of the suicidal sortie to Holland and, in the event, no 12 Group Spitfire squadrons went to France.

By 26 May 1940 it was clear that the Battle for France was lost. On that day the decision was taken for the BEF to retire upon and be evacuated from Dunkirk. From then on, the whole nature of air operations over northern France changed. The RAF now had to provide a protective umbrella for the retreating BEF in addition to covering the actual evacuation. It was now that Dowding committed his Spitfire force to battle over the French coast for the first time.

Dowding's intervention preventing further fighters being sent to France was a matter he barely had time upon which to reflect when this new challenge immediately arose. The problem was that Dunkirk lay fifty miles from 11 Group's closest airfield at Manston. This flight was over the sea, and contact would be over the French coastline. The inherent dangers were obvious, and hardly conducive to preserving precious fighters. Providing continuous fighter patrols from dawn to dusk was impossible, as this would have required every single one of Dowding's fighters – leaving Britain itself vulnerable to attack. Another hugely significant factor in the fighting over Dunkirk would be that the British fighters were unassisted by radar. The System only provided a radar network for the defence of Britain, its stations incapable of gathering data from as far away as Dunkirk and beyond. This is why Dowding knew that the battle ahead would be so exhausting for his pilots: as they could not predict or have early warning of an enemy attack it would be necessary to fly as many standing patrols as possible. Even so, Dowding also knew that given the size of the force he was able to make available – sixteen squadrons – there would be times, howsoever brief, that cover would be unavailable. The man entrusted with Fighter Command's contribution to this operation was the commander of 11 Group: Air Vice-Marshal Park. For what he was about to do, there was no precedent.

Initially, so as to provide cover for as long as possible, Dowding insisted that Park's squadrons patrolled individually. RAF losses had been high, because the German fighters patrolled in substantially greater strength and had greater experience. Park repeatedly requested that his squadrons should at least patrol in pairs, to which Dowding eventually agreed. On 28 May 1940, Park's Spitfire squadrons flew in pairs for the first time. Squadron Leader H.W. 'Tubby' Mermagen, the CO of 222 Squadron, remembered that on that day he 'led the squadron in a wing on its first patrol over the Dunkirk beaches, at 0630 hrs. The sortie lasted two hours and forty-five minutes, a long flight in a Spitfire.'

Unlike his peers, Air Vice-Marshal Park could fly modern fighters – and watched the battle unfold from the vantage point of his personal Hurricane, 'OK1'.

From 29 May 1940, Park employed his squadrons in wings of four. The loss ratio was not reduced, however, as fresh squadrons arrived, without any combat experience of this kind, and suffered accordingly. On that day, three out of five raids were intercepted, but those that got through caused great execution among the soldiers queuing on the beaches below. Poor flying weather hindered both sides the following day, but heavy German attacks over the next two ensured that the beleaguered troops suffered accordingly. The army asked 'Where was the RAF?' Those being bombed on the beaches were unable to see that Park's fighters were engaged above the low cloud and attempting to prevent enemy bombers reaching Dunkirk. In spite of Fighter Command's best efforts, the beaches were so badly hit that on 2 June 1940, the evacuation was switched to night-time. Two days later, Operation DYNAMO was all over; the aim had been to evacuate up to 45,000 troops: the total actually rescued was 340,000. Despite the limitations of the aerial protection provided by Park's fighters, owing to distance and a lack of resources, without their presence the evacuation would have been stopped dead in its tracks.

During DYNAMO the AOC 11 Group had recognised that patrolling in strength was preferable to lone squadrons, despatching pairs of fighter squadrons and ultimately wings of up to four. While this indicates flexible thinking and a thorough appreciation of fighter tactics, it is equally important to understand that in this context these wings were essentially a matter of squadrons crossing the Channel in convoy, ensuring that all units arrived over the battle area in strength before patrolling individually – meaning that in the event of trouble, and there was plenty of it, help was close at hand; as previously discussed, because of the limitations of communication, and deficiencies in training, there was no question of these squadrons fighting cohesively. For our purposes, DYNAMO is significant because Park did not hesitate to recognise and positively react to a circumstance in which the use of a larger formation was preferable to the individual flight or squadron. Following what was a successful operation, Park's personal reputation emerged enhanced, and it was over Dunkirk, from the vantage point of his personal Hurricane, 'OK1', that the tough New Zealander formulated the sound principle with which he would soon fight the Battle of Britain: that it was better to spoil the aim of many, rather than just shoot down a few.

The fighting in France, however, had confirmed just how wrong pre-war thinking had been about the limited value of fighters. The German fighters, especially the Me 109, had ruled the French sky, achieving the aerial superiority necessary to allow bombers to support the army on the ground, and providing the panzers freedom of movement. It was this German aerial umbrella, literally above all else, that won the Battle of France, and similarly the presence of Park's fighters had substantially contributed to the success of DYNAMO. There could now be no doubt of how crucially important fighters were, in defence and offence, and in supporting ground operations. Little wonder, then, that the far-sighted Dowding fought so hard to preserve his precious fighters – which he would not see frittered away on a battle already lost, or on foolhardy tactics in the defence of Britain.

Chapter Five

Bader: 'I must get one of those!'

Among the Spitfire pilots experiencing combat for the first-time during Operation DYNAMO was a certain flight lieutenant; what made this officer unique was that he had no legs. His name was, of course, Douglas Bader, who now becomes central to our tale.

Born in St John's Wood, London, on 21 February 1910, Douglas Robert Steuart Bader was the second son of Frederick and Jessie Bader. Soon after the birth, the new arrival's parents returned to India, where Mr Bader was employed as a civil servant. For the first two years of his life, Douglas was cared for by family on the Isle of Man, joining his parents in 1913, who planned to remain in India indefinitely. Shortly afterwards, however,

Douglas Bader, front row, second right, pictured when a prefect at St Edward's.

Flight Cadet Bader, front centre, captain of RAF Cranwell's cricket team, July 1930. At extreme left, front row, is Flight Cadet Corporal HAV Hogan – later to command 501 (Fighter) Squadron, which served in 11 Group throughout the Battle of Britain, and retired as an air vice-marshal.

Mr Bader decided to return home and study law, settling his family in Kew. The First World War erupted the following year, and Frederick was commissioned into the Royal Engineers (RE), subsequently serving in France. After the war, Major Bader remained in France, initially assisting with reconstruction before working for the War Graves Commission. Sadly, in 1922, he succumbed to a head wound suffered in 1917 and died in Brussels, where he is buried.

After this bereavement, the Baders found themselves in reduced circumstances, leading to a crisis over young Douglas's education. His elder brother, Derick, was already a boarder but funds were insufficient to also provide a private education for Bader junior – and the importance of this cannot be underestimated. These so-called fee-paying 'public' schools were considered training grounds for the future leaders of the nation and captains of industry. Between 1920 and 1940, for example, 68 per cent of Conservative MPs were former public-school boys; those from working-class backgrounds never exceeded a third and were exclusively Labour. Moreover, of 271 civil servants earning over £1,000 per annum in 1939, 190 had public-school backgrounds, as did fifty-six of sixty-two bishops, all but four High Court judges, and 76 per cent of 691 holders of high office in the church, state and industry. Public schools also provided 25 per cent of all university students, markedly dominating Oxford and Cambridge. A public-school background was also required for a commission in the armed forces. The only way forward for Douglas was winning a scholarship – a tall order for a pupil more comfortable on the playing field than classroom. Captain of cricket, rugby and football, Douglas won every race on school sports day and set a record for throwing the cricket ball. Nonetheless, with characteristic self-focus and determination, he won the all-important scholarship to continue his private education at St Edward's School, Oxford.

By this time, Douglas and Derrick's mother had remarried, to the Reverend Ernest Hobbs, a Yorkshire vicar, so the family moved to the large rectory at Sprotborough, a village to the west of Doncaster. Before his father's death, Douglas's aunt, Hazel, had married Flight Lieutenant Cyril Burge RAF, who had flown throughout much of the First World War with the RFC. Unsurprisingly, the young Bader was inspired by his new uncle's tales of aerial derring-do, and in 1923, stayed with the Burges at Cranwell, where Cyril was the RAF College's first adjutant. There Douglas joined flight cadets at games and sat in the cockpit of an Avro 504 biplane. By the end of this visit, the young Bader's mind was set: one day, he would return to Cranwell as a flight cadet himself, and become a pilot in the RAF. Although the selection medical and interview process to become a Cranwell flight cadet was not rigorous, like a public school the fees required were substantial: a non-refundable deposit of £150 upon entry, and £100 per annum for two years. Enthusiasm for aviation and even a burning desire to fly, therefore, counted for nothing: only money could guarantee admission – and again at an amount only available to the top 5.2 per cent of Britain's socio-economic pyramid. Cranwell was, therefore, an extension of the public-school system, and without a public-school background, admission was not an option. Douglas, thanks to his scholarship, had the credentials of St Edwards – but not the money to pay fees.

Towards the end of 1927, the 17-year-old Douglas wrote to his uncle, Cyril Burge, inquiring about the possibility of becoming an RAF officer. The advantage of a public-school background, without which a commission was unachievable, would now pay off. As Sebastian Cox, head of the Air Historical Branch (AHB) confirmed, before the Second World War 'the RAF had no formal definition of leadership. To a degree leadership skills were absorbed rather than taught, and the armed forces reflected the social attitudes of the time which were rather more inclined to assume leadership on the basis of social class.' No one, however, could deny that Douglas had shown an exceptional flare and commitment to captaincy on the sports field, and Burge's response to Douglas's tentative letter was that he was 'just the type they wanted and he would do everything to help'. Burge was certainly well-placed to 'help' his nephew: he was now personal assistant to none other than the CAS, 'Boom' Trenchard, the 'Father of the Royal Air Force'. Nepotism was, of course, a prominent feature in this society and Douglas would now reap the benefits of both a public-school background and a well-placed uncle.

There was, however, a stumbling block to Douglas's admission to Cranwell: fees. Douglas's mother Jessie was adamant that Cranwell was not an option, on the grounds that she disapproved of Douglas flying, and because affording the necessary fees was impossible. Like entry to St Edward's, though, there was a glimmer of hope: annually, Cranwell offered six highly prized cadetships, negating the payment of fees. Competition was fierce, the academic standard high. Characteristically, Douglas applied himself wholeheartedly to the process. In June 1928, Douglas attended the pre-selection interview at Burlington House, off Bond Street, in London – having been briefed on the likely questions and required answers by Burge. It is no coincidence that his score was a seldom achieved 235/250. Rheumatic fever, however, had left Douglas with high blood pressure, requiring rest and a re-examination, which he passed. He was not only in, but had won the fifth of the six cadetships.

The RAF required officers for specific branches: General Duties (flying), Administrative and special duties, Equipment, Accountant, Medical, Dental, Legal and Chaplains. It was with the former category that Douglas was concerned. Trenchard's vision was that all his officers would be pilots, a skill literally over and above the traditional officer function of leading men into battle on land or sea. Ultimately, it proved impractical for all officers to become pilots, but for Douglas and his new colleagues that was their goal. A former interwar flight cadet, 'A.H.E.', described Cranwell and its traditions:

> The life of the College is resumed with alacrity and care at the beginning of term. One day the place will be wearing a wan and neglected air, while the next day everything will be bustle and confusion. The night seems to bring forth cadets in the same way a conjurer produces rabbits from a hat. But as they come, so they depart, yielding place for others in a never-ending stream: each one, however, leaves his impression for good or bad on the College. Some may be forgotten; others

49

will be talked of by terms of the distant future. Yet one and all will retain indelible memories of their sojourn at Cranwell, and will regard the College with an esteem and affection which is of more value than the cosmopolitan camaraderie of greater seats of learning. For the associations of Cranwell are enjoyed only by a privileged few, who are closely bound together by their careers.

A.H.E.'s final sentence is revealing. Douglas was now entering an extension of the world he had experienced to date, one in which the 'old boy network' would later prove a crucial factor. Indeed, his brother-in-law, the wartime fighter ace Wing Commander P.B. 'Laddie' Lucas confirmed that passing out of Cranwell 'opened most doors in the Service and set them climbing the stairway to the stars'.

The course upon which Douglas now embarked was of two years duration. It was a full curriculum, with a great deal of classroom-based study – something which, despite his obvious ability, had never appealed to Douglas. In 1928, Cranwell's first year students flew the Avro 504N biplane, which had a top speed of around 100 mph, progressing the year after to the Armstrong Whitworth Atlas, which was 42 mph faster than the Avro. The Atlas was also currently in service with operational RAF squadrons policing the Empire. There were also a few Fairey Foxes and, for those showing the aptitude to become fighter pilots, Armstrong Whitworth Siskin IIIs. All were single-engine biplanes. Flight Cadet Bader was assigned to Cranwell's 'A' Flight, commanded by Flight Lieutenant Douglas MacFadyen (later Air Chief Marshal Sir Douglas MacFadyen), who recognised Douglas as a natural pilot.

It was on the open roads of Lincolnshire, however, that Douglas's irrepressible bravado was to seek thrills and spills on his motor cycle with a group of Cranwell chums, including one Geoffrey Stephenson, a close friend. Inevitably there were brushes with the police, and this irresponsible behaviour spilled over into College time. Whatever the trouble, Douglas was invariably either the ringleader or in the thick of it. The last straw for staff came when Douglas, the prize cadet, came nineteenth out of twenty-one in the end of first year examinations. His Squadron Commander made it clear that if there was no improvement in industry and attitude, he would ensure that Douglas and his like-minded friends were dismissed. Next, Douglas was sent for by the Commandant, Air Vice-Marshal Frederick Crosby Halahan. Keeping Flight Cadet Bader at attention, the Commandant spoke quietly but decisively; essentially his message was simple: the RAF required men, *not* schoolboys. Humiliated, Douglas knew that Halahan was right, and was ashamed. Not heeding Halahan's advice, Douglas knew, was simply not an option. He knuckled down to his studies. Initially, the staff viewed this change of heart with suspicion but soon regarded it as permanent – which it was.

As ever, Douglas excelled at sport throughout his time at Cranwell. He won all but one boxing bouts, in which he had sparred in a heavier weight than his classification, and achieved a 'blue' in not only boxing, but also rugby, hockey and cricket. A junior cadet, (later Squadron Leader) Rupert 'Lucky' Leigh, considered Douglas 'some kind of god who played every conceivable game and was the best player in every team'. Others disagreed, as fellow cadet (later Air Vice-Marshal) Wilfred Oulton recalled, describing Leigh's 'god' as 'an exhibitionist, not a team player'. Flying, however, was a solo affair – and at this Flight Cadet Bader also excelled. Early on at Cranwell, Douglas had developed an interest in learning more about the successful fighter pilots of the Great War. This, together with his obvious flying ability, particularly in respect of aerobatics, marked him out as a potential fighter pilot. He saw out Year Two flying single-seater Siskin biplane fighters. With a top speed of 156 mph, this was the fastest machine Douglas had yet flown and mastered it with ease. Upon conclusion of the course, on 25 July 1930, his log book was endorsed by Squadron Leader Thomas (for the Commandant) with an 'above average' assessment as a pilot. There is only one higher – 'exceptional' – which is rarely, if ever, given to comparatively inexperienced students. Throughout that final year Douglas maintained his improved attitude and industry, coming second on the course, beaten to the coveted Sword of Honour by his friend Paddy Coote. Flight Cadet Bader's final report noted that he was 'Plucky, capable and headstrong'.

Pilot Officers Bader and Stephenson, to their absolute delight, were both posted as fighter pilots to 23 Squadron at Kenley. If 'A.H.E.'s' words that 'the associations of Cranwell are enjoyed only by a privileged few, who are closely bound together throughout their careers', was not ringing in Douglas's ears as he drove out of Cranwell's gates, they should have been. At various significant junctures throughout his subsequent career he would have occasion to be thankful for sharing this close bond enjoyed by the service's privileged elite.

Pilot Officers Bader and Stephenson reported to 23 Squadron on 25 August 1930. 23 had a fine reputation as a fighter squadron during the First World War, after which it was disbanded, but reformed in 1925. The CO was Squadron Leader Henry Winslow Woollett DSO MC* – a thirty-five

23 Squadron's Pilot Officers Douglas Bader (left) and Geoffrey Stephenson (right) with Flight Lieutenant Harry Day. Bader and Day flew as the RAF aerobatic pair in the 1931 Hendon Air Pageant; Stephenson was reserve.

Victory Sopwith Camel ace. Douglas was posted to 'C' Flight, commanded by 32-year-old Flight Lieutenant Harry Day. Day had seen active service with the Royal Marines (RM), later transferring to the Fleet Air Arm (FAA) until being permanently commissioned into the RAF during 1930. From an august military family, with an uncle who won a VC in the Crimea, and an ancestor who fought aboard Nelson's *Victory* at Trafalgar, Day, like Woollett, was a man of great experience whom Douglas would come to admire. The squadron's base was at Kenley, situated between Croydon and Caterham in Surrey. Kenley had a grass runway and red-brick buildings. The two new pilots were shown into the Officers' Mess, their rooms in the same corridor.

The squadron flew Gloster Gamecock biplane fighters. In addition to flying, sport was also a prominent feature of squadron life. That August, Douglas was selected to play cricket for the RAF. A month later he passed a trial for the famous 'Harlequins' rugby team. Playing centre-three-quarter, the press frequently referred to him as 'brilliant', the best on the field. Naturally Douglas was soon selected to represent the RAF at rugby. He now drove a flash MG sports car. Life could simply not be any better for Pilot Officer Bader:

> It was truly a man's life… We all lived in the Mess, dined-in four nights a week and spent the weekends playing sport.

> There were no women on the Station. We all knew each other,
> went out together, played games together, flew together. Life
> was great, and flying was what we all loved.

At this time, the RAF was only twelve years old, and small enough to possess the air of a very select flying club; an elite, in which Pilot Officer Bader was blissfully happy and completely at home.

With 23 Squadron, Douglas flew biplane fighters, which had no brakes, no flaps, a fixed-pitch, single-bladed wooden propeller, no gyroscopic instruments, no trimming tabs, and fixed undercarriage; the RAF's frontline fighter, the Gloster Gamecock, had a top speed of 156 mph. From April 1931 onwards, Douglas's log book indicates numerous flights practising for the Hendon Air Pageant. Hendon, situated in Colindale, seven miles northwest of Charing Cross in London, was an important centre for aviation at which the RAF held its first annual 'pageant' – an air display – in 1920. To participate in the event was prestigious, and 23 Squadron's pilots trained hard to be selected. Woollett put 'Pricky' Day in charge of the exercise, who was an experienced aerobatic pilot. Day selected Douglas as his No 2 in the RAF aerobatic pairs competition, with Pilot Officer McKenna and Stephenson comprising the second pair, the latter being reserve when Day and Bader represented 23 Squadron in the RAF pairs aerobatic competition. On 19 June 1931, the 23 Squadrons pairs participated in the Andover air show, demonstrating their breath-taking routines. A week later the RAF Display at Hendon took place in glorious weather. An indication of both the event's popularity and the interest in aviation during the interwar years is provided by the volume of people crammed inside the gates: 175,000. The day's finale was a ten-minute aerobatic sequence flown by Day and Bader. Their performance centred on the Royal Box, the 23 Squadron pair won. The next day, the *Times* trumpeted their performance as 'the most thrilling spectacle ever seen in exhibition flying'.

His life entirely fulfilled, at 21 Douglas Bader had already become what would be described today as a celebrity, both in the air and on the sports field. Indeed, his place as fly-half in the full England International rugby squad looked assured. Overflowing with enthusiasm and confidence, Douglas was also in danger – from himself. Having mastered aerobatics, Douglas now turned, according to Lucas,

> to the hard stuff ... such euphoria can only be found close
> to the ground. Low flying, real low flying, right down on the

deck; beat-ups of the girlfriend's house; making the picnic party in the country field run for cover; just for the hell of it; flying upside down… 'with his head almost brushing the grass' – this is the heroin of flying.

Day, however, warned his young stars constantly of the perils associated with unauthorised low flying. On 20 August 1931 – exactly a year since Pilot Officers Bader and Stephenson had reported for duty with 23 Squadron – Day led them on a flight from Kenley to Cramlington, near Newcastle, to perform formation aerobatics at another air show. En route, Douglas dropped out of formation and amused himself by hedge-hopping for an hour – well below the regulation height for low flying. Such irresponsibility, however, incurred Day's wrath; Douglas had been officially warned. Many years later, a Cranwell contemporary, Air Commodore H.W. 'Tubby' Mermagen remembered that Douglas 'was a real show off. He could do everything brilliantly – but he did it very low.'

In July 1931, 23 Squadron phased out its Gamecocks, replacing them with the Bristol Bulldog. This was another open cockpit biplane fighter with a fixed undercarriage, fixed-pitch propeller and twin machine-guns. With a top speed of 176 mph, the Bulldog hardly represented a great leap forward in design and development. The new machine, however, was heavier than the Gamecock and therefore not as manoeuvrable. Half way through a slow roll, for example, the Bulldog lost altitude quickly. The conclusion of such a roll could see the Bulldog 400ft lower than at the starting point. Consequently and sensibly, low-level aerobatics were banned; one pilot ignored this and promptly perished in a fatal flying accident. Following another similarly wasteful and unnecessary death, Day, temporarily commanding 23 Squadron, reminded his pilots that Fighting Area Regulations strictly prescribed the minimum height for aerobatics as 2,000ft – from which height recovering from the Bulldog's vices was not an issue. Day, though, was sympathetic to aerobatic flying, for obvious reasons, and cautioned that if low-level aerobatics were attempted, they should be no lower than 500ft – and beyond the gaze of senior officers. Characteristically, Douglas ignored all of this. In November he was carpeted by Day for beating up the airfield. It was not just the disregard for safe flying practice and regulations that concerned Day. Some members of 23 Squadron resented Douglas, the Cranwellian, thinking him conceited. Stung by the subsequent rebuke for 'showing off', Douglas resolved to calm things down. Life for young Bader, though, was just getting better and better; that month he was selected as fly-half for the Combined Services team. His place as an England international rugby player seemed assured.

According to Lucas, by this time Douglas was 'the best aerobatic pilot in the Royal Air Force'. He was also the victim of his own success. In the wake of his competition-winning Hendon aerobatics came an expectation for him to perform. On the morning of Monday 14 December 1931, 'Pricky' Day authorised Douglas to practise aerobatics. The subsequent flight of an hour and a half increased his total flying hours to 492.20. Later that day, Douglas joined Flying Officer Phillips and Pilot Officer Stephenson on a flight to Woodley's civilian flying club. After lunch, inevitably, the civilian pilots present pressed Douglas to give them an aerobatic display upon leaving. The three fighter pilots took off, having agreed to perform a 'Prince of Wales's feathers'. This involved the central aircraft climbing vertically, while those either side did so slightly to the left and right before peeling away. Douglas occupied the left-hand position, breaking in that direction as expected – but then 'quite unexpectedly headed back to the field at low level'. Douglas's intention was to roll over the airfield at around 125 mph and virtually at zero feet. As he swept across the grass his fixed undercarriage was only 10ft above the ground, his head just 18. The Bulldog was never rolled any faster – so characteristically, Douglas was right on the edge. This was reckless indeed. The little Bulldog rolled right, successfully, the pilot now inverted, his head almost brushing the grass. As the aircraft continued to right itself, speed, as the machine defied gravity, slightly reduced – in this scenario enough to be catastrophic. The reserve of power was not enough to permit correction. An irretrievable slide began – the recklessly slight safety margin gone. Douglas's left wing-tip touched the ground, completely destroying the aircraft's forward trajectory and stability. The biplane was immediately completely uncontrollable, in a fraction of a second the damage done. The airscrew and engine tore loose, bounding across the field, the left wing collapsed, buckling below the fuselage. The right wing literally collapsed onto the open cockpit while the top wing was ripped straight off. Shocked onlookers rushed to the scene, the crash site shrouded in dust and smoke. Meanwhile Pilot Officer Bader, his mangled aircraft crumpled ignominiously around him, lay conscious but gravely injured.

Douglas's right knee was covered in blood, the rudder bar sticking through it, the red stain on his white flying overalls increasing with every pump of his heart, his foot contorted in an abnormal angle. His left leg had been flung backwards, his seat collapsing on top of it. Quickly men gathered about the wreckage, a steward offering Douglas a shot of brandy – which

On 14 December 1931, having previously been warned by Day regarding the danger of low-level, unauthorised, aerobatics, Bader crashed slow-rolling at Woodley airfield. His legs were so badly injured that both had to be amputated.

he immediately declined on the basis that he never drank alcohol – ever. Soon afterwards he passed out. Those onlookers gathered about then began cutting Douglas out of the wreck, laying him on the grass and removing his shoes while the injured aerobatic star passed in and out of consciousness. An ambulance arrived and while Douglas was in it, en route to hospital, an Australian student pilot, Jack Cruttenden, held the femoral artery closed, preventing Douglas bleeding to death. In short order Douglas was being examined by a doctor at the casualty department of the Royal Berkshire

Hospital in Reading. The bones of both legs were nearly severed, the right at the knee, the left shin shattered. Douglas's pulse faded, requiring a heart stimulant. The doctor feared the worst, telling the ward sister, Sister Thornhill, to prepare a warm bed, so as to 'ease the shock … I don't think there's much we can do.' The consultant agreed; operating in Douglas's current state was no option, perhaps if he survived the next few critical hours, but of that there was no realistic prospect. By a coincidental stroke of good fortune, however, Leonard Joyce, considered by many the best practising orthopaedic surgeon in Britain at that time, was operating at Reading that day. Sister Thornhill alerted the great man who was soon at Douglas's bedside. Acknowledging that the young pilot was fit and strong, Joyce agreed to wait and see if the patient recovered sufficiently from shock to survive an operation – that being so, he would do so personally. Information gleaned from the ward suggested to Kenley that Douglas was dying. Harry Day fired off telegrams accordingly to Douglas's mother, Jesse Hobbs, and his uncle, Cyril Burge, the latter only an hour away at Aldershot.

By 2 pm Douglas's pulse and breathing were – incredibly – strong enough for Joyce to operate. From X-rays it was clear that the right leg had to be amputated immediately. Over the shattered left leg Joyce deliberated. Thorough surgery, due to Douglas's critical condition, was impossible. Joyce amputated the right leg, rapidly sealing the wound in the hope of preventing infection. After the procedure Douglas was close to death. By 9 pm, post-operative shock had nearly sapped all of his strength – Joyce knew he was dying and unlikely to survive the night. Cyril Burge was informed and at 2 am summoned to Douglas's room; the time, it was believed, had come. As Burge arrived, however, he was asked to wait; Douglas's pulse had suddenly become marginally stronger. And so it went on, all night and the following day. Although unconscious, Douglas still lingered in this world the following morning – when Joyce told Burge that should he survive another twenty-four hours and infection was kept at bay, he might live, and even the left leg possibly saved. Twenty-four hours later the patient was indeed still breathing – and opened his eyes for the first time since the operation. Joyce was summoned immediately, breaking the news of amputation. Douglas heard but comprehension was slow to follow. Joyce then examined him, confirming that the right leg, or what was left of it, was free from infection – but not so the left, which showed irrevocable signs of septicaemia and gangrene. Joyce was now in a cleft stick; it was unlikely that Douglas would survive another amputation – but given the infection, death was in any case inevitable. The only option was to amputate and hope for the best. Before long Douglas was back in theatre, Joyce removing the infected left leg six inches below the knee. Then Douglas's heart stopped. Adrenalin was immediately administered. The heart restarted. The pulse weak and erratic, Douglas was nonetheless alive. Eighteen hours later he briefly regained consciousness, before slipping back into the netherworld. Six hours later he surfaced once more – the pain from his left leg so intense that not even morphine soothed it. And so it went on, hour upon hour, Douglas drifting in and out of a morphine-induced semi-consciousness, in dreadful pain.

Everyone expected Douglas to die. His mother and uncle remained at the hospital, awaiting the inevitable. Then, the following morning, as Douglas lay in a rare moment of lucid consciousness, a defining moment occurred. Outside his room young nurses hurried by, going about their business. A matron rebuked them, telling them to be quiet, because 'There's a boy dying in there.' This jolted Douglas's fading spirit back into action. Dying? He bloody well wasn't! For all his faults, Douglas Bader was possessed of iron will beyond the comprehension of most. In that moment in which the matron's comment had stung his consciousness into action, Douglas was actually dying. Now he had a battle to fight – the kind of thing he thrived upon. He focused his mind, fighting the unseen power that tried to lure him back to the netherworld – permanently. The pain, however, was such that more morphine was administered. Unconsciousness was inevitable – this time for two whole days – and so began a battle between Douglas and his nurses against death. When he surfaced again more morphine put him out for another two days and nights – throughout which he had but momentary periods of consciousness. Shock was the problem, but Douglas's supreme physical fitness eventually overcame. The coma subsided and he returned to the real world. He remained, however, in tremendous pain and was unaware that his left leg had also been amputated.

Strangely, it was his missing legs, particularly the left, which hurt so much. No one had the heart to tell Douglas that he was now a double amputee – until visited by Squadron Leader Woollett, the CO of 23 Squadron. Complaining profusely of pain from his left leg, Douglas commented that it might be best if it was amputated. Casually, Woollett answered that it had, in fact, been cut off. Douglas heard and understood but, due to the morphine, the impact was lost on him. Back at 23 Squadron, the general feeling was that the loss of both legs for Douglas, the gifted aerobatic pilot and sportsman, was so tragic that death in the accident would have been kinder. There was never any doubt, though, that Douglas Bader was entirely responsible for his own misfortune. Air Vice-Marshal Wilfred Oulton summed up the feelings of the service as a whole: 'I was very sorry, but not surprised.' Later, Douglas wrote in his log book 'X Country Reading. Crashed slow-rolling near ground – Bad show.' Indeed, as he flippantly remarked many years later to Laddie Lucas, 'I just made a balls of it, old boy. That's all there was to it.'

Douglas Bader's life was changed forever as a result of the catastrophic, blameworthy, accident. He now had a whole new challenge; refusing to walk with a stick, he would spend many months recovering and learning to master artificial limbs. This he did, with Herculean determination and courage. Although no action was taken over the accident, Douglas was uncertain of his future in the RAF.

Towards the end of summer 1932, Douglas was invited to spend a weekend with Sir Philip Sassoon, the Under-Secretary of State for Air. Sassoon had been the Member of Parliament for Hythe for some twenty-seven years and entertained his influential circle of friends at one of his homes, either at 45 Park Lane, London, Trent Park or at Port Lympne. It was to the latter that Douglas was invited. Unbeknown to Douglas, Sassoon, who had been present in the Royal Box at Hendon when Day and he had won the aerobatic pairs competition, was an ally and admirer – who had asked to be kept personally updated regarding the amputee's progress. Sassoon was also Honorary Air Commodore of the Auxiliary Air Force's 601 'County of London' Squadron, the 'Millionaires' Mob', which, coincidentally, was undertaking its annual camp at nearby Lympne airfield. Another young officer from 23 Squadron, Peter Ross, was also invited to Port Lympne. Their host arranged that Bader and Ross could fly in 601's Avro 504. When this treat was announced, Douglas was absolutely delighted and could hardly believe it. Needless to say, from his back-seat position it was Douglas, not Ross, who flew the aeroplane up to Kenley, where he made a perfect, three-point, landing. After lunch, Douglas flew back to Lympne, making another perfect landing.

Of flying without legs, Douglas later wrote that,

> Flying an aeroplane presents no difficulty unless it is equipped with foot brakes. Before the war all British aeroplanes were equipped with a rudder control which was either a bar pivoted in the middle (so that pressure by either foot swung the bar) or there were two complete foot pedals which moved up and down. You pushed with your right foot for right rudder and vice-versa. Now, if you place your foot on a bar and push you

can do that from your thigh and your shin without having to depress your foot in relation to your shin. The brakes of aeroplanes in those days were operated from the control column or joystick by means of a lever, rather like that on the handle of a motorcycle. When you depressed the lever and the rudder bar was central, both brakes went on. You obtained differential braking by moving the rudder bar on whichever side you wanted the brake, i.e. right rudder, right brake.

After his trip to Kenley and return to Lympne, Douglas was elated and felt sure that the RAF would allow him to fly again. Indeed, when Sassoon asked to be informed when Douglas had his medical board, the prospect seemed assured.

Soon afterwards, Douglas was ordered to attend an assessment at the Central Medical Establishment (CME), Kingsway. He passed with an A2H rating, which, without legs, could not have been higher. Interestingly, it was noted that his blood pressure was lower due the lack of legs, because the heart had less distance to pump blood around – meaning that without extremities he would be less inclined to black out in dives and steep turns. An A2H rating, however, meant that Douglas couldn't fly solo or overseas. Next stop was the Central Flying School (CFS) – for a formal flying assessment – at Wittering.

Douglas's flying at Wittering was immaculate. The Chief Flying Instructor (CFI), in fact, soon decided that Pilot Officer Bader being there and 'mucking about not being able to go solo' was a pointless exercise. Douglas agreed. The CFI reported to the medical board that Douglas could clearly still fly – resulting in a rapid return call ordering the legless pilot to reattend the CME. There Douglas was surprised not to have to appear before a board of doctors, instead being ushered into the presence of a wing commander. Assuming it to be a mere formality, Douglas entered the room confidently. The words uttered by the officer before him were more crushing than the accident at Woodley: Pilot Officer Bader could not be passed for flying duties because King's Regulations failed to provide for such a circumstance. Unsurprisingly, Douglas was stunned. When his initial astonishment and anger subsided, he began to suspect that the decision had already been made before he had gone to Wittering. Indeed, later he discovered that during his time there an article had appeared in a Sunday newspaper questioning the wisdom of providing a legless man with a flying course. This, the author considered, was a waste of the tax payers' money and unfair on the mothers of sons who had to fly with the individual concerned. Whether this publicity influenced the RAF's decision is unknown, but it may have, and this, coupled with Douglas's 'record of hazardous flying', made his reinstatement as a service pilot 'an unacceptable risk'.

In November 1932, Douglas was posted to RAF Duxford in Cambridgeshire. There 19 Squadron flew Bulldogs, and the Cambridge University Air Squadron (UAS) received instruction. Pilot Officer Bader was given command of the Station's Motor Transport (MT) Section. Douglas, however, refused reclassification as an Administrative or Equipment officer. In April 1933, Pilot Officer Bader was summoned to see Duxford's Acting Station Commander, Squadron Leader Sanderson, the CO of 19 Squadron. Faced with an unenviable task, Sanderson gave Douglas sight of a letter from the Air Ministry. It pulled no punches. The Ministry 'regretted' that as a result of Pilot Officer Bader's last medical board it was no longer possible to employ him in the General Duties Branch. Douglas was to be retired on the grounds of 'ill health'. The only good news was that he would get a service and disability pension. The stark reality that he could no longer remain a pilot in the RAF stunned Douglas. There was, though, a precedent for a legless man being a service pilot; a Captain Drummond had flown in the RFC with two artificial legs. Given that Douglas had the personal support of the Under Secretary-of-State for Air, this end result can only be considered surprising. One explanation has already been offered, that Douglas's reckless flying now made him an unacceptable risk, meaning that in spite of losing his legs, the powers-that-be did not consider him to have learned his lesson – this being borne out by further clashes with authority while running Duxford's MT. So it was that on 30 April 1933, Douglas Bader was formally retired from the RAF.

While working in administration for the Asiatic Petroleum Company (Shell), on 5 October 1933, Douglas married Thelma Edwards. Having mastered golf, with a respectable handicap of nine, Douglas even began playing squash. Thelma noted that Douglas's bouts of depression, which sometimes lasted several days, were becoming both rare and short. Then the Munich Crisis came in 1938. On 12 March 1938, Austria was annexed into the new German Reich – although forbidden by the Versailles Peace Settlement, Britain and France took no action. Hitler then set his sights on absorbing the Sudetenland of Czechoslovakia, which had a large ethnic German population, into the new Germany. Britain's Prime Minister, Neville Chamberlain, knew full-well that Britain was unprepared for war and so, to buy time, pursued a policy of appeasing Hitler. Britain and France, therefore, ceded the Sudetenland to Germany – at the infamous

Munich Conference on 30 September 1938, to which the Czechoslovaks were not invited. When Munich happened, Douglas knew that there was going to be a war. He also realised that the RAF would need all the trained pilots it could muster. Having already proved at Lympne, Duxford and Wittering that he could still fly, in spite of whatever King's Regulations did or did not say, Douglas wrote to the Air Ministry offering his services. The polite response, however, stated that without legs he was still considered a permanent accident risk. Once more, he was offered an administrative role, which again Douglas declined.

Flying was an integral part of Douglas's very being – especially the most exciting aspects of it. During his previous service he had expressed this through aerobatics. Combat flying was an altogether different dimension and one without parallel. Suddenly, the burning ambition to resume the cockpit of a service aircraft rose to the fore again – and this time would not go away. Naturally, after six happy but difficult years, Thelma was against her husband flying again. Douglas, of course, remained in contact with various RAF contemporaries, who talked excitedly of the future and new fighters. Men with whom he worked at Shell were also preparing to do their 'bit'. If there was to be a war, and there was every indication another with Germany was on the horizon, it was intolerable for Douglas to be out of it. He resolved to continually pressurise the Air Ministry, garnering support from friends still in the service and refusing to take no for an answer. Lucas described how,

> Several of the instructors [at Cranwell] in Douglas's time were [now] in positions of influence. Men of the calibre of Boyle, Constantine, MacFadyen and Coningham had obviously been marked out and were on the way up. Additionally there were several among his old contemporaries, close friends like Geoffrey Stephenson and Rupert Leigh, who were in a position to be useful and certainly try to help. Stephenson, a staff officer at the Air Ministry, beavered away for him behind the scenes. Best of all, his first Commandant at Cranwell, Frederick Halahan, was also at the Air Ministry. An air vice-marshal, he carried some responsibility for personnel – not aircrew, but that didn't matter. The important thing was that he was there, in Kingsway, at the centre of things.

It was from this point onwards that the words of the otherwise anonymous Cranwell cadet 'A.H.E.' must have been ringing loudly in Douglas's ears:

'For the associations of Cranwell are enjoyed only by a privileged few, who are closely bound together by their careers.' Indeed, Douglas himself resolved to harness the Cranwell 'Old Boy Network' to his absolute advantage.

Although the British Prime Minister, Neville Chamberlain, had returned from Munich brandishing his famous piece of paper signed by Hitler and supposedly guaranteeing 'peace for our time', the storm clouds of war continued to gather over Czechoslovakia. Appeasement at the Munich Conference, however, gave Hitler confidence that Britain and France would not go to war over Czechoslovakia. On 16 March 1939, therefore, German troops invaded the Czech republic; a week later Slovakia placed itself under German control. There was now no question whatsoever regarding Hitler's wider intentions, convincing Douglas further still that his place was in the cockpit of a Spitfire.

At this time, Geoffrey Stephenson was serving at the Air Ministry and friendly with the personal staff officer to the new Air Member for Personnel, Air Marshal Sir Charles Portal, to whom Douglas wrote – the officer pivotal to Douglas achieving his ambition. 'Peter' Portal had Air Council responsibility for selections and postings. Any decision about Douglas's unique case could only be made by him. As Lucas said, going to the top had 'always been Bader's practice', but having help on the inside was no bad thing. Stephenson's suggestion was that Douglas should be admitted to the new AAF. Portal was largely unmoved, responding to the effect that even a flying capacity in the reserve was impossible during peacetime. There was, however, hope; 'if war came', Portal wrote on 31 August 1939, 'we would almost certainly be only too glad of your services in a flying capacity after a short time if the doctors agreed'. From that point onwards, the prospect of another world war became Douglas Bader's salvation. Indeed, he prayed that war would come – prayers which were answered during the early hours of Friday 1 September 1939, when Hitler invaded Poland.

It was obvious to Douglas that this time, Britain and France would have to go to war over Poland. While Thelma fretted, Douglas eagerly awaited further news. On 2 September he sent Thelma to stay with her parents – anticipating an imminent declaration of war against Nazi Germany and the rapid arrival of German bombers over London. Such was the fear of air attack, in fact, that between June and the first week of September 1939, some 3,750,000 people were evacuated, such movements in the first week of September alone affecting up to a third of Britain's population. It was fully expected that Germany would immediately attempt to deliver the dreaded 'knock-out blow'. News from Poland was dire; the Polish Air Force had been destroyed, largely on the ground, on the campaign's first day, on which the Luftwaffe achieved total aerial superiority. Hitler ignored an ultimatum from Britain and France to withdraw his troops, leading to the long-awaited declaration of war on 3 September 1939. Chamberlain broadcast the far-reaching news to the nation and Commonwealth at 11.15 hrs that Sunday morning. Twelve minutes later the sirens wailed – causing Londoners to fear that Armageddon had arrived. Fortunately this was a false alarm, but Douglas was not among those who sought shelter. Instead, he sat down and wrote to Portal again. He also began 'telephoning and writing peremptory notes to Stephenson and another friend, Hutchinson, at the Air Ministry'. Several weeks passed, during which Douglas promptly had his name removed from the list of those Shell employees exempt from military service, until the Air Ministry responded. That communication took the form of a simple telegram, instructing Douglas to attend Adastral House for a selection board.

Upon arrival, Douglas was shown into the office of none other than Air Vice-Marshal Halahan – his old Cranwell Commandant. Once more a ground job was offered and declined. Douglas's spirited response that only returning to a fighter squadron was acceptable led to Halahan providing his former pupil with a letter for the doctors. It read: 'I have known this officer since he was a cadet at Cranwell under my command. He's the type we want. If he is fit, apart from his legs, I suggest you give him A1B category and leave it to the CFS to assess his flying capabilities.' Douglas's fitness was subsequently not found wanting and he was referred to the CFS. There is no doubt, of course, that Douglas's old Commandant's recommendation was significant. Frustrated, Douglas soon began 'bullying' Stephenson and Hutchinson 'to make someone do something immediately'. On 14 October 1939 a telegram arrived from the CFS, now based at Upavon in Wiltshire, ordering Douglas to attend a test four days later. Not having flown for seven years, unsurprisingly, even for Douglas, nagging doubts regarding his ability to pass the test gnawed away at him during the journey. He need not have worried – Cranwell was about to look after him once more.

The first person Douglas met at Upavon was Joe Cox – with whom he had flown at Duxford after his fateful crash and before leaving the service. They were old chums, and Cox was now a senior instructor at the CFS. Posted to the Refresher Squadron's 'A' Flight, Douglas found the commander to be an old Cranwell chum: Squadron Leader Rupert 'Lucky' Leigh. Junior to Bader at Cranwell, Leigh considered his senior 'to be some sort of God'. This was fortunate indeed; Douglas's flying test was to be taken by Leigh in a North American Harvard monoplane – which had footbrakes. In the event,

Leigh operated the footbrakes, justifying this on the grounds that Douglas would not be flying the American built Harvard operationally and all British service types' brakes were operated by hand. Douglas consequently passed the test with a recommendation from Leigh that he return to the CFS for a refresher course. Douglas could have hoped for no better outcome. He went home to await further orders, which again did not came not quick enough, so soon Douglas was pestering Stephenson and Hutchinson at the Air Ministry again. At the end of November, however, the long-awaited letter from the Air Ministry arrived: Flying Officer Bader was being commissioned not into the AAF or Volunteer Reserve, but back into the regular service – and in a flying capacity. This more than Douglas had dared hoped for.

Restored at last to the active list, on 27 November 1939, Flying Officer Bader reported to Upavon for his Refresher Course – with 500 flying hours recorded in his log book, all on biplanes. The first flight of his resumed career was as a passenger in an Avro Tutor flown by Flight Lieutenant Clarkson. The second was solo – including an *inverted* circuit of the aerodrome. This beggared belief, and failed to impress the CFI, Wing Commander Pringle, who asked Leigh to 'be good enough' to ask Bader 'not to break *all* the flying regulations straightaway'. On 2 December, Douglas flew with Leigh in Harvard N7184. Although he could never solo on this type, due to its footbrakes, because operational RAF fighters were now monoplanes it was imperative that Douglas gained experience of this type. Two days later, he soloed on a monoplane for the first time – not a fighter but a Fairey Battle, a British aircraft with a handbrake. With an enclosed cockpit, retractable undercarriage and a variable pitch propeller, even this comparatively slow light bomber was a very different machine to the biplanes Douglas had flown previously. Another Harvard flight with Leigh followed on 10 December. Then, on 20 December, Flying Officer Bader flew one of the new fighters, Hawker Hurricane L1873, for the first time. In his log book Douglas wrote 'Circuits, landings and low-flying'; he could not have had a better Christmas present. By conclusion of the course, Douglas recorded a total of 5.20 hours on the Hurricane.

At this time, Wing Commander Alfred B. Woodhall was Station Commander and Sector Controller at Duxford:

> One day, Douglas Bader flew over from the CFS in a Hurricane. I was delighted and amazed to see him as I had not done so since his crash. He was in terrific form, and, as it happened, the AOC also came to visit us. I introduced Douglas to the AOC, Air Vice-Marshal Leigh-Mallory, and over lunch Douglas

used all his considerable charm to persuade 'LM' to take him into one of his operational fighter squadrons. After lunch, with the AOC watching, Douglas put on a most finished display of aerobatics, and this finally decided LM. Douglas impressed us all with his terrific personality and his amazing keenness and drive. I have never known his equal. Flying was his supreme passion and his enthusiasm infected us all.

At the CFS, Rupert Leigh described Douglas as 'an exceptionally good pilot' who should be posted to a fighter squadron. Joe Cox agreed: 'When flying with this officer it is quite impossible to even imagine that he has two artificial legs. He is full of confidence and possesses excellent judgement and air sense.... I have never met a more enthusiastic pilot ... he lives for flying.' The CO, Wing Commander George Stainforth, endorsed Douglas's log book as 'Exceptional', a rarely given accolade. With a green light from Upavon, Douglas lost no time in haranguing Stephenson to engineer a posting to his new squadron. Douglas's visit to Duxford, described by Woodhall, timed for when the AOC was lunching there, was no coincidence. Stephenson – a squadron commander – had access to the AOC that day and deftly used the occasion to further his friend's cause. On 7 February 1940, the effect of this string-pulling became evident: Flying Officer Bader was posted to fly Spitfires with Squadron Leader Geoffrey Stephenson's

Although mastering prosthetic legs and passing a flying test, King's Regulations failed to provide for limbless pilots, and so, unable to accept a ground job, Bader left the service in 1933. When war broke out, however, he was declared fit, passed another flying test and recommissioned into the General Duties Branch of the RAF. By this time, his friend Stephenson was commanding 19 Squadron at Duxford, arranging for Bader to visit on the same day the 12 Group AOC, Leigh-Mallory (centre) was lunching with the Station Commander, Wing Commander A.B. 'Woody' Woodhall (left). Bader's display of breath-taking aerobatics sufficiently impressed the AOC to post Flying Officer Bader to Stephenson's 19 Squadron – flying Spitfires.

19 Squadron. The Cranwell 'Old Chums Network' had undoubtedly looked after one of its own.

As Douglas later wrote of his arrival at Duxford: 'Now, modern types consisted of low-wing monoplanes, with retractable undercarriages, wing flaps, constant-speed variable-pitch propellers, blind-flying instruments and radio telephony. None of these things existed when I crashed in 1931.' He was not to fly a Spitfire for a few days, however. Stephenson was away and the squadron operated daily from the coastal station at Horsham St Faith, flying convoy patrols, leaving no serviceable Spitfires at Duxford. While his fellow pilots performed this very necessary task, Douglas, not yet being operational, remained at Duxford, making his first flight with 19 Squadron in a Miles Master. He described this machine as being 'nothing like a Hurricane or Spitfire, for it had a wide undercarriage, was without vice, and was easy to fly. But you sat behind a Rolls-Royce liquid cooled engine, the Master went quite fast and it was fully aerobatic.' It was indeed, as 19 Squadron armourer Fred Roberts remembered: 'Bader's first flight with us was in the station Master, and he beat up the aerodrome in every way.' Ernie French was a member of 'A' Flight's groundcrew:

> When Flying Officer Bader arrived at Duxford from the CFS at Upavon, there was no publicity. He simply joined our squadron as an ordinary pilot. My first sight of him was arriving in his MG. He often took me and other airmen flying in the two-seater Master, making me sit in the front cockpit

19 Squadron was the RAF's first Spitfire squadron, this being a very different and much more advanced aircraft than the biplanes Douglas had previously flown, as a result of which he experienced some difficulty converting to the type, crashing several times.

67

and joking 'French, make sure you start her up before you get in!' These were cross-country flights and he would point out his digs in March and other landmarks.

Douglas's first impression of the Spitfire was that it,

> looked good and was good. But my first reaction was that it was bad for handling on the ground, made taxying difficult since it was not easy to see ahead. It was necessary to swing from side to side to look in front. The view at take-off was restricted in the same way until you were travelling fast enough to lift the tail; only then could you see over the nose. Once accustomed to these minor inconveniences, they were no longer apparent, and once in the air you felt in the first few minutes that here was the aeroplane *par excellence*. The controls were light, positive and synchronised: in fact the aeroplane of one's dreams. It was stable; it flew hands and feet off; yet you could move it quickly and effortlessly into any altitude. You brought it in to land at 75 mph and touched down at 60 – 65 mph. Its maximum speed was 367 mph. You thus had a wide speed range that has not been equalled before or since.

Given the technological differences between the biplanes and the new fighters, Douglas's transition to the Spitfire was not without difficulty. Flying Officer Bader made his first Spitfire flight, in Mk I K9853, on 12 February 1940: 'I sat in the cockpit while a young pilot officer, with little experience, showed me the knobs. He omitted to tell me one important thing about the undercarriage operation which embarrassed me in due course, fortunately without damage.' That 'young pilot officer, with little experience' was, in fact, Pilot Officer Frank Brinsden, who was serving with 19 Squadron *before* it received Spitfires on 4 August 1938:

> I feel free to elaborate on this comment as Douglas raised the matter and I was there. Any 'young pilot officer with little experience' on 19 Squadron assigned to brief Douglas Bader would actually have been flying Spitfires since October 1938. By early February 1940, when Bader came on the scene, that pilot officer would have been qualified to fly operationally by both day and night. Is such a pilot officer therefore likely to have

omitted from the briefing the rather important matter of raising the undercarriage? In any case the crew room had an ample supply of Pilot's Handling Notes and anyone who embarked upon his first solo in such a (for that time) radical aircraft without fully understanding its controls was a complete bloody fool! It must be remembered that the biplanes with which Bader had previously been familiar had a fixed undercarriage. Although he had flown a handful of hours in a Hurricane, retractable undercarts remained relatively new to him.

It was both typical and offensive that Douglas should blame his own mistake on another. It would not, though, be the only one he would make. At the time, Air Vice-Marshal Michael Lyne was a Cranwell graduate and another young pilot officer on 19 Squadron:-

By March 1940 the weather was better but we now had Flying Officer Douglas Bader to contend with. He was very brave and determined but having a hard time getting to grips with the Spitfire, a far more advanced machine than the biplanes he had flown previously. He particularly experienced problems in cloud. More than once my friend, Watson, and I were lent to Bader as a formation by the CO, but emerged from cloud faithfully following our leader only to find ourselves in a steep diving turn!

Douglas was not only having a hard time with the Spitfire, but also fitting back into squadron life as a comparatively junior officer – his rank not being commensurate with either his age or contemporaries. Douglas was nearly 30; his Cranwell friends were largely squadron leaders, whereas his years out in the wilderness meant that he was just a flying officer – senior only in rank to a pilot officer. So here was Douglas Bader, the Cranwell graduate and famous aerobatic champion, a very junior officer in a fighter squadron commanded by his best friend, an exact contemporary. Those pilots of equal or junior rank were 20-odd year olds – even his flight commander in 'A' Flight, the quiet and intellectual Flight Lieutenant Brian Lane was only 23.

During a dummy interception of Wellington bombers, Douglas hit a tree while chasing a low-flying bomber. Characteristically he blamed his leader, complaining to his CO, 'That silly clot led me into a tree.' Stephenson's response was, 'Well, you're the silly clot. It's up to you to see where you're going. He can't fly the aeroplane for you.' Douglas was simply unable to acknowledge his own mistakes, or play second-fiddle to anyone – and certainly not a young 20-odd-year-old. Douglas was unable to cope with being 19 Squadron's 'sprog' pilot. He did not see that as his place – which was commanding a fighter squadron.

During early 1940, in addition to providing convoy patrols, 19 Squadron rehearsed Fighting Area Attacks. Douglas, however, disagreed with the Air Fighting Manual and considered the air exercises completely unrealistic. For years he had read the memoirs of Great War fighter aces, and firmly believed that height, sun, getting in close and independent action would win the day – not the rigid formation attacks endorsed by Fighter Command. Instead of attacking in an orderly fashion from the same direction, Douglas argued that fighters attacking from all angles would be more effective. Future events confirmed that the tacticians were wrong – but only because Hitler's unprecedented conquest of France placed southern England within range of his single-engine fighters. This meant that there would be an enormous amount of fighter-versus-fighter combat – which, contrary to the experts' pre-war belief, *was* possible. Douglas's take on fighter tactics was that once battle was joined, each pilot should act independently and attack as he saw fit – not be bound to a set-piece, rehearsed, attack that in reality would be impossible due to the enemy's evasive action and return fire. In this area of argument, he was more right than wrong. Douglas remonstrated with Stephenson over tactics, but whatever 19 Squadron's CO thought, he had no brief to deviate from the stipulated tactics – which relied upon team work and not the individual. As ever, Douglas remained convinced that he was right. The inability for independent action and his disagreement with Stephenson, though, exasperated him further still. He had much to thank Stephenson for, but was becoming increasingly unhappy on 19 Squadron. Indeed, Douglas openly told his CO, 'Look, I don't feel happy flying behind these younger chaps. I'm more experienced and older, although I've not so many hours on Spitfires.' The fact was, Douglas was unhappy as a team player – unless he was captain of it.

Again, though, 'the associations of Cranwell' were to rescue him. Another significant officer at Duxford was also a Cranwellian, Squadron Leader H.W. 'Tubby' Mermagen, CO of 222 Squadron:

> When I was commanding 222 Squadron at Duxford, which had recently exchanged twin-engine Blenheims for Spitfires, Douglas Bader, a personal friend, was serving alongside us in 19 Squadron. However, he was finding it difficult to serve

Struggling to serve under his friend Stephenson, and officers younger than he, Bader persuaded fellow Cranwellian Squadron Leader H.W. 'Tubby' Mermagen to take him as a flight commander in his 222 Squadron, also based at Duxford.

under Geoffrey Stephenson, with whom he had once shared equal rank at Kenley before his accident. Bader knew that I had a flight commander suspected as being 'lacking in moral fibre' and whom I wished rid of. Bader therefore asked me if I would approach the AOC, Leigh-Mallory, regarding the possibility of him being transferred to 222 on promotion to acting flight lieutenant and becoming a flight commander. The AOC agreed.

Douglas, of course, had already personally met Leigh-Mallory, at the meeting ironically arranged by Stephenson. Wing Commander Woodhall had been present on that occasion and commented that:

> As a spectator, I was intrigued to see the impact that Douglas had on the AOC – and vice-versa. Air Vice-Marshal and Flying Officer, rank did not enter into it, they were two of a kind – born leaders. They were both men who were respected by all and were affectionately esteemed by most. Their attraction for each other was immediate and their friendship was, I am sure, established at that first meeting.

Woodhall – Duxford's Station Commander – was also impressed by Flying Officer Bader during that far-reaching visit to Duxford:-

> I had not seen Douglas since his crash, and in his maturity appealed to me very strongly. Such was his zest for living and

flying that one forgot his artificial legs. He ignored them, and so did everyone else. His prowess at golf and squash was such that very few people on the Station were a match for him in either game.

Woodhall supported Mermagen's formal recommendation that Douglas replace his suspect flight commander.

By this time, the Spitfire's original fixed-pitch propeller – as fitted to the old biplanes – had been replaced by the De Havilland two-pitch airscrew. 'Pitch' refers to the angle at which the propeller blade cuts into the air. The effect of changing pitch is akin to changing gear in a car. This development also caused Douglas difficulty, as Air Vice-Marshal Lyne described:

> On 31 March 1940, Douglas was leading our section of three Spitfires on a convoy patrol. We went off downwind on the shortest run at Horsham. Douglas, however, forgot to put the airscrew into fine pitch for take-off and cartwheeled across the main road and into a ploughed field. Watson and I stuck with him until the last minute but then pulled up and away on emergency power. I remember only just clearing the hedge and seeing clods of earth flying high overhead from my leader's Spitfire. Bader broke a pair of artificial legs in the accident, in fact, and had to send away for a new pair.

The Spitfire concerned, K9858, was written off. It was an extremely stupid mistake, drawing a rebuke from Squadron Leader Stephenson – and a 'snarled' response from Flying Officer Bader. It is surprising, therefore, that on the same day, Squadron Leader Stephenson wrote in Douglas's log book 'Ability as a Spitfire Pilot Exceptional'. Although Douglas was concerned that bending another Spitfire could (and should, perhaps) have jeopardised the rapid promotion and transfer he sought, unsurprisingly, given Woodhall's account, the AOC's approval was assured. When interviewed by Leigh-Mallory, Douglas made no excuse for the accident – how could he? The AOC agreed – there was none – but still promptly promoted Douglas to acting flight lieutenant, posting him to 222 Squadron. As Wing Commander Brinsden said: 'Although we all admired Douglas, I wasn't the only pilot not sorry to see him go.' Clearly, 19 Squadron had simply been a stepping-stone to better things: on 16 April 1940, Flight Lieutenant Bader took command of 222 Squadron's 'A' Flight.

Douglas continued to expound his own contrary theories on air fighting. He also remained unable to behave responsibly in the air, continuing to engage in unauthorised low-level aerobatics. He had now, though, made progress in his ambition to catch up his contemporaries – but still had a way to go; in early May 1940, Rupert Leigh, promoted to squadron leader, brought his own Spitfire Squadron, 66, to Duxford. For now, though, commanding 'A' Flight of 222 Squadron on the usual round of convoy patrols and training flights would have to do.

At 0300 hrs on 28 May 1940, Flight Lieutenant Douglas Bader was awoken by his batman; at 0400 hrs 222 Squadron was to fly to and operate from Martlesham Heath – in 11 Group. Air Vice-Marshal Park was concentrating even more Spitfire squadrons in the south-east, ready to operate across the Channel during Operation DYNAMO. Mermagen and his pilots did not know this, however, as they took off, bleary eyed, and flew to their destination, near Felixstowe in Suffolk. Biggin Hill's 92 Squadron was already there and had seen action – losing the CO, Squadron Leader Roger Bushell, on the unit's second patrol. Bushell's senior flight commander, Flight Lieutenant Robert Stanford Tuck, found himself in temporary command. Upon landing, Douglas marched up to Tuck and demanded to know 'the score'. Tuck's response was to rebuke Flight Lieutenant Bader for not having tucked the loose end of his silk scarf into his tunic – which, in the event of bailing out, could have snagged on something. Indeed, Tuck's first impression of the 'obstreperous man' was that he was 'too cocky and ought to be taken down a few pegs'.

92 and 222 Squadrons flew together on 28 May 1940, with Tuck and the former squadron leading. Mermagen's pilots flew in the stipulated vics of three, while Tuck led 92 in loose well-spaced pairs. It was clear by now that Fighter Command's tacticians really had got it wrong – as Douglas had charged. The presence of the German single-seater fighter, the Me 109, had changed everything. As Douglas had predicted, in practice the formation attacks stipulated by Air Ministry had proved useless. Although the Spitfire, hitherto preserved by Dowding for home defence, was only now meeting the Me 109 for the first time, the RAF pilots were learning quickly.

No Me 109s, or indeed any other enemy aircraft, were encountered on Douglas's first patrol over the French coast. During the return flight, 222 Squadron was diverted to the Kentish coastal station at Manston. After refuelling it was off to Duxford, from where Mermagen was ordered to take his pilots to Hornchurch. From that sector station the Spitfire pilots of 54 and 65 Squadrons had already been in action for several days, their place in the line now being taken by 222 and 41 Squadrons. In the Mess that night, Douglas spoke to some of the outgoing pilots of their experiences – and learned that all, without exception, totally agreed with his assessment of the area attacks insisted upon by Fighter Command. The suicidal impracticality of these had become immediately apparent, leading to their instant rejection. The problem now faced, though, was that new formations and tactics literally had to be worked out on the job – and a very dangerous one it was, considering the massive advantage in combat experience enjoyed by the enemy's fighter pilots.

On 29 May 1940, 222 Squadron was up again, running head-on into a gaggle of twin-engine Me 110s, which broke for cloud out of the Spitfires' guns' range. Mermagen, however, managed to hit one, chalking up 222's first combat victory. The next two days saw Mermagen's pilots patrol uneventfully. Of events on 1 June 1940, Douglas later wrote that:

> We were all flying around up and down the coast near Dunkirk, looking for enemy aircraft which seemed also to be milling around with no particular cohesion. The sea from Dunkirk to Dover during those days of the evacuation looked like any coastal road in England on a bank holiday. It was solid with shipping. One felt one could walk across it without getting one's feet wet, or that's what it looked like from the air. There were naval escort vessels, sailing dinghies, rowing-boats, paddle-steamers, indeed every floating device known in this country. They were all taking British soldiers from Dunkirk back home. The oil-tanks just inside the harbour were ablaze, and you could identify Dunkirk from the Thames estuary by this huge pall of black smoke rising straight up in a windless sky. Our ships were being bombed by enemy aeroplanes up to about half way across the Channel and troops on the beaches were suffering the same attention. There were also German aircraft inland, strafing the remnants of the BEF fighting their way to the port.
>
> I was flying along at 3,000ft when an Me 109 appeared straight in front of me at about the same speed and going in the same direction. Like me, he must have been a beginner, because he stayed there while I shot him down, and I didn't get him with the first burst.

With 222 Squadron, Flight Lieutenant Bader scored his first victories during the Dunkirk evacuation, and is pictured here at Hornchurch during that operation (centre); with cap is another ace, Flight Lieutenant Robert Stanford Tuck of 92 Squadron.

Mermagen recalled their return from this particular sortie:

> When we landed, Douglas stomped over to me and enthused 'I got five for certain, Tubby, old boy!' Now this was the first time we had met Me 109s, which were damn good aeroplanes, and everything happened very quickly indeed. To be certain of having destroyed five enemy aircraft in such circumstances was impossible. I said 'You're a bloody liar, Bader!' We credited him with one destroyed. Nevertheless, Bader was generally easy to keep in order, as it were, and had already proved to be an excellent flight commander.

Douglas was also credited, in fact, with damaging an Me 110. 222 Squadron was up again later that day, Douglas writing of that sortie 'Attacked two He 111s. Killed one rear gunner and damaged machine.' Of this operation, Douglas wrote:

> A day or two later I saw a Dornier bombing one of our ships. He was about a mile away and I rushed at him with the throttle wide open, giving myself just enough time for a hurried burst which silenced the rear-gunner. I had to pull up very quickly to avoid a collision. Thinking about it later that evening I got

75

the message which every fighter pilot assimilates early in his career – if he hopes for a career at all. It is this: overtake your target slowly and relax before you start shooting; you will never get him in a hurry.

By 4 June 1940, the Dunkirk evacuation was over. During this vicious air fighting, Douglas had seen combat – and scored his first successes against the enemy. The RAF's experience over France had also confirmed his belief that the tacticians had got it wrong. Fortunately these deficiencies had been discovered just in time for a certain amount of positive adjustment before the enemy's crucial aerial assault on Britain itself. Douglas was even more convinced now that the experience of Great War fighter pilots held true: he who has the height advantage controls the battle, he who has the sun behind him achieves surprise – and he who gets in very close hits his target. Flight Lieutenant Bader was not, of course, the only pilot to have realised this – but he doubtless expounded his theories loudest.

On 12 June 1940, Air Vice-Marshal Leigh-Mallory visited the Sector Operations Room at Duxford. It is no surprise that Leigh-Mallory favourite Douglas flew the Spitfire required for a radio-test demonstrated to the AOC. The following night, though, Douglas crashed another Spitfire; Mermagen: 'On that occasion Douglas came in far too high and far too fast. He went through a hedge. I drove over to pick him up and he was ranting, shouting that the flarepath was incorrectly laid out. I thought "Well, look at that, what a total lack of humility, he's blaming someone else now!"' The Spitfire was badly damaged. Nonetheless, Mermagen was a fan:

> Douglas carried out several operational sorties under my command and displayed exceptional leadership qualities; he was a fine Spitfire pilot. He used to come stomping into dispersal saying 'Come on chaps, get out of the way, I want a cup of coffee', barging everyone else aside, but the chaps loved him for it, he was a real morale booster.

By now, though, having ingratiated himself to his AOC, Douglas had been earmarked for better things.

Wing Commander Woodhall:

> Soon after the Fall of France, Leigh-Mallory rang me to say that 242 (Canadian) Squadron was reporting to Coltishall and

would be under the operational control of my Duxford Sector. He told me that the squadron had had a tough time in France, and that the groundcrews had only just been evacuated via Cherbourg thanks to the resourcefulness of their adjutant, Flight Lieutenant Peter MacDonald MP. Their own CO had left them to their own devices after the pilots had landed in England, and the Squadron, led by Flying Officer Stan Turner, had landed at Coltishall with nothing but the uniforms they were wearing. Tools, spare kit, baggage, the lot, had been abandoned.

'LM said "I've got to find them a new squadron commander but he's got to be good, because these chaps are Canadians and they've had a rough time. They are browned off with authority and need a good leader – any suggestions?'

'At once I said "What about Douglas Bader?"'

'LM replied "I thought you'd say that. I think you are right."'

Air Commodore Mermagen:

By the time Bader was promoted to command 242 Squadron, a Canadian unit suffering from poor morale, he was known personally to the AOC, Air Vice-Marshal Leigh-Mallory, who knew of his record and had particular respect for the way in which he had dealt with both the crash and amputations. I had spoken to Leigh-Mallory on several occasions, confirming that Bader was an 'above average' Spitfire pilot, a most mature character and quite an outstanding personality in Fighter Command. I feel certain that my high opinion of Douglas Bader helped him achieve such rapid promotion which he rightly deserved and was proven by his later service record.

Acting Squadron Leader Bader had now caught up his Cranwell contemporaries – in just four months. Indeed, just eight weeks ago he had been a lowly flying officer. During his years in the wilderness such a scenario had been unimaginable. Now Douglas could really get to work – and drove off on 23 June 1940 from Kirton to Coltishall, relishing the prospect:

The AOC told me that the Two-Hundred-and-Forty-Second (Canadian) Squadron was a pretty brassed-off bunch; they lacked discipline and he thought that I might be some use in getting the thing straight. So I rushed off, thinking that this would be absolutely splendid!

The following morning, Douglas was delighted to find that Coltishall's resident Spitfire squadron, 66, was commanded by an old friend: Squadron Leader Rupert 'Lucky' Leigh. Breakfast was followed by an interview with the Station Commander, Wing Commander 'Bike' Biesiegel, who briefed Douglas on his new command. 242 Squadron had been formed at Church Fenton on 30 October 1939, the first Canadian squadron to do so. It had arrived at Coltishall only a short time before Squadron Leader Bader, having been severely mauled during the Battle of France. When the blitzkrieg began, the squadron had been operating with 1 Squadron at Châteaudun, from which it rapidly withdrew to Le Mans. By the campaign's conclusion what was left of 242 Squadron was at Nantes, without effective leadership, cohesion – or even its ground personnel, which were somewhere between Le Mans and the coast with the adjutant, Flight Lieutenant Peter 'Boozy Mac' MacDonald MP. There had certainly been a crisis of leadership in France, so far as this particular fighter squadron was concerned. The CO, a French Canadian, had a background in Training Command – not as a fighter leader. In the face of Hitler's onslaught inspirational leadership was required – but not the CO or his flight commanders had the ability to provide it. The outcome was inevitable; only nine pilots survived the Fall of France. Douglas clearly had work to do, in order to restore morale and gain 242 Squadron's confidence – for all his faults, it was exactly this kind of challenge that brought out the best in Douglas Bader:

> I found myself … in conjunction with my adjutant, an elderly gentleman of the finest class who had been Member for the Isle of Wight for the past plus 500 years, and had fought in World War One, he took me into a dispersal hut where these chaps were lying about on beds, wearing Mae Wests and flying clothes, and all reading comic strips. He said 'Gentlemen, this is your new Squadron Commander, Squadron Leader Bader' – and for some extraordinary reason, because I had been trained at the RAF College Cranwell, I thought they might stand up. In fact some of them lowered their comics, looked over the top, obviously didn't care for what they saw, put the comics back

After Dunkirk, Bader was promoted to acting squadron leader and posted to command 242 Squadron, flying Hurricanes at Coltishall. Demoralised after a hard time in France, Bader restored morale and by the Battle of Britain's start 242 was fully operational.

> up and went on reading! There was one chap lying with his back to me. He actually turned over, had a look, then turned back again and went on reading! I then told the adjutant that I wanted to see all of the pilots in my office.

During the interval, of an hour and ten minutes, 242 Squadron's new CO took off in Hurricane P2967 on what he described in his log book as 'Practice on type'. More accurately this was a breath-taking display of low-level aerobatics – intended to impress upon the disgruntled pilots that, even without legs, their new CO was no passenger and that things had very much changed.

> They arrived and I gave them what I thought was a reasonable three-minute talk. When finished I said 'Has anybody got anything to say?' There was a long silence, then, from the back of the room a voice said 'Horseshit!' Again, they hadn't taught me at Cranwell what to do in such a situation. As I was getting rather red around the neck and face, and was about to make a bloody fool of myself, the same voice added 'Sir!'

Above and below: Back as a team captain, Squadron Leader Bader was in his element…

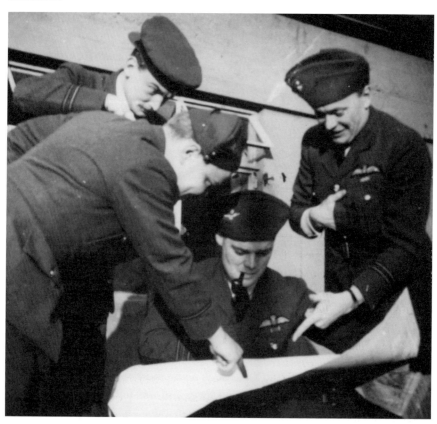

A lively discussion then ensued, in which Douglas was enlightened as to why morale was so poor; even the pilots' clothes, left behind in France, had yet to be replaced, and neither had they been paid for some time. Immediately recognising the urgent need for strong leadership in all aspects, Douglas firstly sent his pilots clothes-shopping in Norwich, personally guaranteeing payment, then established a new command team: Flight Lieutenant Eric Ball was brought in from 19 Squadron to command 'A' Flight, and Flight Lieutenant George Powell-Sheddon, a Cranwellian, came from the Fighter Command Pool to command 'B' Flight. There was already another young British officer flying with 242 Squadron, Pilot Officer Denis Crowley-Milling. An Old Malvernian who had joined the RAFVR, 'Crow' remembered that:

> When he received command of 242 Squadron, Douglas Bader was approaching 30 while the rest of us were around 20 or 21. After France we were in a bad state, but less than a month after Douglas took command the squadron was fully operational – and our morale was high. Fear was always there, of course, but Bader was afraid of nothing. Through personal example and constant encouragement he helped us all conquer our anxieties. You always felt perfectly safe when flying with Douglas Bader. For me, his arrival at Coltishall was the start of eighteen exciting months of operational flying together, an unforgettable experience which helped shape my subsequent career.

In addition to 242 Squadron's pilots' problems, its Hurricanes had suffered too; although eighteen new aircraft were on charge, no spare parts or tools were on the inventory. Douglas's next port of call was the Squadron's Engineering Officer, Warrant Officer Bernard 'Knocker' West. For the next few days, Douglas berated Coltishall's Stores Officer, but his forthright demands for equipment fell upon deaf ears. After a week of this, West informed his CO that stores had cited an obscure regulation confirming a three-month wait before fresh equipment could be ordered. Justifiably on this occasion, Douglas was absolutely furious. In response, on 4 July 1940, he sent an unprecedented signal to 12 Group HQ: '242 Squadron now operational as regards pilots but non-operational repeat non-operational as regards equipment.' He then lurched into the Station Commander's office and showed the flimsy to him. A heated scene ensued, and West could not believe his eyes when he read the signal shortly afterwards. What Douglas failed to tell his boss, but not Mr West, was that a copy had also been sent to

Fighter Command HQ. The response came that evening from the latter. An unhelpful squadron leader concluded by pointing out that Dowding himself was 'furious' – before having the phone virtually rammed down his ear. Two days later Douglas was carpeted before the AOC-in-C himself: Air Chief Marshal Sir Hugh Dowding. Suffice it to say that Douglas got his way; the obstructive stores officer found himself removed from his cushy HQ post, and 242 Squadron's much-needed equipment was soon arriving. To the previously lack-lustre squadron, it was as if Squadron Leader Bader was super-charged and could do *anything*.

Of Douglas's dismissive view of administration, however, 'Woody' Woodhall wrote that:

> Douglas was very apt to cut corners and ignore regulations or interpret them his own way in order to get on with the war. On one occasion when he had offended against some rule, I was given orders from a higher authority to reprove him. He was ordered to report to my office, and when he stumped in and saluted with his usual cheerful grin he noticed that I was wearing my cap and did not tell him to sit down, indicating an official interview. Douglas stood to attention and with an impish grin said 'Woody, you're not going to be rotten to me, are you?' What could I do but laugh, then tell him to sit down? Needless to say the reproof <u>was</u> passed to him as a joke – but the fact that it was passed on proved quite effective. The administrative and operational tasks and problems increased daily, and hampered as we were by a set of peacetime rules and regulations, designed as they were in the main to prevent petty pilfering, it is not surprising that everyone trying to do his job had to cut the red tape in order to get on with the war. In this Douglas Bader and I saw eye-to-eye, and I can state that we backed each other up loyally in this matter of tape-cutting. LM, our AOC, was always on our side too, which was very comforting!

Hard task master though Douglas was, he was in his element and would defend any member of 242 Squadron to the hilt, if necessary:

> I felt they were *mine*, all the pilots and troops. I used to get furious if anyone said anything about them or did anything to them, and I arranged with Norwich Police that they never

put my chaps on a charge but sent the matter to me to deal with. I was tough with them myself, but always closed ranks if anyone else tried to interfere. I suppose I was unreasonable in my attitude to the squadron, but it was an obsession with me and I would not brook interference.

Incredibly, this stance even extended to the Station Commander. When several of 242 Squadron's groundcrew contravened blackout restrictions, Biesegel's punishment was making them sleep in a hangar. This, however, was done without reference to 242 Squadron's CO, who, furious, stormed into the wing commander's office and called him 'a bastard'. Such insubordination was, and is, unthinkable. In the face of such a determined verbal assault the Station Commander backed down – no one, it seemed, could resist the sheer force of Douglas Bader's incredible personality.

On 18 June 1940, Winston Churchill had stirred the nation's spirit with his usually inspirational rhetoric, making perfectly clear what lay ahead:

> The Battle of France is over. I expect that the Battle of Britain is about to begin…. The whole fury and might of the enemy must very soon be turned on us. Hitler knows that he will have to break us in this island or lose the war. If we can stand up to him, all Europe may be free and the life of the world may move forward into broad, sunlit uplands. But if we fail, then the whole world, including the United States, including all that we have known and cared for, will sink into the abyss of a new Dark Age, made more sinister by the lights of perverted science. Let us therefore brace ourselves to our duties, and so bear ourselves that if the British Empire and its Commonwealth should last for a thousand years, men will still say 'This was their finest hour'.

The Battle of Britain predicted by Churchill began on 10 July 1940 – just one day after Squadron Leader Bader declared 242 Squadron fully operational.

Since the Fall of France, the Luftwaffe had amassed its units in France in preparation for a determined aerial assault upon England. Wresting aerial supremacy from the RAF had but one purpose: to facilitate the seaborne invasion of England. Although the Air Ministry decided that Churchill's anticipated 'Battle of Britain' began on 10 July 1940, the two fighter forces had clashed over Channel convoys since 2 July. With convoys frequently chugging around the Wash, Coltishall's squadrons found themselves flying numerous patrols over the supply ships. On 11 July 1940, Douglas attacked, in very bad weather, a Do 17 which escaped in cloud, but was later reported to have crashed in the sea off Cromer. The media made much of this victory by the anonymous legless squadron commander. Already, though, the facts were becoming distorted. An example of this appeared in Worcestershire's *Malvern Gazette* in July 1940, aimed at encouraging donations to the town's Spitfire Fund:

> Remember the story of the young pilot who lost his legs in a crash? Fitted with artificial legs he argued his way back into the RAF; argued his way through the medical boards; argued his way into a squadron, and one day, quite recently, he went up alone and shot a *Dornier* down into the sea. Did he say 'I've given the country my legs; why should I now be expected to give them my neck?' Not a bit! Like all those gallant lads he was ready to give the extra. God bless them for it.

Now Douglas's tenacity and bravery are beyond dispute – but he had certainly not 'given the country my legs'. The circumstances of his crash during peacetime are well documented and by Douglas's own admission was his own fault. This, then, is a prime example of how Douglas was already beginning to be used to raise morale. A legless fighter pilot was inspirational stuff, at a time when the nation needed heroes. The fact was that Douglas Bader's usefulness and contribution to the war effort actually far exceeded fighting the hot war from a Hurricane cockpit – he was, in short, a propagandist's dream and would increasingly find himself used in that direction.

Interestingly, on 20 and 24 July, 66 and 242 Squadrons practised 'wing exercises'. As we have seen, Dowding had already stated that a single squadron would be the largest tactical formation, although training to date had revolved around the flight of just six aircraft. It is difficult to understand, therefore, why 12 Group squadrons were practising in this way – but indicates an early leaning towards large formations, even if contrary to the AOC-in-C's view.

On 29 July 1940, 19 Squadron's 'B' Flight was scrambled, according to the Squadron's Operations Record Book (ORB), 'in a big alarm at Coltishall, when all available squadrons left the ground'. Interestingly, the Spitfires flew in three sections of two – not the stipulated vic of three;

some squadrons were clearly learning fast. The 12 Group Controller was responding to an attack on a convoy off Harwich; 66 Squadron engaged and destroyed two raiders, but 19 and 242 Squadrons made no contact. Incredibly, 12 Group had scrambled thirty fighters to meet this threat – leaving Coltishall defended by a single flight. The wisdom of such a deployment appears questionable – but is further evidence of the attitude in 12 Group towards large formations. Indeed, Wing Commander David Cox was a sergeant pilot with 19 Squadron at the time, and remembered that in June 1940, Leigh-Mallory visited the Squadron, 'who, stabbing his finger at a map on the wall, exclaimed "My fighters will be here, here and here!", from which I now deduce that he always had in mind to intercept the enemy in numbers…'.

Also, on 29 July 1940, the DCAS, Air Vice-Marshal Sholto Douglas, ordered Fighter, Bomber and Coastal Command to make strong attacks against E-Boat bases on the Channel coast, Luftwaffe coastal airfields and gun batteries. Attacks on airfields were to be made immediately after German aircraft had landed following raiding England. The constant enemy air activity over the Pas-de-Calais, however, was making it difficult to anticipate when a raid was forming up, until the German formation struck out across the Channel, and owing to the speeds involved, at that point the Germans were just five minutes from Dover – putting into sharp focus the problems 11 Group had with effecting rapid intercepts. Indeed, the time from a raid being identified and it recrossing the French coast was usually only around thirty minutes. To strike when the German bombers landed, therefore, RAF bomber squadrons would have to be brought to a state of immediate readiness whenever a raid appeared likely. Furthermore, immediately after meeting such an attack, 11 Group would find it difficult to provide sufficient fighters to cover such a counter-attack.

Leigh-Mallory was keen to support this scheme, and despatched 19 Squadron's 'B' Flight to operate from Eastchurch alongside the Spitfires of Wittering's 266 Squadron. At this time, 19 Squadron was trialling the cannon-armed Spitfire Mk IB in an attempt to provide the Spitfire parity with the 20mm Oerlikon-armed Me 109E. Leigh-Mallory intended for 19 Squadron to strafe E-Boats with their cannon, and together with 266 Squadron provide fighter escort to Fairey Battle bombers 'on a beat up of the other side'. The heavy daylight losses to the Battle force in France, however, should already have been sufficient to indicate the folly of such a plan. Fortunately, Dowding's current SASO, Air Vice-Marshal Douglas Evill, having previously served as Bomber Command's SASO, recognised the difficulties involved. After conferring with Air Vice-Marshal Park, Evill concluded that such a policy would be both impractical and imprudent; far better to counter-attack in strength, following extensive reconnaissance. Fortunately, thanks to Evill, Leigh-Mallory's proposed 'beat up' never went ahead – but is clear evidence of Leigh-Mallory and Sholto Douglas already working closely together.

On 31 July 1940, 19 Squadron had occasion to celebrate when Flight Lieutenant Brian Lane, the commander of 'A' Flight, was awarded the DFC. Flight Lieutenant Wallace 'Jock' Cunningham was a pilot officer in Lane's 'A' Flight, and recalled:

> We were lying in the sun at Coltishall along with Douglas Bader and other 242 Squadron pilots. It was before our involvement in the Battle of Britain proper, but Brian had already received a 'gong' for his good leadership of the squadron and general activities at Dunkirk. There was some banter going on and Douglas asked Brian 'What's *that*?' in his usual cocky fashion, thrusting his pipe at Brian's DFC ribbon. '*I* must get one of *those*!' said Bader – and, as we all know, he went on and did just that.

Throughout the latter half of August 1940, the tempo of battle increased over southern England, while for 12 Group's squadrons the battle, such as it was, wore on with little action beyond the monotonous round of convoy protection patrols and chasing the odd raider.

And that is really when problems began.

Chapter Six

'... we were frequently scrambled too late ...'

The Battle of Britain was now really hotting up over the 11 Group area, extensive aerial reconnaissance being followed by heavy attacks on shipping, ports and installations, radar stations and, crucially, Fighter Command's airfields. The main difficulty for Air Vice-Marshal Park and his controllers was identifying diversionary attacks, so as to preserve sufficient reserves to meet the main raid when it came. To intercept coastal attacks, virtually all squadrons at readiness were maintained at forward aerodromes, such as Lympne, Hawkinge, Rochford and Manston, and great vigilance was required to prevent these precious fighters being destroyed on the ground. Park's tactic was to despatch half his available fighters (including all his superior Spitfires) against enemy fighters, the remainder against the bombers. 11 Group clearly had a very difficult balancing act to both maintain a high state of preparedness and pick the right moment to engage. 12 Group's squadrons, however, remained largely occupied with mundane convoy protection patrols and chasing lone raiders.

At Coltishall, Squadron Leader Douglas Bader was bereft, unable to accept that his was a lesser part in what was clearly a critical and historic aerial conflict. The comparative inactivity, the constant hanging around and waiting up in 12 Group was unbearable. Constantly he berated his AOC, imploring Air Vice-Marshal Leigh-Mallory to send 242 Squadron to reinforce 11 Group.

Air Marshal Sir Denis Crowley-Milling:

> Naturally Douglas wanted to get we of 242 Squadron into the action. He used to say 'Why don't they get us airborne when the Germans are building up over the Pas-de-Calais?' He felt that we could then proceed south and meet the enemy formation on the way in.

An extraordinary set of snapshots from the album of Air Marshal Sir Denis Crowley-Milling, showing 242 Squadron idly awaiting the call to scramble at Coltishall. Bader was like a caged tiger, exasperated and being unable to play a key role in the ongoing battle further South.

Douglas's idea, however, was impractical, for a variety of reasons. RDF, for example, was unable to identify when a raid was 'building up' due to the constantly high level of enemy air traffic over the Pas-de-Calais. The only real indication was when a raid began moving out from the French coast – by which time, given the distance involved, it was too late to commit 12 Group's squadrons as he suggested. In addition to having its own geographic area of responsibility, a crucial function of 12 Group's fighters was to protect 11 Group's airfields while Park's fighters were engaged further forward. Moreover, controllers could never be sure if or when a heavy attack would develop against the industrial midlands and the north. The far-sighted merit of maintaining a strong fighter presence throughout the country – instead of simply in the south – was vividly confirmed on 15 August 1940, when a large raiding force attacked northern England from bases in Norway. Seven Fighter Command squadrons, including several from 12 Group, mauled the enemy without loss. The action was the absolute vindication of Dowding's policy. Curiously, given his previous over-reaction to the Harwich threat, Leigh-Mallory only responded to this huge attack with eighteen fighters. Exasperatingly for Douglas, 242 Squadron was situated too far south to be of assistance.

So heavy were the attacks on southern England too that day, though, that 11 Group requested assistance from 12 Group; Wing Commander David Cox:

19 Squadron was scrambled from the Duxford Sector to intercept a raid on Martlesham Heath airfield, near Ipswich. This raid was mounted by some twenty-five Me 110s of Erprobungsgruppe 210, led by their brilliant Kommodore, Erich Rubensdorfer. The enemy's approach went completely undetected until they were only a few minutes from their target. Only three Hurricanes of 17 Squadron managed to get from Martlesham before the 110s arrived. Our chances of intercepting the raid, however, were nil – taking into account that the distance from our airfield at Fowlmere to Martlesham was sixty air miles. Taking an optimistic speed for our Spitfires of 300 mph, it would take twelve minutes from take-off to reach Martlesham. I doubt that at our altitude, 2,000ft, our cannon-armed Spitfires were capable of that speed, as its maximum speed was not reached until 19,000ft. I would suggest that 280 mph was the maximum possible speed for height, but even at 300 mph the squadron could not achieve the impossible.

Left: Wing Commander Woodhall shared Bader's view that 12 Group should reinforce 11 Group and attack in strength.

Below: 12 Group failed, however, to prevent 11 Group's airfields north of the Thames being bombed, infuriating Air Vice-Marshal Park and sparking a row between the two groups.

Air Vice-Marshal Park, however, was incensed by 12 Group's failure to protect his airfields. This was unfair – no one was at fault, in fact. This was a well-executed raid on a coastal airfield, which was all over in minutes. Again, time, speed and distance was the issue.

The following day, 16 August 1940, Flight Lieutenant Lane led his Spitfires of 19 Squadron's 'A' Flight into action against a formation of ZG 26 Me 110s off Harwich. In spite of the Spitfires' cannon stoppages, three 110s were claimed destroyed and one probable – a remarkably accurate assessment, in fact, given that the actual enemy losses were two destroyed and one damaged. That day, Douglas intercepted two 'X-Raids', but both transpired to be friendly aircraft. His mounting frustration can only be imagined – and it was 19, not his own 242, Squadron that was now easily the most combat experienced unit in 12 Group.

Down south, the battle raged, 11 Group's airfields beginning to take a battering. Park gave his controllers very clear instructions regarding how he wanted the battle fought – emphasising that in order to preserve their fighters, only the minimum number of squadrons were to be engaged, and that if necessary, in order to protect the 11 Group airfields of Debden, North Weald and Hornchurch, reinforcements to patrol and protect them should be requested directly from 12 Group or via Fighter Command HQ. Previous accounts have often accused 11 Group of 'hogging' the Battle of Britain – but clearly that was not the case. Park was simply adhering to Dowding's strategy – which included being reinforced, whenever necessary, by 12 Group. Later, Park reported upon the employment of RAF fighters during the period 8–18 August 1940, concluding that:

> Results [of air combat] were satisfactory ... as much of this fighting took place over the sea, casualties were higher than they would have been if over land. The results of air combat were good because the enemy fighters were frequently too high to protect the bombers ... our fighter defences proved too good for the enemy, because on 18 August the Germans withdrew their dive-bombers, Ju 87s, and there was a break of five days in intensive operations.

On 17 August 1940, 310 (Czech) Squadron became operational at Duxford. The Czechs rapidly became popular and earned respect.

Wing Commander 'Woody' Woodhall:

> Most of the Czechs had reported in French uniform, having fought with the French until France fell. Upon arrival they spoke little English and had to be converted onto Hurricanes. They were therefore provided an English squadron commander, Squadron Leader Douglas Blackwood, and English flight commanders, namely Flight Lieutenants Sinclair and Jeffries, in addition to an English flying instructor and interpreter. The Czech CO was Squadron Leader Sacha Hess, who was quite famous in Czech air force circles. Much older than the rest, at 45, he was a first-class pilot and a dedicated fighter.

After some success on 30 August 1940, enabling Bader to opine that he, although only recently returned to the service, knew best, Leigh-Mallory authorised the creation of a 'Duxford Wing', firstly of three squadrons, the Hurricanes of 242 and the British-led Czechoslovaks of 310 Squadron…

… and the Spitfires of 19 Squadron based at Fowlmere.

Our first problem was to overcome the language difficulty, so I rang the BBC with the result that the interpreter and I spent a day at Broadcasting House where we recorded a series of orders, first in English followed by Czech, covering everything from 'Scramble' to 'Pancake'. The BBC quickly sent us several copies of these records, and in a very short time the Czechs were conversant with orders in English alone.

310 Squadron had a spare Hurricane (needless to say the oldest and slowest) which was always at my disposal, and as a result, albeit on the few occasions when I could spare the time from my other duties as Station Commander and Sector Controller, I flew on operations with the squadron as rear-end Charlie.

Squadron Leader Douglas Blackwood:

I cannot speak highly enough of the Czechs' fighting qualities, although they did not always know what was expected of them; they were very keen on attacking enemy aircraft whenever they saw them, no matter what the circumstances.

Flight Lieutenant Gordon Sinclair:

I have nothing but praise for my fellow Czech pilots who were a wonderful bunch of people, totally determined to kill Germans. They went about this task with great enthusiasm and courage, and I found it tremendously comforting in battle to be surrounded by such pilots!

Corporal Bill Kirk was a clerk attached to 310 Squadron:

The Czechs were first class and anxious to have a go. It became a tradition for British personnel serving with 310 Squadron to replace our top tunic buttons with a Czech Air Force example. I was among the personnel sent to form 310, and our office processed all the admin from leave passes to Air Ministry orders. Working hours were unspecified, you just went to work until the job was done. I lived in the barrack block at Duxford and we all got on famously with the Czechs. They were always keeping fit, playing volley ball, and were very keen generally.

For us on the ground it was tremendously exciting knowing that our aircraft were going into action, and upon return we all looked anxiously for those Hurricanes with blown gun port patches, indicating that the guns had been fired. It could also be distressing, talking to a chap in the Mess only for him to be a 'goner' the next day. Our office was almost on the airfield, so we were very close to the pilots and aircraft. They were exciting times.

Pilot Officer 'Teddy' Morten:

I received my commission in late June 1940, and was posted to RAF Duxford for supernumerary duties in Operations. The VR letters on my tunic still shone brightly, they were so new. Several of us arrived together, including an elderly pilot officer who was a retired solicitor. We were all introduced to the Station Commander, Wing Commander Woodhall, who noticed that the old lawyer was wearing a Boer War medal ribbon but none from the Great War. When asked where his 1914–18 ribbons were, the old boy replied that he had been too old for active service in that conflict! In view of his obviously extensive life experience, the Wing Commander made him Assistant Adjutant to 19 Squadron, to help the Adjutant write casualty letters.

At that time, the Duxford Sector Controllers were Wing Commander Woodhall, Squadron Leader K.C. Horn (who had commanded a Strutter squadron in the Great War and whose brother was a successful Sopwith Camel squadron commander), Squadron Leader Marsden, Squadron Leader Stanley Cooper, and Squadron Leader Livivosk. As dawn broke each day, if on duty at Ops 'B', the Controller would be resting (i.e. asleep and only to be disturbed if necessary). Straight after dawn I would telephone Wing Commander Woodhall on his direct line and inform him of the situation over southern England. There was dire trouble if ever 'Woody' wasn't given this brief first!

As an embryonic controller, a 'Wingless Wonder' or 'Penguin', I always made it my business to get to know as many pilots as possible, so as to gain their trust and understand the problems they faced in the air. All of us on the ground, of course, wanted to help them as much as possible.

The WAAF plotters in Duxford's Operations Room were known as 'Woody's Beauty Chorus'.

Jill 'Half Pint' Pepper:

> In 12 Group there were long periods with little action, so we got plenty of time to chat to the Observer Corps on our headphones. Voices, however, can be very misleading and we often got a shock when meeting the bloke in person!
>
> After Dunkirk things got livelier and we were kept busy on our watches, concentration and calmness being essential to get the plotting right. The planes went up and it was always exciting when we heard 'Tally Ho!' over the intercom. We felt then that we were doing our bit to help stop the bloody Huns. It was sad, though, when some of our aircraft failed to return, even if we did not know the pilots personally.
>
> There were often dances in the big hangar and whenever I hear 'In the Mood' I'm back there again and can see the Station Controller, Wing Commander Woodhall, complete with monocle, playing his saxophone with great enthusiasm!

On 19 August 1940, Air Vice-Marshal Park took stock of the battle to date and issued a memorandum to his controllers in 11 Group:

> a) Despatch fighters to engage large enemy formations over land or within gliding distance of the coast. During the next two or three weeks, we cannot afford to lose pilots through forced landings in the sea;
>
> b) Avoid sending fighters out over the sea to intercept reconnaissance aircraft or small formations of enemy fighters;
>
> c) Despatch a pair of fighters to intercept single reconnaissance aircraft that come inland. If clouds are favourable, put a patrol one or two fighters over an aerodrome which the enemy are approaching in clouds;

d) Against mass attacks coming inland, dispatch a minimum number of squadrons to engage enemy fighters. Our main objective is to engage enemy bombers, particularly those approaching under the lowest cloud layer;

e) If all our squadrons around London are off the ground engaging mass attacks, ask No 12 Group or Command Controller to provide squadrons to patrol aerodromes Debden, North Weald, Hornchurch;

f) If heavy attacks have crossed the coast and are proceeding towards aerodromes, put a squadron or even the Sector Training Flight, to patrol under clouds over every sector aerodrome;

g) No 303 (Polish) Squadron can provide two sections for patrol of inland aerodromes, especially while the older squadrons are on the ground refuelling when enemy formations are flying overland;

h) No 1 (Canadian) Squadron can be used in the same manner by day as other fighter squadrons.

These new instructions made clear how the battle was to be fought. They also provide clarity concerning any allegation that 11 Group was hogging the battle deliberately. It was not. Park was complying perfectly with the System and clearly not only receptive to requesting reinforcements from 12 Group, that was an important component of the overall plan. Coincidentally, on the same day, five bombs were dropped on Coltishall, damaging a new hangar and killing two men. Although a nuisance raid by a solitary aircraft, this underlined the defensive commitment north of the 11 Group area.

On 21 August 1940, the Luftwaffe maintained pressure on the beleaguered defenders by making numerous scattered raids across a broad front. A number of raiders were active over Norfolk. While returning with his Section to Coltishall upon conclusion of another training flight, Douglas heard his friend Squadron Leader Rupert Leigh of 66 Squadron being vectored to intercept an 'X-Raid'. Without having been instructed by the Controller to do so, Squadron Leader Bader broke away and headed south-east – towards Yarmouth and the action. Arriving before the Spitfires, Douglas peered through a thin veil of cloud at 8,000ft and saw the now familiar silhouette of a Do 17. Climbing through the 'clag', the raider's sharp-eyed rear gunner spotted and opened fire on the rapidly closing Hurricane. Douglas briefly returned fire, the 'Flying

Pencil' subsequently disappearing into thick cloud. Although believing he had hit the bomber, Douglas made no combat claim. Concurrently with Douglas's combat, 242 Squadron's Blue Section was also in action close-by; Sub-Lieutenant Gardner, Flight Lieutenant Powell-Sheddon and Pilot Officer Latta sharing the destruction of a 2/KG 2 Do 17 which crashed at Conifer Hill, Starston. Five other Dorniers were also confirmed destroyed over eastern England or off its coastline that day by 56 and 611 Squadrons. Several days later, Douglas was informed by the Coltishall Intelligence Officer that the body of a Do 17 crewman had been recovered from the sea in the area of his inconclusive combat; the dead enemy airman's watch had stopped at the time concerned: 1215 hrs. On that basis, the CO of 242 Squadron was credited with having destroyed this bomber.

On 26 August 1940, Park reported to HQ Fighter Command:-

> ... the heaviest casualties to pilots and aircraft were experienced among reinforcing squadrons that had been formed in the North since the outbreak of war. During the past two months' fighting over our own territory, our former experience has been confirmed, as will be seen from the figures given below.

> 2. In order to keep our casualties in pilots and fighter aircraft to a minimum, especially during the next critical month, it is strongly recommended that only highly trained and experienced eight-gun fighter squadrons be sent from northern groups to exchange with depleted squadrons in the South of England, because of the German practice of employing fighter screens and close escorts to mass formations of bombers in this part of the country.

> 3. The marked difference in results shown in the table below can hardly be due to the difference in standard of fighting efficiency of northern groups. It is thought probably to be due to the fact that 13 Group have always made a practice of selecting squadrons for temporary duty in the South from among their most experienced squadrons, because of the appreciation of the heavy fighting up to date in the South of England:

Squadron	Period under 11 Grp	Enemy Aircraft Destroyed	Own Casualties			Total
			Kld.	Msg.	Wnd.	
41	26/7 – 8/8	13	–	1	–	1 (13 Group)
152	12/7 – 4/8	4	–	–	1	1 (13 Group)
602	17/8 – date	26	–	1	1	2 (13 Group)
266	12/8 – 21/8	9	2	4	–	6 (12 Group)
616	19/8 – date	8	–	6	1	7 (12 Group)

4. Sector commanders have commented favourably on the high standard of flying and fighting efficiency of several squadrons of 13 Group that have been sent South on exchange or on temporary duty during the past few months.

Park added that during the Dunkirk fighting, the northern groups had considered 11 Group 'a good training ground in air fighting for less experienced squadrons … the practice proved expensive in pilots and aircraft in the instance of newly formed squadrons'.

More recent research provides updated statistics:

Squadron	Period under 11 Grp	Own Casualties				Total
		Kld.	Msg.	Wnd.	POW	
41	26/7 – 8/8	–	1	1	–	2
152	12/7 – 4/8	–	1	1	–	2
602	17/8 – 26/8	–	–	4	–	4
266	12/8 – 21/8	4	2	2	–	6
616	19/8 – 26/8	2	1	4	1	7

It is also interesting to note when these squadrons were formed and received their Spitfires:

Squadron	Date Formed or reformed	Date Spitfires received
41	RF 1/4/39	1/39
152	RF 2/10/39	12/39
602 (AAF)	F 12/9/25	5/39
266	RF 30/10/39	1/40
616 (AAF)	F 1/11/38	10/39

'... WE WERE FREQUENTLY SCRAMBLED TOO LATE ...'

The Fighter Command Order of Battle on 8 August 1940, details squadrons in 12 Group, providing for a deeper analysis:

Squadron	Date Formed or reformed	Rec'd monoplane fighters	Length of monoplane operating to August 1940
73	RF 15/3/37	7/38 (Hurricane)	2 years, 1 month
19	RF 1/4/23	8/38 (Spitfire)	2 years
46	RF 3/3/36	3/39 (Hurricane)	1 year, 6 months
611 (AAF)	F 10/2/36	5/39 (Spitfire)	1 year, 3 months
616 (AAF)	F 1/11/38	10/39 (Spitfire)	10 months
66	RF 20/7/36	10/39 (Spitfire)	10 months
266	RF 30/10/39	1/40 (Spitfire)	8 months
242	RF 30/10/39	2/40 (Hurricane)	6 months
229	RF 4/10/39	3/40 (Hurricane)	5 months
222	RF 4/10/39	3/40 (Spitfire)	5 months

This exercise illuminates just how little experience most squadrons had on their new Spitfires and Hurricanes. Dowding's system of rotating squadrons in and out of the primary combat area provided for squadrons there being maintained largely at full-strength. Replenished squadrons, though, lacked one crucial factor: actual combat experience, and were at their most vulnerable upon return to 11 Group. Interestingly, in sending 266 and 616 Squadrons to 11 Group, Leigh-Mallory was not providing his most experienced fighter units, but his joint fifth and sixth. Indeed, at no time during the Battle of Britain would he send either 19 or 242 Squadrons to 11 Group. As our tale unfolds, the reader will appreciate that had 242 Squadron been sent south, the need to write this book is unlikely to have arisen.

Returning to 26 August 1940, the day saw yet more heavy fighting over the south-east. Between 1430 and 1443 hrs, three German formations, comprising sixty, twenty and twelve aircraft, had assembled over Dunkirk. By 1450 hrs these raiders were all over the eastern approaches to the Dover Straits and bound for the Thames Estuary. Shortly before 1500 hrs, two of these raids were crossing Kent's north-east corner, their target clearly being the airfields north of the Thames Estuary. Eight 11 Group squadrons were scrambled – and help requested from 12 Group. Consequently at 1515 hrs, Flight Lieutenant Wilf Clouston of 19 Squadron led 'All available aircraft in air' from Fowlmere, the Duxford satellite. At nearby

Duxford, Squadron Leader Sacha Hess took off with the Hurricanes of his 310 Squadron. Quarter of an hour before, however, combat had been joined over Whitstable, from which point on the defenders fought a running battle between the Isle of Sheppey and Colchester. Only the most northern raiding force, though, was intercepted before bombing its target – Debden airfield. 310 Squadron, originally instructed to patrol North Weald, was vectored to Debden, arriving in time to attack the enemy and destroy two bombers. 19 Squadron, however, 'did not contact the enemy'.

Sergeant David Cox flew on that sortie in Flying Officer Brinsden's Green Section:

> 19 Squadron were told to patrol Debden at 10,000ft, to intercept a raid on that airfield. The actual raid came in at 1,000ft – and as 19 were at 10,000ft above 10/10ths cloud, saw nothing of the raid. It appears that the Observer Corps reported the E/A coming in at 1,000ft but the 11 Group Controller thought this a mistake and consequently told 19 to patrol at 10,000ft. The later report was that 'the Spitfires from Fowlmere were slow at getting off the ground'. This was certainly not the case.

The official Air Historical Branch narrative, however, insists that 'the Germans approached the airfield above the clouds, which were from between 5,000–7,000ft, and then glided through them to attack'. Even if that was so and the Germans did not come in and attack from 1,000ft, the point was when 19 Squadron arrived, having been scrambled only five minutes before Debden was bombed, the Germans had already descended into the cloud, bombed Debden and disappeared. The distance between Fowlmere and Debden is forty miles. Even taking a speed of 300 mph, it would take thirteen minutes for 19 Squadron to reach Debden. Air Vice-Marshal Park was furious that, again, 12 Group had failed to prevent an all-important sector station being damaged, but this, it would appear, was due to 19 Squadron having been scrambled too late – because 11 Group asked for assistance too late, and unanticipated German tactics owing to the band of cloud.

Pilot Officer 'Teddy' Morten, Ops 'B' Controller, Duxford:

> The 11 Group Controller definitely called for 12 Group too late. By the end of August there was a certain amount

Above: 19 Squadron's exceptional CO, Squadron Leader Brian Lane DFC, seated in left-hand corner, beneath window, with a 'gaggle' of 19 and 616 Squadron pilots at Fowlmere in September 1940.

Right: Flight Lieutenant H.E. 'Teddy' Morten, an Ops 'B' Controller at Duxford – who well-remembers the Duxford Wing failing to patrol as instructed, instead undertaking free-roving fighter sweeps over Kent, throwing the defences into confusion. On one occasion Bader and Woodhall kept up such a volume of radio traffic that 11 Group was unable to break in and urgently vector the wing to North Weald – which was bombed with loss of life.

of hostility between the respective operations rooms. 11 Group accused us of always being too late; we said they always called for us too late. Whenever 12 Group squadrons arrived after the action we would have to suffer sarcastic remarks from the 11 Group Controller – so the situation was not good.

Wing Commander 'Woody' Woodhall:

> we were frequently scrambled too late because we were not allowed to fly over 11 Group unless asked for by them. It was frustrating to see an enemy raid plotted on our board, obviously going for a target in 11 Group, then to wait on the ground, pilots in their cockpits, for fifteen or twenty minutes – and finally be scrambled too late to get into the fight.
>
> In those early days, the RDF information was not very accurate, particularly regarding height and numbers of aircraft, and of course there was a time lag of several minutes before the information reached the Sector Operations Room. The Sector Controller therefore had to use intelligent guesswork to direct his fighters on an intercepting course and also to position them up-sun of the enemy. To begin with, the operations table in 12 Group only extended to the north bank of the Thames, and enemy plots were only passed to us when they reached this point. In 11 Group, however, plots were received while the enemy was still over France. Command Operations Room had the whole picture, of course, but in my opinion there was never enough liaison between 11 and 12 Groups.
>
> Luckily, Wing Commander Victor Beamish, the sector commander at North Weald, was a good friend of mine, so I extended our operations table to the south as far into France as St Omer. As soon as North Weald was informed of enemy activity we kept the tie-line telephone open, and plots were passed from North Weald to us at Duxford. In that way we obtained earlier warning, but in spite of this we were frequently scrambled too late because we were not allowed to fly over 11 Group unless asked for by them. It was frustrating to see an enemy raid plotted on our board, obviously going for a target in 11 Group, then to wait on the ground, with the pilots in their cockpits, for fifteen or twenty minutes – and finally be scrambled too late to get into the fight.

On 27 August 1940, an angry Air Vice-Marshal Park issued instructions to 11 Group controllers concerning 'Reinforcement from 10 and 12 Groups'. While 10 Group had provided every assistance and fully cooperated, Park charged that 'the same desire' had not been shown by 12 Group, despatching their squadrons to locations other than that instructed by the 11 Group controller – leading to failures to intercept the enemy. On two occasions, the 11 Group Commander charged, referring to the incidents involving 19 Squadron on both 19 and 26 August, 'our airfields were heavily bombed'. In both cases, however, the available evidence firmly points to 19 Squadron having made all haste to exactly where instructed – but arriving late owing to time and distance. Park continued that when offers of help had proactively been extended by 12 Group, Leigh-Mallory's fighters had not patrolled where requested. From this point on, therefore, 11 Group Controllers were ordered to direct requests for 12 Group assistance only when incoming raids were 160 plus, and not talk direct to 12 Group HQ at Hucknall but to the Command Controller at Fighter Command HQ. Park decided that such a system would mean 'obtaining assistance' would be 'a little slower', but would ensure that 12 Group's fighters 'are in fact placed where they can be of most assistance'. Park also wrote and complained about 12 Group to Fighter Command's SASO, Air Vice-Marshal Evill – who did nothing. Had he placed the matter before Dowding, and had the AOC-in-C intervened decisively at this stage, subsequent sorry events would not have happened. It is safe to say, however, that it was on this date that relations between 11 and 12 Groups broke down.

This was a time of real crisis and great stress, so Air Vice-Marshal Park's reaction is understandable. His subsequent report made clear the situation with his airfields:

> Contrary to general belief and official reports, the enemy's bombing attacks by day did extensive damage to five of our forward aerodromes, and to six of our seven sector stations. The damage to forward aerodromes was so severe that Manston and Lympne were on several occasions for days quite unfit for operating fighters.
>
> Biggin Hill was so severely damaged that only one squadron could operate from there, and the remaining two squadrons had to be placed under the control of adjacent sectors for over a week. Had the enemy continued his heavy attacks against the adjacent sectors and knocked out their operations rooms or telephone communications, the fighter defences of London would have been in a parlous state during the last critical phase, when heavy attacks have been directed against the capital.

The sector operations rooms have on three occasions been put out of action, either by direct hits or by damage to GPO cables, and all sectors took into use their emergency operations rooms, which were not only too small to house the essential personnel, but had never been provided with the proper scale of GPO landlines to enable normal operations of three squadrons per sector. In view of this grave deficiency, arrangements were made to establish alternative sector operations rooms within five miles of each aerodrome, and work is now proceeding on the highest priority.

At several important aerodromes and sectors, enemy bombing has put out of action the station's organisation by destroying telephone communications, buildings etc. Fortunately the enemy switched his raids from aerodromes onto industrial and other objectives, and gave a short respite during which the station organisation at bombed aerodromes was completely reorganised.

The attacks on our fighter aerodromes soon proved that the Air Ministry's arrangements for labour and equipment to quickly repair aerodrome surfaces were absolutely inadequate, and this has been the subject of numerous signals and letters during the last four weeks.

On this occasion, Dowding did not support Park's criticism of the Air Ministry, stating in his covering report, 'although the scale of attack certainly exceeded the capacity of the works organisation existing at the outset, this was rapidly strengthened, and I do not wish to express any dissatisfaction with the measures taken to effect this improvement.' Park's report, however, offended the DCAS, Air Vice-Marshal Douglas, convincing him that the commander of 11 Group should be replaced. It was not a good move.

On 28 August 1940, Leigh-Mallory began sending 611 Squadron's Spitfires from Digby to the Duxford sector, to operate out of Fowlmere with those of 19 Squadron; the Hurricanes of the new Czech 310 Squadron remained at readiness at nearby Duxford. Duxford was 12 Group's closest station to London and therefore offered the greatest chance of action. The move may also have been to increase the chances of 12 Group successfully responding to an assistance shout from 11 Group by placing more fighters closer to the action. Meanwhile, 66 and 242 Squadrons remained relatively inactive further north at Coltishall. For Douglas, this situation was absolutely intolerable. He was beside himself. His squadron had trained hard, drawn blood, and was bursting with high morale. Feeling like a caged tiger, he sulked and ranted to anyone who would listen about Fighter Command's apparent stupidity in not committing 242 Squadron to the battle raging further south.

Across the Channel, following heavy bomber losses, Reichsmarschall Göring had insisted that his fighters provide an inflexible close-escort service – and concentrated them in the Pas-de-Calais. For the renewed assault, this gave Generalfeldmarschall Kesselring an apparently overwhelming number of fighters for the great daylight battles over England that lay ahead. For Douglas Bader, the wait for the action he so craved was nearly over.

Chapter Seven

'Heartiest congratulations on a first class show. Well done 242'

30 August 1940 would be a significant day for Squadron Leader Bader, to say the least.

Up with the lark that morning, Major Adolf Galland's Me 109 pilots of JG 26 flew an early 'freie' hunt over Kent, which the defenders sensibly ignored, as was a similar sweep. It was obvious to the defenders that this would be a day of high activity. At 1100 hrs forty He 111s and thirty Do 17s, escorted by nearly 100 fighters, were incoming over the Kentish coast. 151 Squadron was first to react to the threat, destroying two bombers but losing two Hurricanes and pilots, one being the Squadron's new CO, Squadron Leader Eric 'Whizzy' King.

222 Squadron's Spitfires were patrolling over Gravesend, but were bounced by Me 109s; Sergeant Iain Hutchinson:

> It was the first time we had engaged the enemy since our arrival at Hornchurch only the previous day, and was the usual scenario: the Me 109s were higher and knew exactly what they were doing, while we were just learning the ropes. I didn't even see the one that hit me.

Fortunately Sergeant Hutchinson, who was unhurt, managed to crash land his Spitfire near Hornchurch.

According to the 222 Squadron ORB, 'the squadron was very positively engaged in operations and flew three patrols during the day. Sergeant Johnson was killed, Flight Lieutenant Matheson and Sergeant Edridge were wounded.' During those three sorties, No 222 lost a total of six Spitfires destroyed and three damaged in yet another example of a 'green' squadron being roughly handled while still adjusting to the completely different tempo of combat over southern England.

Another squadron, 603, fresh to 11 Group was also in action, over Deal; the CO, Squadron Leader Denholm, was shot down and baled out, as was Sergeant Sarre later in the day.

The Hurricanes of 253 Squadron were also new to 11 Group, having arrived at Kenley from Prestwick only the day before. During this morning's fighting, this similarly 'green' squadron suffered three Hurricanes damaged and three destroyed. Two pilots were killed; Pilot Officer David Jenkins was machine-gunned by German fighters while hanging beneath his parachute, and 19-year-old Pilot Officer Colin Francis was posted missing (the latter would not be found until forty-one years after the Battle of Britain, when his aircraft and remains were recovered from a field at Wrotham in Kent). That afternoon, the squadron lost another pilot killed and two more aircraft damaged.

Me 109s also gave 616 Squadron trouble, which had already taken a battering; over West Malling, Me 109s attacked the squadron head-on, shooting down Pilot Officer Jack Bell, who was killed, and Sergeant Hopewell's Spitfire was damaged when he overshot the runway upon returning to Kenley.

As these raids withdrew, fresh waves of enemy fighters and bombers were incoming at twenty minute intervals, provoking further combat. Indeed, the scale of fighting was such that Air Vice-Marshal Leigh-Mallory, whose 19 and 310 Squadrons were patrolling over the 11 Group airfields of Debden and Biggin Hill, decided to send one of Coltishall's squadrons to Duxford, where it would remain at readiness. Squadron Leader Douglas Bader's 242 Squadron, therefore, at last flew south to Duxford – but while en route was for some unknown reason recalled. Douglas, who had brooded, sulked and stormed about 12 Group's lack of action, was fuming. Upon return, he immediately harangued the Controller over the phone, who, a short while later, ordered 242 Squadron off again. Arriving at Duxford without further incident, Bader and his Canadians settled down to await the call for action that they were so desperate for.

At 1600 hrs, 300 plus enemy aircraft were reported over Kent and the Thames Estuary, the raiders splitting up to attack the airfields at Kenley, North Weald, Hornchurch, Debden, Lympne, Detling and Biggin Hill. At 1620 hrs, sixty He 111s of I/KG 1 and II/KG 53, escorted by Me 110s, crossed the coast north of the Thames. Anticipating an attack on the Sector Stations in that area, the 11 Group Controller requested reinforcements from 12 Group. At 1623 hrs, therefore, Wing Commander Woodhall scrambled 242 Squadron, Squadron Leader Bader leading fourteen Hurricanes off from Duxford with orders to patrol North Weald at 15,000ft.

The enemy formation next showed its true intention; I/KG 1 headed for the Vauxhall Motor Works and aerodrome at Luton, while II/KG 53, being the larger of the two raiding parties, began to fight its way to the Handley Page aircraft factory at Radlett. At 1625 hrs, 56 Squadron was scrambled from North Weald, and 1 Squadron from Northolt. At 1655 hrs, two Spitfires of 222 Squadron were sent up from Hornchurch, while Squadron Leader Harry Hogan's 501 Squadron's Hurricanes had already scrambled from Gravesend. At 1650 hrs, while flying east over Chatham, 501 Squadron sighted a large force of He 111s, sub-divided into staffeln, each in an arrowhead pattern. According to the Squadron's combat report:

> The bombers were at 15,000ft and flying West, South of the Thames Estuary towards London. Stepped up behind them were formations of Me 109s and 110s. The enemy aircraft turned north over Southend, and the squadron circled around them, attacking the second vic head-on. This broke up, and one He 111 jettisoned its bombs. Another was pursued by two of our fighters and landed on the water near the *Girdler* lightship. Another crashed in Southend. Our aircraft were not attacked by fighters, which were some distance behind.

Shortly after take-off, 1 Squadron sighted six enemy aircraft 'north of London', which it prepared to attack, but fortunately recognised them as Blenheims before any gun buttons were thumbed. Upon breaking away, Squadron Leader Pemberton's pilots saw the enemy formation; thirty to forty bombers protected by a similar number of fighters, in no standard formation from 12,000 to 25,000ft. 1 Squadron's subsequent attack was carried out with each pilot acting independently; Sergeant Merchant:

> I was No 2 of Red Section and upon sighting enemy followed my Section Leader in line astern. After attacking a Do 17, which was in company with another E/A, an Me 110 dived on me from astern. Breaking away, I shook him off, and then saw ahead a single He 111K. Climbing and going ahead, I attacked from the beam. On the second attack the port engine stopped. At this moment a Hurricane from another squadron dived on the rear of the He 111 and got in a burst. Again attacking from the front I got in a long burst, and a man jumped by parachute. A further two parachutists jumped after about one minute, as I put in another burst. The aircraft dived down and crashed in the middle of a road near a cemetery to the east of Southend.

HEARTIEST CONGRATULATIONS ON A FIRST CLASS SHOW

The He 111 claimed by Sergeant Marchant crashed at Lifstan Way, Southend; it was the same raider claimed by 501 Squadron, so this is a prime example of how one actual enemy loss became two, as it were, and so on.

1 Squadron's Pilot Officer Pat Hancock:

> I pursued the main body of enemy aircraft. One He 111 was lagging behind. I gained height and prepared to attack it. Before doing so, however, a Spitfire did an astern attack of about five seconds duration. I then went in and fired several long bursts at each engine in turn. I observed smoke, oil and flames coming from each engine. I did not follow the aircraft to the ground as a vic of Me 110s appeared to be attacking me. I evaded them and returned to base.

Again, the He 111 attacked by Hancock is believed to have been that which came to grief at Lifstan Way. The Spitfire mentioned was no doubt one of the two 222 Squadron machines involved: Flying Officer Cutts and Sergeant Davis also claimed a He 111 'probable' in that area.

1 Squadron's Sergeant Clowes also claimed an He 111 that 'emitted smoke and some flames', reporting that on his second pass the bomber's 'perspex nose exploded', although this too was the Lifstan Way raider. Another shared kill was the 5/KG 53 He 111 that crashed at Colne Engaine, near Halstead: this bomber was first attacked and damaged by 1 Squadron's Pilot Officer Matthews before being finished off by 56 Squadron's Flight Lieutenant Gracie (the North Weald sector commander, that indomitable Irishman Wing Commander Victor Beamish, was flying with 56 Squadron and claimed an Me 110 'probable' during this engagement). 1 Squadron's CO, Squadron Leader Pemberton, attacked an Me 110 'in company with a Hurricane of LE squadron', which was one of two 110s that crashed at Ponders End, to the east of Enfield. 'LE' were the code letters of Squadron Leader Bader's No 242 Squadron. This is significant.

Romantic and exaggerated accounts of this action claim that 242 Squadron was ordered to patrol North Weald at 15,000ft but instead climbed to 19,000ft, Bader flying twenty miles west of his allotted position so as to have the sun behind him. Consequently attacking from the sun, 242 Squadron executed the perfect 'bounce'. The 242 Squadron combat report, however, offers a slightly different view:

> Squadron 242 was ordered at 1623 hrs from Duxford to patrol North Weald at 15,000ft on a vector 190°, just north of North

Weald. They received a vector of 340°. Three aircraft were noticed to the right of the formation, so the Squadron Leader detached Blue Section to investigate.

These three aircraft were almost certainly some of the Blenheims reported by 1 Squadron, and the changing vector was in response to the enemy's changing course. The Coltishall Intelligence Officer, Flight Lieutenant Maybaum, continued his report:

> Green Leader then drew attention to a large enemy formation on their left so the rest of the squadron turned and saw a vast number of aeroplanes flying in an easterly direction. These were recognised to be from 70 – 100 E/A, twin-engine and in tight formation, stepped up at 12,000ft, after which there was a gap of 1,000ft, then another swarm of twin-engine machines stepped up from about 15,000ft to 20,000ft.

The foregoing report indicates that Squadron Leader Bader actually complied with instructions, his own report confirming this, adding that '242 Squadron had the height advantage on the lower group and as it was obviously impossible to attack all the enemy it was decided to attack down sun on the lower group.'

Maybaum's report continued:

> Green Section were ordered to attack the top of the lower formation; Red and Yellow Sections were ordered into line astern. It seemed impossible to order any formation attack. The Squadron Leader dived straight into the middle of the formation closely followed by Red Two and Red Three; the packed formation broke up and a dogfight ensued. Squadron Leader Bader saw three Me 110s do climbing turns to the left and three to the right. Their tactics appeared to be to climb in turns until they were nearly stalling above the tail of Squadron Leader Bader's aircraft. Squadron Leader Bader fired a short burst into the Me 110 at practically point-blank range and the E/A burst into flames and disintegrated almost immediately. Squadron Leader Bader continued his zoom and saw another Me 110 below and so turned in behind it and got a very easy shot at about 100 to 150 yards range. After the E/A had

received Squadron Leader Bader's first burst of from two to four seconds, the enemy pilot avoided further action by putting the stick violently forwards and backwards.

Squadron Leader Bader got in another burst and saw pieces of the enemy's starboard wing fly off; then the whole starboard wing went on fire and the E/A went down burning in a spiral dive. Squadron Leader Bader then saw in his mirror another Me 110; he did a quick turn and noticed five or six white streams coming out of forward-firing guns; the E/A immediately put his nose down and was lost, but subsequently seen far below. Squadron Leader Bader saw nothing around him, called Duxford and was told to land.

Red Two, Pilot Officer Willie McKnight, went into attack with Squadron Leader Bader; he got behind an Me 110 and opened fire at 100 yards, enemy aircraft bursting into flames and crashing. After a beam attack on a formation of He 111s, Red Two turned the tables on an Me 110, which had attacked him from behind, chasing the enemy machine from 10,000 to 1,000ft. From just 30 yards, McKnight opened fire; the 110 crashed at Enfield Sewage Farm, Ponders End. After the initial Section attack, Red Three, Pilot Officer Denis Crowley-Milling, damaged an He 111, which Pilot Officer Hart confirmed having seen go down in flames. Yellow One, Flight Lieutenant Ball, emptied a third of his ammunition into an Me 110, which Pilot Officer Stansfield also attacked, the 110 going down with both engines on fire, and so it went on, with many more claims by 242 Squadron's elated pilots.

This was what Squadron Leader Bader and 242 Squadron had been desperately waiting for: an opportunity to engage the enemy in numbers. As indicated by the foregoing, however, there were other squadrons involved in this combat, which also recorded victories. Due to the high numbers of engaging fighters, various pilots had independently attacked and claimed the same German aircraft, which became duplicated on the balance sheet. In the heat of the moment, however, the relatively inexperienced 242 Squadron had been oblivious to the presence of other RAF fighters and so believed that 242, and 242 alone, was responsible for this successful interception. In total, 242 Squadron claimed seven Me 110s destroyed and three probables, and five He 111s destroyed. At the time, these claims were accepted unconditionally and without question, it being the result that Squadron Leader Bader and Air Vice-Marshal Leigh-Mallory craved. Indeed, the AOC 12 Group signalled the Squadron: 'Heartiest congratulations on a first class show. Well done 242.' The CAS added his congratulations: 'Magnificent fighting. You are well on top of the enemy and obviously the fine Canadian traditions of the last war are safe in your hands.' It was, in fact, an unprecedented signal.

The Under-Secretary of State for Air sent a similar message. Certainly the destruction of twelve enemy aircraft for no loss would have been remarkable – had it been accurate. There was clearly more afoot here. 242 Squadron was Canadian; although loyal to the Crown, Canada had not rushed to join Britain in declaring war on Nazi Germany, debating the issue for a further week, the country's mood differing markedly to that of 1914. Just as their legless commander was newsworthy, so too was 242 Squadron important to the propagandists. This was the propagandists' first opportunity to trumpet the contribution of Canadian fighter pilots.

Sebastian Cox confirms that:

> Air Intelligence, perhaps because of its relative inexperience in the field, was certainly too ready to accept RAF claims at face value. In the period 8 August to 16 August 1940, the defences claimed 501 enemy aircraft confirmed as destroyed, and a further 231 probably destroyed, when the actual scale of loss was only 283.

The romantic legend surrounding the story of Douglas Bader also claims that the raid in question was turned about by 242 Squadron before it reached the Handley Page factory. This is not true. The majority of RAF fighters, low on ammunition and fuel, actually disengaged some ten miles before the bombers reached their target where, hampered by accurate and heavy AA fire, the bombardiers' aim was poor; little damage was caused and work on the new Halifax bomber was unaffected (the other raiding force, however, hit the Vauxhall works hard, killing fifty-three people).

From Douglas's perspective the world must have been aglow. As far as he and his pilots were concerned, they alone had broken up a determined enemy attack and inflicted numerous losses upon the raiders without loss. 11 Group squadrons did not make claims like this, leading Douglas to conclude that he, above all others, including both Air Chief Marshal Dowding and Air Vice-Marshal Park, had got the right idea. Feverishly, he set pen to paper, scribbling a report on the action entitled 'Fighter Tactics v Escort and Bomber Formations'. Given that 11 Group's squadrons had been in action daily, sometimes several times a day and often against even bigger enemy formations, this is astonishing. Douglas wrote:

> At the suggestion of the Intelligence Officer I am writing a report on the tactics employed on 30 August against a large formation of enemy bombers and twin-engine escort fighters. It has been suggested this report may be of interest in view of the warning signal from 11 Group of increased casualties suffered in that Group due to enemy tactics of tight formation with bombers and escort fighters intermingled, and the good fortune enjoyed by 242 Squadron of complete immunity from damage to aeroplanes or personnel. In regard to the second point it must be appreciated that luck definitely played a part since any squadron leaving an engagement without any damage cannot claim all credit for cleverness in flying etc. ...
>
> It appears that bombers escorted by twin-engine fighters can be dispersed by shock tactics of the sudden arrival of a Hurricane or Spitfire in their midst, preferably out of the sun...
> It was anticipated (and the fight in question proved it) that if a squadron of Hurricanes or Spitfires met a large enemy bomber formation (provided there were no single-engine fighter escorts) the Hurricanes or Spitfires would have the advantage (in spite of numerical inferiority) if the enemy formation could be broken up, and provided the squadron started with the height advantage. In any case, the primary object is achieved if the formation is broken because it ruins the enemy's chance of accurate bombing, and even if one's own squadron's successes in E/A shot down is slight, the E/A are scattered in small groups or singly and other fighters which are certain to be at hand can pounce of them.

Douglas concluded that 'as far as 242 Squadron is concerned the attacking and fighting conditions were very favourable.' They were indeed. Not only had the Controller perfectly positioned the Hurricanes to strike from the sun, but, perhaps even more importantly, there were no Me 109s engaged. Flying very high, the 109s would undoubtedly have bounced the Hurricanes lower down – possibly with disastrous consequences.

Douglas later described subsequent events:

When we were writing up our combat reports afterwards, Leigh-Mallory rang me up and said 'Congratulations, Bader, on the Squadron's performance today'.

I said 'Thank you very much, Sir, but if we'd had more aeroplanes then we would have shot down a whole lot more.' He asked what I meant and I explained that with more fighters our results would have been even better. He said 'Look, I'd like to talk to you about this', so I flew over to 12 Group HQ at Hucknall and told the AOC what I thought. He agreed and created the 'Duxford Wing', under my leadership and comprising 19, 242 and 310 Squadrons. Leigh-Mallory said to try the idea and see what we could do.

Leigh-Mallory, of course, had been told by Dowding on a number of occasions regarding how he expected squadrons to be deployed. That Leigh-Mallory had a penchant for large formations has already been demonstrated. Given 242 Squadron's apparently all-conquering victory of 30 August 1940, and the newsworthy Squadron Leader Bader's huge enthusiasm for his idea, Leigh-Mallory clearly saw the prospect of a 12 Group wing as a means of getting his squadrons into the battle proper – even if such tactics were contrary to the System and the requirements of his AOC-in-C. That he was prepared to go ahead with this indicates a level of confidence, suggesting the level of Leigh-Mallory's political support at the Air Ministry – not least from the CAS and DCAS. There was much more to this decision than Douglas's simple explanation to Lucas: 'We were learning…. We were all learning. That was the point.' That may well have been the case for Squadron Leader Douglas Bader, only recently returned to the service, but it did not apply to Dowding and Park – who knew exactly what they were about and had immense experience. Brave as a lion though he undoubtedly was, and an immense inspiration to many, Douglas was in this instance as naïve as he could be arrogant.

That 242 Squadron wildly over-claimed on 30 August 1940 is a demonstrable fact, possibly in the ratio of 4:1. The attack was not, therefore, as successful as believed. Moreover, not one 242 Squadron report on the action mentions the presence of fighters from other RAF squadrons. This could well be because in their high state of excitement in what was their first major action, 242 Squadron's inexperienced pilots simply failed to register them. We know, however, from official records – and in particular personal combat reports from various 11 Group pilots, some of substantial experience, that other Hurricanes and Spitfires successfully engaged. In fact, over fifty RAF fighters were actually engaged, collectively destroying a total of nine enemy aircraft. Given that fifty fighters were actually committed to that battle, Squadron Leader Bader's theory, therefore, that more fighters (than just 242 Squadron) would have executed greater damage was simply incorrect. This action and Douglas's theory, however, underpinned the remainder of his own personal 'hot' war – and had far-reaching consequences for Fighter Command as a whole.

Chapter Eight

'It was windy work, make no mistake'

On 31 August 1940, a day after 242 Squadron's apparently all-conquering engagement over Hatfield, the Duxford Sector was bombed, including Fowlmere, as was 11 Group's nearby Debden airfield – just the kind of attacks north of the Thames Fighter Command also had to be alert for. As it was, the bombs rained down on Fowlmere just after 0800 hrs, Wing Commander David Cox recalling that 19 Squadron was 'caught on the hop!' Some Spitfires managed to get off, but both Flying Officers Coward and Brinsden were shot down, baling out, and Pilot Officer Ray Aeberhardt was shot-up and killed landing without flaps. While 19 Squadron was engaged, Squadron Leader Bader led 242 Squadron to patrol Duxford, but saw no action, and neither did 310 Squadron, which scrambled immediately. Tellingly, Douglas recorded in his log book that at lunchtime 242 Squadron had uneventfully 'Patrolled London District'. At 1300 hrs, however, 310 Squadron was formally despatched to patrol the 11 Group Hornchurch Sector Station, north of the Thames, and together with 11 Group units attacked a formation of Dornier bombers escorted by Me 109 and 110 fighters. This was actually the unit's first combat, in which one Me 109 was claimed destroyed, and two damaged, offset against the loss of two Hurricanes, the pilot of one of which, Pilot Officer Sterbacek, remains missing to this day.

Wing Commander Woodhall:

> I met the Czechs on their return to the airfield and spoke with Squadron Leader Sacha Hess; he had disabled a Do 17 over Epping Forest which made a wheels-up forced landing in a field. He followed it down with the intention of making certain that no one got out of it alive. He saw three Germans climb out, who, when they realised Sacha was diving on them, held up their hands. To quote his own words: 'I hesitate, then it was too

116

late, so I go round again to make sure I kill them – they wave
something white – again I do not shoot – then (disgustedly)
I think it is no use – I am become too bloody British!'

Hess had good reason to desire revenge that day; he had recently received
notification that his wife and daughter had been killed by the Germans.

611 Squadron had again flown from Digby to Duxford, before landing
patrolling Feltwell. Before returning home that day, Squadron Leader
Jimmy McComb's pilots had flown two more uneventful patrols, one over
Duxford, the other over north-east London.

The following day, 611 Squadron's 'A' Flight relieved 46 Squadron's
detached flight at Ternhill in Shropshire, leaving 'B' Flight as the only
operational day fighters in the Digby Sector. Again, 242 Squadron patrolled
from Duxford, without incident.

During the first week of September 1940, the Luftwaffe continued
pounding 11 Group's airfields. Throughout this time, Park frequently
called for and received cooperation from Air Vice-Marshal Brand's
10 Group – whose squadrons at Middle Wallop were well positioned
to patrol aerodromes and aircraft factories south of London. The
relationship between 11 and 12 Groups, however, remained unchanged,
although the patrols by 12 Group squadrons over London and Hornchurch
the previous day suggest that 11 Group was requesting and receiving
assistance from 12.

On 2 September 1940, 242 Squadron remained at Coltishall, flying
further fruitless patrols. Such was the case over the next few days.

On 6 September, Air Vice-Marshal Leigh-Mallory, following
consultation with Squadron Leader Bader, ordered that in future 19, 242
and 310 Squadrons would operate from Duxford as a wing. This was a
purely parochial arrangement without consultation with HQ Fighter
Command. As we have seen, training had revolved around the flight, not
even a squadron as a whole, which was the largest tactical formation Air
Chief Marshal Dowding considered practical. Over Dunkirk, though, Air
Vice-Marshal Park had his squadrons travel together, in convoy, across the
sea to patrol the French coast – but these were not wings in the true sense
of the word, not least because, owing to the TR9D radio's limitations, inter-
squadron communication was impossible, and so, therefore, was command
and control of any formation larger than a squadron. Nonetheless, Air Vice-
Marshal Park had already realised that it was wise to use his precious Spitfire
squadrons in pairs, as a high-altitude umbrella, protecting the Hurricanes

which were better-suited to operating lower down, against bombers at medium altitude. Indeed, Park reported that:

> As the enemy penetrated further inland, we adopted the tactics of meeting enemy formations in pairs of squadrons, while calling on 10 and 12 Groups to provide close cover for our aerodromes near London and for suburban aircraft factories west of London. This arrangement enabled us to meet the enemy further forward in greater strength while giving a measure of close protection against enemy raids which might elude us at various heights. On some occasions it therefore became practicable to detail a wing of two Spitfire squadrons to engage escorting enemy fighters while a wing of Hurricanes engaged the bombers.

In this context, clearly a 'wing' is a pair of squadrons, representing flexible thinking on Park's part and again confirming that he was not averse to using larger formations than a flight or squadron when the tactical circumstances required the enemy to be met in greater strength. Conversely, the 12 Group three squadron wing was a purely maverick scenario, arising out of a misconception concerning the combat on 30 August 1940, and the burning ambition of the 12 Group AOC and 242 Squadron's swashbuckling CO to play a more prominent role in the fighting. Clearly, then, for our purposes, 6 September 1940 is a significant date.

On the morning of 7 September, codename CROMWELL was broadcast: invasion imminent. That morning, Douglas led 242 Squadron to Duxford, in readiness for the initial operation of what became variously known as the 'Big Wing', the 'Duxford Wing' or the '12 Group Wing', and even the 'Bader Wing'. Douglas himself once explained the thinking behind this idea:

> 'Woody' would ring me up and say that the Germans were building up over the Pas-de-Calais, and I remember saying 'Well why the hell don't we go off now and get the buggers while they're forming up?' You see the bombers would come from their bases in France and orbit the Pas-de-Calais, that area around Calais and Boulogne, and the fighters would then take off from their airfields within that area, such as Wissant and St Omer. Of course the fighters have very short range, not

more than forty-five minutes. They would climb up and join the bombers and then the whole armada would set course over the Channel. If our Duxford Wing had got off when they were building up, we'd have got about seventy miles south of base, probably down to the Canterbury area, and we had got them there, on the way in. We would have been at the right height and therefore have controlled the battle.

The new formation's first patrol was an uneventful sortie over the 11 Group airfields of Hornchurch and North Weald. Douglas, naturally, led with 242 Squadron in the van, followed by the Czech Hurricanes of 310, while 19 Squadron's Spitfires, with their superior performance, provided top cover. 19 Squadron, in fact, commented that flying in such strength of numbers was a 'most comforting feeling indeed'. Equally 'comforting' was the fact that the squadron had been re-equipped with machine-gun armed Spitfire Mk IAs, the pilots having lost all confidence in the cannon-armed Mk IBs, owing to frequent stoppages.

Wing Commander Gordon Sinclair was a flight commander with 310 Squadron:

> There was never any possibility of three or more squadrons taking off from Duxford together and receiving battle orders from a wing leader while airborne. Our R/T sets, TR9s, were not up to it, but in any case, such a situation never arose or was even contemplated. Each squadron acted on its own, down to flight or section level, and we received information regarding the whereabouts of enemy aircraft from the Duxford Operations Room, based upon advice they had received from the relevant RDF station. Douglas Bader was a natural leader of men, but I never heard of the other squadrons' COs operating in the Duxford Sector agreeing to his leadership in the air.

Douglas elaborated on the impossibility of communicating with the wing himself:-

> Only the squadron commanders were on the same frequency. We had four buttons on the VHF in those days, which we had received just before the Battle of Britain. It was ridiculous, anyway, trying to tune this thing with someone shooting up

your backside! Anyway, the other pilots each had their own squadron frequency. The Controller would talk to me on my frequency, but to talk to the chaps I would have to keep changing frequency from squadron to squadron. Later, of course, we got it so that we were all on the same frequency. When we were above the enemy I would say 'Diving, diving now, attacking now', and my Section of three would go down – followed by everyone else. As soon as we had made one pass, though, our formation was broken up. My objective was to get the wing into the right position, then say 'Attacking now', after which it was up to them. They awaited my order, every man knew what he had to do, but the wing was impossible for me to control after that point.

Wing Commander Douglas Blackwood was the English CO of 310 Squadron at the time:

The Big Wing thing was all started by Douglas Bader, who of course had a Cranwell background so naturally became leader. At the time, I was younger than he and had received command of 310 Squadron only shortly before Douglas received 242. Certainly among the three squadrons initially involved, Douglas was the senior squadron commander; Brian Lane had only just received command of 19 Squadron, so although he had the most combat experience he was the Sector's most junior squadron leader. When Douglas suggested the wing, as he was senior we just automatically assumed that he would lead. He was a *very* forceful character, of course, so even if we had wanted to it would have been *impossible* to argue with him! An example of this occurred when we were all together at Duxford many years later during the making of *Battle of Britain*. Douglas was there as a consultant but would not stop interfering with the shoot. In the end the Director said 'I'm making this film, not you' – and ordered him off the set. That was Douglas to a 'T'.

In 1940, his ideas regarding the Big Wing had the support of Duxford's Station Commander, Wing Commander Woodhall, but even he could not have stood up to Douglas if ever it had come to that. Douglas just said 'I'm doing this' – and that was that. There was no doubt, however, that Douglas Bader was a very brave man and it was because of the way he had conquered his disabilities caused by the crash in 1931 that he became popular with his acquaintances. His 242 Squadron pilots would have followed him anywhere. We are talking, after all, about a man who played squash well and had a low golf handicap despite having no legs! We never did any practice sorties as a wing, we just went off on an operational patrol together one day with Douglas leading.

The Battle of Britain had now been raging for nearly two months, yet there was still no sign of the Hurricanes and Spitfires being beaten. Having concentrated his fighters in the Pas-de-Calais, Reichsmarschall Göring was continually thwarted in his desire to destroy Fighter Command en masse by Park's careful preservation of his force. Instead of committing large numbers of fighters to battle – as Leigh-Mallory now intended – Park mainly attacked in penny-packet formations and kept his aircraft well dispersed. The Luftwaffe, however, due to 'over-confidence and poor intelligence', were fighting, argued Cox, 'an ill-directed campaign, which breached a fundamental principle of war – maintenance of the aim'. Already the aim had changed several times and, at what was a vital moment, considering the battering 11 Group's airfields had received, was about to change again.

On the night of 24 August 1940, Bomber Command had attacked Berlin – Hitler immediately seizing upon this as justification for changing tack once more and ordering an all-out assault upon London. In previous campaigns the Poles and Dutch had surrendered after the bombing of their main centres of population, and the Danes had done so simply at the threat of it. Hitler hoped, therefore, that the same would be true of Britain. Göring believed that round-the-clock bombing of London would exhaust Fighter Command and considered London to be the only target capable of forcing Dowding to commit his entire force to battle. Göring now personally assumed command of the campaign. The first major attack of this latest phase began at 1635 hrs on Saturday, 7 September 1940. Standing on the French cliffs at Cap Gris-Nez, Göring and his entourage marvelled at Germany's aerial might as 350 black-crossed warplanes roared overhead towards London. The approach of this aerial armada – the largest unleashed against England thus far – was anxiously monitored by 11 Group, which naturally assumed that sector stations were again the target. At 1617 hrs, eleven squadrons were scrambled, and by 1630 hrs all of Park's twenty-one squadrons were airborne.

At 1645 hrs the Duxford Wing was scrambled to patrol North Weald at 10,000ft. Douglas, however, climbed the wing 5,000ft higher – arriving over the allocated patrol line at 15,000ft. To the east, anti-aircraft fire alerted the 12 Group pilots to an enemy formation at 20,000ft – 5,000ft higher than themselves. The enemy climbed over their rendezvous points and throughout the outward-bound journey across the Channel – the escorting Me 109s frequently incoming very high indeed, often, in fact, just beneath the stratosphere. He who has the advantage of height – and sun – controlled the battle, so, knowing this, it is difficult to understand why the Duxford Wing was instructed to patrol at the suicidal height of 10,000ft. Upon sighting the enemy from his allocated patrol line, Douglas requested permission from Duxford Control to engage – which was granted. Immediately, this highlights the problem of communication, and why the System simply did not provide for tactical control of 12 Group's wing by 11 Group – over whose area the Duxford Wing now operated. The 11 Group Controller had no means of communicating directly with the 12 Group formation leader – and it is unlikely that Duxford referred to 11 Group before giving Douglas permission to leave his allocated patrol line and engage. Certain previous commentators have charged that Douglas failed to comply with instructions, left his patrol line in search of the enemy, thereby failing to protect North Weald. Clearly this is not the case. Any fault lay with the 12 Group Controller, who we assume to have been Wing Commander Woodhall.

The main German formation was at 20,000ft – but typically the Me 109s were another 5,000ft higher – giving the enemy escorts a 10,000ft height advantage on the Duxford Wing. Douglas later wrote that his wing had been 'alerted late' – hence why the wing was now in an extremely tactically disadvantaged position. More accurately, the wing had been poorly positioned height-wise – and had Douglas not used his own initiative and climbed that extra 5,000ft, that disadvantage would have been greater still. These two immediate problems of height and control emphasise from the outset the difficulties involved for both 11 and 12 Groups where operating the Duxford Wing was concerned. The System had simply not provided for this unexpected scenario.

Climbing at full throttle to at least get level with the Germans, the element of surprise was lost. Unsurprisingly, given the difference in performance between the Spitfires and slower Hurricanes, the wing became 'straggled out so that full weight could not be pressed home'. The wing had certainly lost 'cohesion' – but the reason for that was not the fault of either Duxford's Controller or Squadron Leader Bader. Inevitably, the German fighter escort fell on the thirty-six Duxford fighters; Douglas: 'To be attacked by an enemy fighter when you are climbing is fatal if your opponent is experienced. You are flying slowly and are thus virtually unmanouevrable, as well as being a sitting target for an opponent flying above you and flying faster.' Douglas climbed flat-out and turned left to cut off the enemy. Confirming how 'straggled out' his formation was, the only other fighter to arrive with him was Douglas's Red Two, Sub-Lieutenant Cork:

> Squadron Leader Bader gave a very short beam burst at about 100 yards at E/A which were then flying section of three line astern in a large rectangle. Then, accompanied by Red Two, gave short bursts at the middle E/A of back section. The E/A started smoking preparatory to catching fire. Squadron Leader Bader did not notice result which was later confirmed by Pilot Officer Turner as diving down in flames from the back of the bomber formation. At the time of Squadron Leader Bader's attack on the Me 110, a yellow-nosed Me 109 was noticed reflected in his mirror, and he turned to avoid the E/A. Big bang was heard by him in the cockpit of his Hurricane. An explosive bullet came through the right-hand side of the fuselage, touching map case and knocking off corner of the undercarriage selector quadrant and finished up against the petrol priming pump. Squadron Leader Bader executed a steep diving turn and found a lone Me 110 below him, which he attacked from straight astern and above him, and saw E/A go into a steepish straight dive finishing up in flames in a field just north of railway line turning approximately East (West of Wickford, due North of Thameshaven).

According to the 242 Squadron combat report:

> Red Two, sighted E/A to East and above. He climbed to meet E/A and carried out beam attack on the leading section of bombers, firing at a Do 215 on the tail-end of the formation. Port engine burst into flames after two short bursts and crashed vertically. Red Two was then attacked by E/A from rear and

hit in starboard mainplane. He broke away downwards and backwards, nearly colliding head-on with an Me 110. Red Two gave short burst before pulling away and saw front cabin of 110 break up and machine go into vertical dive. Two of the crew baled out. While Red Two was following E/A down, E/A was stalling and diving. An Me 109 attacked Red Two from the rear, one shot from the E/A going through the side of Red Two's hood, hitting bottom of reflector sight and bullet-proof windscreen. Red Two received a number of glass splinters in his eyes so broke away downwards with half roll and lost sight of E/A.

Red Three, Pilot Officer Crowley-Milling, attacked an Me 110, setting its port engine ablaze before being attacked by an Me 109. One cannon shell smashed into the Hurricane's radiator, and others hit the aileron and pilot's seat. Air Marshal Crowley-Milling remembered:

What the official report doesn't mention is that my windscreen was also shattered by a cannon shell. Fortunately we had armoured glass, which was laminated, a couple of inches thick, which saved my life. I managed to put the Hurricane down at Stow Maries. It was all pretty traumatic but at least I was personally unscathed!

The Me 110 that Pilot Officer Crowley-Milling accounted for, jointly with Green Four, Sub-Lieutenant R.E. Gardner, crashed at Little Burstead. Again, the Squadron Combat Report continues:

Blue One (F/Lt Powell-Sheddon) climbed to 22,000ft to engage e/a but did not engage for some 10 minutes. He finally chased an Me 109 which was itself chasing a Hurricane. Both swerved in front of Blue One, about 100 yards away. Blue One gave a quick deflection burst at e/a as it passed. E/a turned left and again crossed Blue One's path at same range. Blue One gave another burst and hit e/a's tail. Blue One then got a third burst from above and behind at a range of 50 yards, bullets hitting e/a from which pieces came off. Blue One got into e/a slipstream, ceased fire and got out slightly to one side and fired again at e/a which then hung in the air for a few seconds

Squadron Leader Bader first led his new Wing into action over London on 7 September 1940, but was bounced by enemy fighters while clawing for height. The young and impressionable Pilot Officer Crowley-Milling, who worshipped his swashbuckling leader, was shot-up, forced-landing his Hurricane at Stow Maries – his armoured glass windscreen having stopped an enemy machine-gun bullet.

Crowley-Milling's Hurricane, 'LE-H', P3715.

and then fell forward in a vertical dive, smoke pouring from the starboard wing and fuselage. E/a disappeared into black smoke over Thameshaven.

Meanwhile, as Squadron Leader Brian Lane climbed No 19 Squadron's Spitfires, an Me 110, which was being attacked by two Hurricanes of 310 Squadron, flashed in front of 'A' Flight, which, with Lane leading, sped off in pursuit. All five pilots subsequently fired at the hapless 110, which crashed near a railway line, one mile east of Hornchurch. This aircraft belonged to Stab II/ZG 2, which was escorting He 111s of KG 53. One crew member was killed when his parachute failed, the other landed safely in a field only to be captured by two elderly women from a nearby house! After the combat, 'A' Flight was split up, so Squadron Leader Lane, Flight Lieutenant Lawson and Sergeant Jennings, having lost contact with the ongoing air battle, returned to Fowlmere.

The other pilots of No 19 Squadron, however, were still engaged. Red Three, Pilot Officer Cunningham, blacked out after breaking off the pursuit of the Me 110 destroyed by 'A' Flight, came too and joined up with a squadron of Hurricanes heading south-eastwards. At 1720 hrs, these fighters executed a front-quarter attack on twenty He 111s at 20,000ft. Pilot Officer Cunningham's Spitfire hurtled through the bombers, in an attempt to break their formation, before singling out a particular Heinkel which caught fire and lost height. After a further attack, Cunningham last saw the raider ten miles inland from Deal, but after only a short burst at another vic of He 111s his ammunition was expended.

After attacking the Me 110 with the rest of 'A' Flight, Flight Sergeant George 'Grumpy' Unwin found himself alone at 4,000ft. Climbing under full boost to 25,000ft he saw 'a Hurricane squadron going somewhere in a hurry' and followed them. Suddenly three separate enemy formations, comprising thirty bombers each, appeared with their inevitable close fighter escort.

Flight Sergeant George 'Grumpy' Unwin:

> I was surrounded by Me 109s and ended up fighting a running battle between Ramsgate and west London. The usual fight ensued, during which I definitely hit at least five of them but only two were shot down, both in flames. I then climbed for a breather and shadowed the third enemy formation when I saw a fourth arriving. By this time two of the other three formations had turned north and the other went straight in a

westerly direction. The leading formation turned east and I was at 25,000ft and above them. As there did not appear to be any of their escorts left, I dived on the rear vic and gave them the rest of my ammunition, about 50 rounds in each gun, and from 450, closing to fifty yards range. The bomber at which I fired wobbled a bit but otherwise carried on. Without ammunition I returned to Fowlmere.

When Squadron Leader Bader tally ho'd and led 242 Squadron to attack the bombers, Squadron Leader Blackwood led 310 Squadron in a charge at the enemy fighters. After the initial Squadron attack in line astern, the Czechs were split up, acting independently or in pairs. Over Canterbury Sergeant Furst attacked a 1/LG 2 Me 109, which, although the pilot managed to bale out, exploded in mid-air; the Czech then struck against an Me 110 of 6/ZG 2 which ditched in the Channel off Birchington. The exchange was far from one-sided, however. One of 310 Squadron's Czechs was badly burned, his Hurricane a write-off while another was damaged.

Back at Duxford, 242 Squadron's Pilot Officer John Benzie was missing, later confirmed to have been killed. Douglas: 'it was windy work, let there be no mistake. On landing I rang the Operations Room in a fury, to be told that we had been sent off as soon as 11 Group had called for us at Duxford.'

As explained, the question of height was the critical factor in this engagement, and 11 Group's order for the Duxford Wing to patrol at 10,000ft was questionable indeed. The intention, however, had not been for the wing to attack the incoming enemy, so the 11 Group Controller was not, in fact, instructing 12 Group to intercept these. Nonetheless, had the wing stayed put and patrolled nearby North Weald at 10,000ft, not only would it have invited attack from above, but what that would have achieved on this occasion, given the size of the enemy attack and that its objectives had already become obvious, is also questionable.

Assistance had also been provided by 10 Group Spitfires: Wing Commander Bob Doe:

after 234 Squadron was scrambled from Middle Wallop, I climbed like mad in an attempt to avoid the trauma of the previous two raids where I had been at a disadvantage from the very start, and managed to reach London at a reasonable altitude where I could have a go at the bombers on my terms.

At the time, Flight Lieutenant Keith Lawrence, a New Zealander, was another experienced and successful fighter pilot also serving with 234 Squadron:

> On the question of 10 Group providing support to 11 Group, I would say that whenever we were vectored to the Brooklands area, we climbed to 20,000ft, so as to reach the patrol line at a reasonable altitude before action. My recollections of Middle Wallop scrambles in August and September 1940 is that they were generally ordered in good time for us to climb to an appropriate height for interception while en route.

Flight Lieutenant David Crook, a Spitfire pilot in 10 Group's 609 Squadron:

> In the next week or two we flew up to London almost every day, sometimes twice a day, in order to give the overworked London squadrons a helping hand. They certainly needed it; the weight and intensity of these raids exceeded anything I had seen before.

Flight Lieutenant Roger Hall was also flying Spitfires in 10 Group, with 152 Squadron:

> We saw our own fighters, the 11 Group squadrons and some from 12 Group in the Midlands, climbing up from the North. There seemed to be quite a number of us. They too were black dots, climbing in groups of twelve, or thirty-six in wing formation. Most of them were Hurricanes. We were soon engaged with Me 109s, the combat lasting about fifteen minutes. When it was over, we were scattered all over Kent. As London blazed, the smoke from the docks being visible for miles, I recalled for a moment Mr Baldwin's prophecy, not a sanguine one, made to the House of Commons some five years before when he said that the bomber would always get through. Now it was doing just that.

Clearly, there were no cooperation issues between 10 and 11 Groups.

The allegation that the Duxford Wing were always called for late by 11 Group, however, would become a vexing issue. Wing Commander Douglas Blackwood:

> I think that we should have been requested earlier as that would have enabled us to climb out to sea and then attack high

128

over the Thames Estuary. But I think that *everyone* was doing their best, we were all learning. 11 Group felt it was their responsibility to defend London, without 12 Group interfering.

Clearly, though, that was not the case, because 11 Group had no hesitation in calling upon Air Vice-Marshal Brand's 10 Group, as evidenced by the foregoing first-hand accounts.

The limitations of RDF and the System, however, meant that it was not just squadrons in 12 Group which complained about being scrambled late; Air Commodore Peter Brothers was then an experienced flight commander serving in 11 Group:

> Until 9 September 1940 I flew with 32 Squadron. During our time at coastal aerodromes at Hawkinge and Manston, or even Biggin Hill, which was further inland, we were often scrambled late. The Controller obviously had to ensure that it was the real thing and not a 'spoof' to get us airborne and catch us while refuelling. This was frustrating as at such forward bases there was so little time anyway.

For reasons beyond the control of those directing the battle, this would remain an irresolvable difficulty. Douglas himself once expressed his own thoughts on the time factor:

> Some ignorant people have stated in print that the wing took a long time to get off the ground. Not so. As the two Hurricane squadrons got off the ground from Duxford, the Spitfires did so from Fowlmere. There was no time wasted in forming up. I just set course and kept going, and everyone else just formated on my lead. We took off in sections of three, in line abreast, and as soon as the first three were getting towards the far hedge then the next three would be taxying into position and so on. There was no orbit. I used to get off the ground and get absolutely right on course. The chaps then joined me, the Spitfires staying 5,000ft above us. I usually set the pace to climb at 140 mph. We reckoned to be at the Thames Estuary at about 20,000ft, which was forty-eight miles away. There was no time lost through us getting off. Once we were off, we were off, there was no milling about, all this was done on the climb and en route. No time lost. The leader is the fellow who sets

the pace, to give the blokes at the back time to settle down and so on. Obviously, a squadron in a hurry was faster than a wing because the leader has less blokes to worry about. I used to go on at Leigh-Mallory about why we couldn't get off early and be down there, but he said, 'Look, we can't go until Air Vice-Marshal Park requests us. Do please remember, Bader, that they've got plenty of problems down there without us adding to them.'

Woodhall also supported Douglas's view that information from the controller should be provide to assist – not restrict – the leader in the air:

Douglas had made an intimate study of the fighter tactics developed by famous pilots like McCudden, Ball and Bishop in the First World War and was a great believer in the advantages of making the correct use of the sun, and first gaining superior height. As I saw it, my job as Sector Controller was to vector the fighter leader on a course and to a height which would place him above and up-sun of the enemy, and keep him informed of the enemy's position, course and speed as accurately as possible from the information we had on the operations table. As soon as our fighter leader sighted the enemy, it was over to him.

Although the Duxford Wing's first action on 7 September 1940 had been 'windy work' provoking Douglas's 'fury', the squadrons involved made the following combat claims:

242 Squadron: 10 destroyed, 2 probables, 5 damaged.
310 Squadron: 5/3/3
19 Squadron: 5 destroyed.

Wing Total: 20/3/6

The Wing's losses:

242 Squadron: 1 pilot killed, 2 Hurricanes damaged.
310 Squadron: 1 pilot badly burned and Hurricane destroyed, another damaged.
19 Squadron: 0

The Luftwaffe actually lost a *total* of forty aircraft on operations this date – seventeen of which either crashed in England or close enough to the coast for their crews to be captured or bodies recovered. From the evidence available it is difficult to confirm more than six kills by 242 Squadron, suggesting an over-claiming ratio of 3:1. Once more, though, the claims of Douglas and his pilots appear to have been accepted without question. The question of verifying combat claims would, in fact, vex both sides throughout the Battle of Britain. Accurate intelligence regarding losses and claims was, of course, crucial to both evaluating enemy strength and the success of one's own tactics – but was very difficult to accurately confirm. For example, between 8 and 16 August 1940 the defences claimed 501 enemy aircraft destroyed and 231 probables – when the actual German loss was 283. Inevitably, however, the Duxford Wing's tally on 7 September 1940 generated further congratulatory signals from both Leigh-Mallory and the Secretary of State for Air, Sir Archibald Sinclair. Woodhall was certainly convinced that the wing's claims were accurate: 'Bader and the intelligence officers checked these figures very carefully – with me.' They were wrong.

On that fateful 'Black Saturday', 7 September 1940, the date on which Squadron Leader Bader first led the Duxford Wing into action, Londoners had witnessed combat on a hitherto unseen scale. Through sheer weight of numbers the Germans had reached their target, starting huge fires in the docklands and East End. Vast areas were devastated and nearly 1,800 Londoners lost their lives. Late that evening, Air Vice-Marshal Park was airborne over the blazing capital in his personal Hurricane, 'OK1'. It was a sight that the tough New Zealander would vividly remember:-

> It was burning all down the river. It was a horrid sight. But I looked down and said 'Thank God for that', because I knew that the Nazis had switched their attack from our fighter stations, thinking they were knocked out. They weren't, but they were pretty groggy.

The day's action had cost the *Luftwaffe* forty aircraft, but Fighter Command had lost twenty-seven, with fourteen more pilots killed – and casualties were now an increasing concern at Fighter Command HQ. That afternoon, Dowding called an urgent meeting at Bentley Priory to decide upon measures for 'going downhill' in an economical manner, providing for a rapid climb back. When losses decreed, depleted squadrons in 11 Group were replaced by those from other groups, which were at full-strength. Casualties meant a

Above, below and opposite: On 21 September 1940, the official Air Ministry photographer Stanley Devon visited Duxford, taking these iconic photographs of Squadron Leader Bader and 242 Squadron. By this time the wing's combat claims were substantial, convincing many powerful service chiefs and politicians that Dowding and Park had got it wrong, while Leigh-Mallory, Woodhall and 'young Bader' had it right.

deficiency in combat experience, and that was the problem. The DCAS, Air Vice-Marshal Douglas, felt that Dowding was being overly 'pessimistic'. Dowding, conversely, was bemused by Douglas's apparent inability to grasp the difference between a trained and a combat-ready pilot. And in any case, there were insufficient pilots, trained, combat experienced or otherwise. Dowding's SASO, Air Vice-Marshal Evill, provided figures confirming that in the four weeks ending 4 September 1940, casualties totalled 338, whereas during that period the OTUs had only converted 280 pilots. Air Vice-Marshal Park pointed out that in 11 Group casualties were approaching 100 a week. Losing patience, Dowding snapped at the DCAS, 'You must realise that we *are* going downhill.' Douglas's response was to suggest creation of a fourth OTU, but Evill interjected, pointing out the impracticality of this suggestion, because it would take too long. Dowding also observed that another training unit would be a further drain on precious resources. The solution – arrived at by Dowding and Park – was the 'Stabilising Scheme'.

This categorised fighter squadrons as 'A', 'B' or 'C' units. 'A' were those in the frontline, maintained with a minimum strength of sixteen operational pilots; 'B' were those being rested, with up to six combat-ready pilots, who could be called upon if necessary. 'C' were those currently rebuilding after

Dowding's Senior Air Staff Officer at Bentley Priory was Air Vice-Marshal Douglas Evill – who failed to act upon Park's complaint about 12 Group's lack of cooperation. Had he acted decisively at that point, much later trouble and angst would have been avoided.

suffering losses and were unlikely to be called to battle. With a minimum quota of three combat-ready pilots, the latter units were to provide operational experience to pilots fresh from OTU, away from the combat zone. Once these new pilots were considered combat ready, they could be posted to 'A' or 'B' squadrons further south.

When the minutes of the 'Going Downhill' conference were provided to the DCAS, he objected, claiming that the minutes misrepresented him, casting him in the role of 'Mutt', a foolish music-hall comedian who asked stupid questions. Fighter Command's SASO, Evill, replied that the minutes were virtually verbatim. Dowding and Park stood firm in the belief that their use of resources was sound, and, especially at such a time of crisis, had no time for Air Ministry incompetence or politics. Unfortunately, they failed to appreciate that their open contempt for the DCAS at this conference had placed them in grave danger from the enemy within…

Above and right: Dowding had responsibility for the whole Command and defending the entire country, so unlike Leigh-Mallory did not have a parochial view. The Air Chief Marshal is pictured with the King and Queen during their visit to Bentley Priory, and on another occasion with the King.

Chapter Nine

Battle for London:
'... thoughtful wishing'

After this initial wing action, Air Vice-Marshal Leigh-Mallory, Wing Commander Woodhall and Squadron Leader Bader were convinced that with some fine-tuning, the Duxford Wing would positively contribute to the battle being fought over 11 Group.

The following day, 242 Squadron despatched a servicing party from Coltishall by road to remain at Duxford. No action was forthcoming for the Duxford Wing that day, however. At 1635 hrs on 9 September 1940, it was clear that a major attack was incoming when some 300 German aircraft approached the English coastline between North Foreland and Dover – heading for London. At 1650 hrs, Squadron Leader McComb's 611 Squadron 'B' Flight was scrambled from Duxford to patrol North Weald, firstly below cloud-base, then at 27,000ft. Although a distant enemy formation was sighted, wisely McComb remained on his allotted patrol line. The Duxford Wing was not scrambled until 1700 hrs – the time-lapse of twenty-five minutes adding weight to arguments that on occasions 11 Group called for help too late. That said, it was always a difficult call, not knowing whether another, perhaps heavier, raid would be launched north of the Thames and at the 12 Group area, so it would have been rash to request assistance at trouble's first sign.

When the call for reinforcement came on this occasion, it was for the Duxford Wing to patrol North Weald at 20,000ft. According to Brickhill, the instruction Douglas received from Woodhall, however, was '*Will* you patrol between North Weald and Hornchurch, angels twenty?' This 'order', if true, was open to personal interpretation by the Duxford formation leader. Douglas disagreed that the way to protect airfields was to patrol above them. He believed that the bombers should be intercepted while approaching their target. Consequently he ignored both the given height by climbing to 22,000ft, and led the wing south-west, over London. According to

310 Squadron, a large enemy formation was sighted, 'South of the Thames Estuary, heading north-west... The attack was delivered South of London.' This was, of course, exactly the scenario Dowding and Park had sought to avoid. The sector stations north of the Thames were now unprotected – and yet the possibility of a threat against them could not be discounted. If evidence exists confirming that 12 Group was on occasion called for too late, this demonstrated that 12 Group's contribution was self-serving; it was hardly likely to improve relations between the two groups.

The usual confused fight developed. Although 310 Squadron reported attacking 'Do 215s', it actually became embroiled with Me 110s and He 111s, the latter of KG 1 and Farnborough bound. During the initial charge, Flight Lieutenant Gordon Sinclair collided with Flying Officer Johnnie Boulton; the former safely took to his parachute but the 20-year-old Boulton was killed. His Hurricane, in fact, collided in turn with an Me 110 of 9/ZG 76 which crashed at Woodmanstone – some thirty miles south-west of North Weald. The Me 110 attacked by Flying Officer Bergman and Pilot Officer Fejfar exploded over Worcester Park; Pilot Officer Zimprich fired at a 3/KG 1 He 111 already engaged by 607 Squadron's Sergeant Burnell-Phillips, the bomber forced-landed near Sundridge.

Given their Spitfires' superior performance at high altitude (see *How the Spitfire Won the Battle of Britain*, Dilip Sarkar, Amberley Publishing, 2010), 19 Squadron had been detailed to protect 242 and 310 Squadrons from high-flying German fighters. Having climbed to 23,000ft, the Spitfires were soon in action, subsequently making various claims. Pilot Officer Wallace Cunningham left an Me 109 'enveloped in flames'; the German crashed at Ditcham. Sergeant David Cox left another diving in flames. Sub-Lieutenant Giles 'Admiral' Blake, however, pursued the raiders across the Channel, leaving an He 111 with both engines stopped and descending seawards.

When the wing attacked, Douglas himself fired a long burst at the leading He 111, which he left 'turning on its back', later writing in his log book that he had 'Got the leader in flames'. Pilot Officer Willie McKnight claimed a Dornier in flames and the destruction of an escorting fighter. Flight Lieutenant Ball also claimed an Me 109 flamer.

Upon conclusion of this engagement, the wing's squadrons claimed as follows:

19 Squadron: 5 (& 2 shared) destroyed, 3 probables, 0 damaged.
310 Squadron: 3/3/1.

242 Squadron: 10 destroyed.

Wing total: 20 (& 2 shared) destroyed, 6/2

The Wing's losses:

242 Squadron: 1 pilot killed, 2 Hurricanes lost.
310 Squadron: 1 pilot killed, 2 Hurricanes lost.
19 Squadron: 2 Spitfires damaged.

The wing score of twenty destroyed and two shared, along with six probables and two damaged, made impressive reading. Soon, 242 Squadron received further congratulatory signals from Leigh-Mallory and the CAS. Those in high places were becoming increasingly convinced that 12 Group had got it right. The reality, however, was that the enemy lost but twenty-seven aircraft in action over England that day – only four of them having definitely been destroyed by the Duxford Wing (and another through the collision with Boulton). The available evidence, therefore, suggests that on this occasion the wing over-claimed by some 5:1, it being noteworthy that 242 Squadron's claims were consistently and substantially higher than the other squadrons.

On 9 September 1940, there were changes in 12 Group's order of battle. On 3 September, 616 Squadron had been relieved at Kenley, only eight of its original pilots flying away to Coltishall. Six days later, 616 Squadron withdrew further north, to Kirton-in-Lindsey, categorised a 'C' unit, being replaced at Coltishall by 74 Squadron. Between June and August, 74 had flown from the Hornchurch sector in 11 Group, then, after a brief stay at Wittering, had rested and received replacements at Kirton. Now, a 'B' unit, Squadron Leader Adolph Gysbert 'Sailor' Malan rotated his 74 Squadron with Squadron Leader Billy Burton's 616. It was a clever system – which worked. 74, of course, was a famous squadron, their South African leader already a legend in Fighter Command and a leading ace.

The following day, Douglas flew to 12 Group HQ for an hour-long interview with Leigh-Mallory. The AOC listened while the legless squadron commander explained his belief that it was the formation leader who should decide when and where to attack – not the controller – on the grounds that height information received from RDF was frequently inaccurate and that, in any case, the controller could not see the enemy personally. This, however, was absolutely and completely contrary to Fighter Command's System. According to Brickhill, Leigh-Mallory agreed with Douglas and said, 'I'll put this to the right people and in the mean-time you might as well carry on with your theory. It seems to work.' So convinced, in fact, was Leigh-Mallory that 12 Group knew better than both Air Chief Marshal Dowding and Air Vice-Marshal Park that he added two more squadrons to the Duxford Wing. This was now not just a wing, but a *big* wing of five squadrons – a 12 Group Corps d'élite indeed. Nothing could have been more contrary to how Dowding had expressly ordered the battle to be fought. Even Douglas himself was 'startled'.

On this dull day, there were no major raids. 611 Squadron had again flown from Digby to Fowlmere, where they were joined by fourteen 74 Squadron Spitfires. 242 Squadron, in their leader's absence, remained at Coltishall. Apart from a section of 611 Squadron aircraft investigating an X-Raid over 12 Group, which transpired to be friendly, the Duxford Sector squadrons were not called upon.

On 11 September 1940, 242 Squadron again remained at Coltishall, in fact whenever the CO was absent, as he still was, the unit did not proceed to Duxford. Again, Squadron Leader Malan led 74 Squadron to join 19 and 611 Squadrons at Fowlmere. One flight of 266 Squadron, now a 'B' unit, although officially based at Wittering, had operated from 242 Squadron's dispersal at Coltishall for the last three days, also flew to Fowlmere. At Duxford, the Polish Hurricanes of 302 'Poznan' Squadron were also on readiness for the first time, putting three Spitfire and two Hurricane squadrons, some fifty fighters in all, at the Sector Controller's disposal.

Like the Czechoslovaks, the Poles were continuing the fight with the RAF. 302 Squadron had been formed at Leconfield on 13 July 1940, like 310 Squadron operating a 'double-banking' system with Polish shadowing English-speaking officers. For example, while the Polish CO was Squadron Leader Mieczyslaw Mumler, his British counterpart was Squadron Leader W.A.J. 'Jack' Satchell. The Poles had been operational since 19 August 1940, and eagerly looked forward to action.

On this day, poor weather in the morning once more dictated that the enemy's main assault was delayed until afternoon. At 1500 hrs, the He 111s of I & II/KG 26 left their French bases, bound for England. After rendezvousing with their 200-strong fighter escort, the bombers headed up the Thames Estuary to London. From 1530 hrs onwards, Fighter Command squadrons attacked the enemy formation but was unable to reach the bombers until after their bombs began exploding in the docklands below. The Me 110 escorts withdrew southwards, where they formed a defensive circle over Croydon, covering the bombers' shortest exit route: out over the coast between Dover and Dungeness. Inaccurate routing on the approach, however, led to the Me 109s expending too much fuel and a substantial number of the escorting fighters had to break off and return to France. This left the Heinkels with little protection and, unsurprisingly, they suffered heavy losses: ten were shot down and twelve more damaged.

At 1530 hours, Squadron Leader Brian Lane led eight Spitfires of his own 19 Squadron, together with six of 266, off from Fowlmere as the lead unit in an all-Spitfire wing, the other squadrons being Squadron Leader 'Sailor' Malan's 74 and Squadron Leader Jimmy McComb's 611. Lane's instructions were to patrol in a southerly direction towards the Thames Estuary. At about 1550 hrs, while flying at 20,000ft over south-east London, the Spitfires sighted 100 enemy aircraft approaching them from the south. 74 and 611 Squadrons executed a left-hand turn, attacking on the beam of the enemy formation. Squadron Leader Lane led 19 Squadron in a head-on charge against the He 111s. Sergeant Bernard 'Jimmy' Jennings fired at an He 111 during Lane's initial charge, but later attacked the rearmost machine of fifteen Me 110s. The Spitfire pilot reported that, 'this one fell back from the rest of the formation with smoke pouring out of his starboard engine. I did another attack from above and behind and he crashed in a wood, south of the Ashford railway line between Sittingbourne and Maidstone'.

Flight Sergeant George 'Grumpy' Unwin:

> I was at about 20,000ft, flying my usual Spitfire, P9546, QV-H, and I suddenly saw this lone Dornier. How he was on his own I'll never know, but he was off home. So I went after him. Now the drill against a Dornier was he had a dustbin rear gunner, a dustbin hanging down below the fuselage and so you had to fix him first before closing in for the aircraft. This I did, very cleverly of course. I could see him shooting at me and so closed in and gave him a burst and shot him up. At least I thought I had, I'll never know to this day whether I did or didn't, or whether someone took his place. Because as I closed right in on him and started shooting I saw his rear gunner shooting back at me, the little red sparks you could see. I didn't pay much attention to it, thinking that after a quick spray from the spread of my guns he would stop. I carried on firing for quite a while, when suddenly I was covered in smoke. To my horror a hole appeared in my windscreen – I was leaning forward of course, one did to peer through the gunsight which was fortunately in the middle of a

piece of armour plated, bullet resistant glass about an inch and a half. A hole appeared in front of my face. I thought, 'Good God I must be dead, or something' – no blood, no nothing, but I'm covered in smoke, I thought I was on fire. So I whipped the hood back, undid my straps and started to get out.

By this time I'd broken away, I was going downhill. I was halfway out of the cockpit when I suddenly saw that the smoke was coming from the top of the engine through the engine cowling which is where the glycol pipe is, the coolant pipe. The smoke was a really browny colour, it wasn't black smoke. I could smell it too, it was glycol. So I got back in and strapped myself in again, leaving the hood open, still going downhill in case somebody was following me. Then I started looking for a field, finding one to land in near Brentwood in Essex. In those days you were supposed to get it down without hurting the aircraft. So I waited until I'd found my field and got down to about a thousand feet, dropped the undercarriage and did a forced landing in this field which had a few cows in it. Quite a big field, it was. No trouble at all.

I hadn't even got out of the cockpit before a jeep with a young subaltern and two soldiers with fixed bayonets came roaring through the gate. As soon as they saw it was one of ours they changed their attitude. I got a screwdriver from one of the soldiers and we took the top off, and there it was – a bullet had gone through the glycol pipe. As I had first served in the RAF as an engineering apprentice at Halton before the war, my technical knowledge was good, and so I knew what needed to be done to get me airborne again. The soldiers took me to North Weald, where I got help from a fitter plus spares and repaired the aircraft, which I flew back to Duxford two days later. The windscreen, however, could not be repaired on station and so P9546 was sent off to a Maintenance Unit (MU).

In what was 611 Squadron's first engagement of a massed formation, Squadron Leader McComb's pilots had also been in the battle's midst; Sergeant 'Sandy' Levenson attacked several enemy aircraft, including a 'Ju 88' which he actually flew alongside as the raider lost height. As he did so, his Spitfire was hit by AA fire and as black smoke poured from beneath the instrument panel he broke off to force-land near Kenley. A nearby searchlight post then informed Levenson that the bomber concerned had crashed in flames a few miles south of Kenley. This was an He 111 of 3/KG26 which came down at Lingfield; the same Heinkel also featured in the combat reports of at least eight other RAF fighter pilots. The Squadron's Sergeant F.E.R. Shepherd, however, baled out over Croydon with his parachute in flames and was killed, his Spitfire crashing onto an air raid shelter, killing two civilians. 266 Squadron made no combat claims but lost a Spitfire, Pilot Officer Roach baling out safely over Billericay.

In this action, this all-Spitfire wing claimed as follows:

> 19 Squadron: 4/6/2
> 74 Squadron: 5/2/3
> 266 Squadron: 0/0/4
> 611 Squadron: 2/3/0

> Wing total: 11/11/9

> The Wing's losses:

> 19 Squadron: 1 Spitfire damaged, pilot safe.
> 74 Squadron: Nil.
> 266 Squadron: 1 Spitfire lost, pilot safe.
> 611 Squadron, 1 Spitfire lost, pilot killed.

Such a confused air battle was this, involving so many aircraft, that it is impossible to identify with certainty any more than three of the wing's claims.

After this combat, Malan returned with 74 Squadron to Coltishall, and did not operate with the Duxford Wing again, despite remaining there until 15 October 1940, on which date the unit returned to 11 Group for another frontline tour.

Why 12 Group decided to operate an all-Spitfire wing to this day is unknown. The two Hurricane squadrons, 302 and 310, remained on readiness at Duxford, with the Czechs patrolling North Weald uneventfully that evening.

Air Vice-Marshal Park later reported upon the enemy's tactics during this phase:

> The normal attack was formations of long-range bombers, escorted by strong formations of fighters as experienced in the previous phase of operations up to 10 September 1940.

Bombing attacks were mostly high-level, with only a few at medium altitudes.

Method of Attack

The enemy has attempted in this phase to draw our fighter patrols off from his bombers by high altitude diversions, as he had attempted to do, unsuccessfully, prior to 10 September. Increasingly high fighter screens were sent inland to draw off and contain our fighters, while the bomber formations, closely escorted by further fighters, endeavoured to sweep in some 6,000 – 10,000 feet below.

The majority of attacks approached in two or three waves at varying intervals of time, on a much wider front and at heights varying between 16,000 and 20,000 feet for bomber formations. Small formations sometimes broke off from the main raid immediately fighter opposition was encountered and, descending to lower altitude, made clever use of cloud cover to attack objectives in the London area. Owing to extreme difficulty in reporting the tracks of these split raids, they frequently reached their objectives without effective interruption, and sometimes made their escape to the coast without being engaged.

As our success against these bombers increased, there was a noticeable increase in the ratio of enemy fighters to bombers, the ratio in the later part of the phase being about four fighters to one bomber.

Employment of Enemy Fighters

The favourite practice was to send a very high fighter screen over Kent from 15–45 minutes ahead of bomber attacks, presumably to draw up our fighter squadrons and exhaust their petrol before the main attack crossed the coast. At other times the high fighter screen arrived only a few minutes in advance of the bomber formations with close escort. Fighter escorts normally consisted of two parts: (a) a big formation above and to the flank or in rear of the bombers, and (b) smaller formations of fighters formating with the bombers on the same level or slightly below. The latter formations endeavoured to prevent head-on attacks by our fighters against the incoming bombers.

Regarding the deployment of 11 Group's squadrons, Park added:

> The general plan adopted was to engage the enemy high fighter
> screen with pairs of Spitfire squadrons from Hornchurch and
> Biggin Hill, half-way between London and the coast, and so
> enable Hurricane squadrons from London sectors to attack
> bomber formations and their close escort before they reached
> the line of fighter aerodromes East and South of London. The
> remaining time to intercept the first wave of the attack by
> climbing in pairs formed a third and inner screen by patrolling
> along the line of aerodromes East and South of London. The
> fighter squadrons from Debden, Tangmere, and sometimes
> Northolt, were employed in wings or three squadrons in pairs
> to form a screen south-east of London to intercept the third
> wave of the attack coming inland, also to mop up retreating
> formations of the earlier waves. The Spitfire squadrons were
> redisposed so as to concentrate three squadrons at each
> of Hornchurch and Biggin Hill. The primary role of these
> squadrons was to engage and drive back the enemy high fighter
> screen, and so protect the Hurricane squadrons, whose task
> was to attack close escorts and then the bomber formations, all
> of which flew at much lower attitude.

This response reflects a flexible approach – not a fixed mindset, especially
regarding formation-size and the fact that the Spitfire's high-altitude facility
meant that the type performed a crucial function. Regarding 11 Group's use
of wings, Park added that:

> When early warning had given adequate time, and cloud
> conditions were suitable, squadrons were employed in wings
> of three against enemy bomber formations and their close
> escort. Being located outside the area normally patrolled by
> enemy fighter screens, the squadrons from Debden, Northolt
> and Tangmere were not infrequently employed in wings of
> three squadrons. These wings were successful in engaging
> retreating bomber formations, which normally lost their escort
> before reaching London, because of the vigorous action of
> Spitfire and Hurricane squadrons working in pairs against
> incoming raids.

Experience showed that even small wings of three squadrons were not effective against high fighter patrols, and the Spitfire squadrons were therefore used in pairs.

Again, though, the limitations of aerial radio telephony meant that these 11 Group wings were really only arriving over the battle area together, before fighting independently. Also, three squadrons were only operating against bombers at medium altitude, while pairs of Spitfire units patrolled at high altitude. The important thing to appreciate, and which becomes relevant shortly, is that the 11 Group sector controllers and Observer Corps were aware of the existence, position and intention of these friendly formations.

At Debden, the Hurricane-equipped 17 and 73 Squadrons flew together as a wing; on 11 September 1940 this formation, patrolling over the Thames Estuary and intercepting Me 110s of ZG26, claiming five destroyed, off-set against one Hurricane written-off and two more damaged. This increase in formation size was well-thought out and confirmed by Park's 'Instruction to Controllers No 16', issued on 11 September 1940:

Readiness Squadrons
Despatch in pairs to engage first wave of enemy. Spitfires against fighter screen, and Hurricanes against bombers and close escort.

Available 15 Squadrons
a) Bring to Readiness in pairs;
b) Despatch in pairs to engage second wave.

Available 30 Squadrons
a) Bring to Readiness;
b) Despatch singly to protect aircraft factories or sector aerodromes, or to reinforce squadrons already in the air.

If there is a third wave and it is necessary to despatch these squadrons, they should be sent in pairs as follows:

Debden and North Weald squadrons together.
Hornchurch and Biggin Hill squadrons together.
Kenley and Northolt squadrons together.

Tangmere Squadrons

When not required to protect the Portsmouth-Southampton area in conjunction with 10 Group squadrons, the Tangmere squadrons should be employed within Kenley or back Tangmere Sector to engage enemy formations that approach London from the South, or endeavour to pass round the South of London to attack aircraft factories at Kingston, Brooklands and Langley.

Whenever time permits, the Readiness squadrons and the Available 15 squadron should be despatched to work as a pair after having rendezvoused at base.

Rendezvous of squadrons

The Group Controller must name the base over which pairs of squadrons are to rendezvous, as they normally occupy separate aerodromes within a Sector. Sector Controllers should inform Group Controller immediately a pair of squadrons have rendezvoused over any given point. Group Controller should then detail these squadrons to a raid and leave the rest to Sector.

Selection of Squadron to lead a pair of squadrons

The detailing of the directing squadron should be done by the Sector Controller, who should know which squadron is best suited to lead. Sector controllers must also repeat to the squadron being led all orders issued to the directing squadron in case these units become separated by clouds. Sector commanders must impress upon squadron commanders the importance of leading squadrons in a pair joining up and maintaining contact with the squadron being led.

On the same day, 10 Group had again reinforced 11 Group. Among Air Vice-Marshal Brand's squadrons was 238, freshly returned to Middle Wallop from a two-month sojourn at Cornwall's St Eval airfield. On this day, 238 Squadron lost three Hurricanes: two pilots were missing, the other wounded. Yet again, the sudden change in the tempo of battle had been traumatic. Air Commodore Harry Fenton commanded 238 Squadron at the time:

> We had a daily routine: rise before first light, at about 0330 hrs, have a coffee and then go to dispersal, spending the

day there and being scrambled in either section or squadron strength. We shared Middle Wallop with 609 Squadron, with whom we took it in turns to spend every third day down at Warmwell, undertaking convoy protection patrols. That was during the early days, but I was shot down and wounded on 8 August 1940, returning to the squadron on 12 September. By that time, 238 had been back at Middle Wallop for two days but had already lost two pilots, both missing from action over 11 Group: David Hughes, an able flight commander, and Duszynski, a Pole whom I had not even met. The tempo of combat had completely changed.

Among Fenton's pilots was Sergeant Gordon Batt:

When we returned to Middle Wallop in September, the size of the German formations had increased: the bomber formation was usually fifty-sixty strong, in an oblong block and close formation, and above them were Me 110s, and Me 109s higher still. To counter this we often flew accompanied by one of Wallop's Spitfire squadrons. Our CO was the senior squadron commander and so we usually led, our Hurricanes attacking the bombers while the Spitfires held off the escort. It certainly did my morale a lot of good; God and Hitler know what it did to theirs! The only snag was that as 238 was first to attack, I never had the opportunity to look back – there must have been chaos!

Towards the end of August and throughout September, we were frequently called to the West of the London area. The Controller would give us a commentary regarding what was going on generally, and while holding off at 20,000ft, we could hear him directing 11 Group's squadrons into action. From our position West of London, we could see ack-ack bursting over the capital, and condensation trails of the Spitfires, Hurricanes and Me 109s. The boys of 11 Group were obviously holding their own and we were sensibly being held in reserve. When we were vectored, the Controller would say something like: '25 Bandits, Angels 20, heading straight for you, they're all yours!' It really was slick control. All of the sorties, though, were quite frightening and fraught with danger!

Indeed, Air Vice-Marshal Park reported favourably upon the cooperation received from 10 Group:

> During this phase of heavy attacks on the London area, there were occasionally heavy diversionary attacks on the Portsmouth area, when 10 Group rendered invaluable assistance by despatching squadrons singly or in pairs to reinforce Tangmere Sector. During mass attacks over London, valuable reinforcements were provided by 10 Group for the close protection of aircraft factories and airfields West and south-west of London. These squadrons several times intercepted bomber formations that had broken away from the main raids and endeavoured, without escort, to attack aircraft factories and aerodromes, making use of cloud cover.

12 September 1940 saw poor weather, cold and rain. 19 and 611 Squadrons stood by at Fowlmere, while 242 Squadron joined 302 and 310 Squadrons on readiness at Duxford. The following day was similar, with little flying. The weather improved slightly on 14 September; at 1550 hrs Squadron Leader Douglas Bader led a four-squadron wing over London, at 23,000ft, but without event. The same squadrons, 19, 302 and 310, followed 242 on another patrol that evening. The Wing's instructions were to patrol north of the Thames Estuary – but the evidence confirmed what the Big Wing was already acting as an independent entity; according to the 19 Squadron ORB, Douglas had led the 12 Group 'Balbo' over 'Kent and almost France'.

Flight Lieutenant 'Teddy' Morten:

> On one of the many occasions on which Bader tackled me in the Mess regarding the 'Hun in the sun' etc he said 'Morty, you know that yesterday you told the wing to patrol North Weald at Angels Twenty?'
>
> 'Yes', I said.
>
> 'Well, d'ya know where we were upon reaching required height?'
>
> 'No', I said.
>
> 'Over *Reading*! We were looking down on the patrol area, up sun and all eyes skinned!'
>
> I found this astonishing. How could the battle be fought if controllers didn't know where their aircraft were?

Morten was right. Only able to communicate with the 12 Group Duxford Sector Controller, here was the Duxford Wing roaming freely over the 11 Group area, confusing the defences and Observer Corps. Squadron Leader Bader, it seemed, was gaining confidence to operate as he wished.

Another eye-witness was Group Captain (then Wing Commander) Thomas Long, who was one of three officers selected by Park to control the air component of the Dunkirk evacuation, after which he had served as an 11 Group Controller; writing in 1961, he recalled that:

> On one occasion I had specifically asked 12 Group to have their Balbo patrol over London, from North Weald to Kenley.... Knowing that we had no operational control over it, as 'LM' simply refused to allow us to give a single order to his favourite Balbo, I asked the Observer Corps to plot this Balbo on this occasion. The WAAF and RAF plotters were amazed to see what transpired. From Duxford ... the plots took them right out to Lowestoft then turned South and entered the Thames Estuary East of Southend! By then, they were in the midst of a small ragged formation of German enemy aircraft beating it to France. I told the AOC, Keith Park, who took due note. What happened about it, I don't know.

13 September 1940 was another wet and dreary day with little flying. 611 Squadron was at Fowlmere and sent two sections off to investigate an X-Raid, but the Spitfires were recalled almost immediately. 242 Squadron was at Duxford, uneventfully patrolling over London and North Weald.

14 September 1940 was, however, a significant date for Squadron Leader Bader, who was appointed to the DSO. The citation read:

> This officer has displayed gallantry and leadership of the highest order. During three recent engagements he has led his Squadron with such skill and ability that thirty-three enemy aircraft have been destroyed. In the course of these engagements Squadron Leader Bader has added to previous successes by destroying six enemy aircraft.

While no one could deny that Douglas had 'displayed gallantry and leadership of the highest order', 242 Squadron's victory tally, we now know, was highly questionable. Given that Flight Lieutenant Eric Ball, commander of 242 Squadron's 'A' Flight, received the DFC that day, there was nonetheless just cause for celebration that night – although Bader himself never drank alcohol.

By 1100 hrs on Sunday 15 September 1940, it was obvious, given enemy air traffic over the Pas-de-Calais, that a very big attack was imminent. Surprisingly, however, the enemy formation took thirty minutes to form up and sally forth across the Channel. This delay provided 11 Group time to scramble ten squadrons – which were now being deployed in pairs, with Spitfires providing Hurricanes protection against the high-flying Me 109s – and request reinforcements from both 10 and 12 Groups. At 1125 hrs, 19, 242, 302 and 310 Squadrons were scrambled from Duxford, being joined en route to North Weald by 611 Squadron. At 1133 hrs, the first German formation crossed the coast between Dover and North Folkestone, followed three minutes later by two more incoming over Dover and South Foreland. The enemy proceeded on a dog-leg course, flying first towards the Thames Estuary, then south or south-west to Kent's north coast, and finally west to Maidstone before approaching the capital. The raiders' targets were gasworks, industrial targets and docks in the London area. Ready to meet this new assault were 312 Spitfires and Hurricanes.

310 Squadron's diary confirmed the Big Wing's deployment:

> The Squadron, with the CO leading, took off at 1130 hrs to patrol North Weald. The Squadron … was flying in a wing formation by sections in line astern, with 242 Squadron in the van. It had been arranged that the Spitfires (19 and 611 Squadrons) would attack the fighter escort, the Hurricanes (242, 302 and 310 Squadrons) tackling the bombers.

Needless to say, this five-squadron strong 12 Group force did not patrol North Weald as instructed. Douglas led the wing towards London, from the north. At 1209 hrs, anti-aircraft fire alerted the wing to twenty-four incoming Do 17s of KG 76 – to the south, over Brixton. Two 11 Group Hurricane squadrons, 257 and 504, were already attacking the bombers head-on at 16,000ft. The Big Wing was at 20,000ft and up-sun; Douglas later said that the bombers were 'without a single fighter to escort them. This time, for a change, we outnumbered the Hun.' His combat report reads:

> Saw two squadrons pass underneath us in formation, travelling NW in purposeful manner, then saw AA bursts

so turned 12 Group wing and saw E/A 3,000ft below to the NW. Managed perfect approach with 19 and 611 between our Hurricanes and sun, and E/A below and down-sun. Arrived over E/A formation of twenty – forty Do 17. Noticed Me 109 dive out of sun and warned our Spitfires to look out. Me 109 broke away and climbed SE.

About to attack E/A which were turning left-handed, i.e. to West and South, when I noticed Spitfires and Hurricanes (11 Group?) chasing them. Was compelled to wait for friendly fighters and dived down with leading Section in formation onto last section of three E/A. Pilot Officer Campbell took left-handed Do 17, I took middle one, Sub-Lieutenant Cork the right-hand one, which had lost ground on outside of turn. Opened fire at 100 yards in steep dive and saw a large flash behind starboard motor of *Dornier* as wing caught fire. Must have hit petrol pipe or tank. Pulled up, overshot and pulled up steeply. Then carried on and attacked another Do 17 but had to break away to avoid Spitfire. The sky was then full of Spitfires and Hurricanes, queuing up and pushing each other out of the way to get at the Dorniers, which for once were outnumbered.

I squirted at odd Dorniers at close-range as they came into my sights but could not hold them in my sights for fear of collision with other Spitfires and Hurricanes.

Saw collision between Spitfire and Do 17, which wrecked both aeroplanes. Finally ran out of ammunition chasing crippled and smoking Do 17 into cloud.

Douglas later wrote that:

This time, for a change, we outnumbered the Hun, and, believe me, no more than eight got home from that party. At one time you could see planes going down on fire all over the place, and the sky seemed full of parachutes. It was sudden death that morning, for our fighters shot them to blazes.

One unfortunate German rear-gunner baled out of the Do 17 I attacked, but his parachute caught on the tail. There he was, swinging helplessly, with the aircraft swooping and diving and staggering all over the sky, being pulled about by the man hanging by his parachute from the tail. That bomber went crashing into the Thames Estuary, with the swinging gunner still there.

Just about the same time, one of my boys saw a similar thing in another Do 17, though this time the gunner who tried to bale out had his parachute caught before it opened. It caught in the hood, and our pilot saw the other two members of the crew crawl up to set him free. He was swinging from his packed parachute until they pushed him clear. Then they jumped after him, and their plane went into the water with a terrific smack. I've always thought it was a pretty stout effort on the part of those two Huns who refused to leave their pal fastened to the doomed aircraft.

One of KG 76's Dorniers was flown by Feldwebel Wilhelm Raab, a veteran of the campaigns in both Poland and France, in addition to numerous sorties over England. High above Brixton, Raab's bomber was attacked by numerous RAF fighter pilots: first Sergeant Tyrer of 46 Squadron, then Flight Lieutenant Rimmer of 229 Squadron, and both Flight Lieutenant Peter Brothers and Pilot Officer Mortimer of 257 Squadron. As the *Dornier* dived for cloud cover, Flight Lieutenant Powell-Sheddon and Pilot Officer Tamblyn of No 242 Squadron attacked next. The CO of 19 Squadron, Squadron Leader Brian Lane, then also saw and attacked the Dornier, at first unaware of the attack in progress by the Hurricanes; realising that he had 'jumped the queue', he followed the Hurricanes and took his turn to fire. Lane was unable to tell, however, whether he or the two 242 Squadron Hurricanes were responsible for the hits he could see on Raab's aircraft. Descending at 100ft per minute, the Dornier dropped out of the cloud and, after being attacked by even more fighters, Raab ordered his crew to bale out before tumbling into space himself. At 1230 hrs, Squadron Leader Lane watched the pilotless bomber narrowly miss a house, and explode on impact at Underriver, south of Sevenoaks in Kent. Raab's fate certainly confirms the 310 Squadron statement that on this day 'no individual pilot could claim one bird as his own'.

KG 76 had certainly suffered at the hands of Fighter Command, six of their number crashing on English soil. Among these was probably the most famous German casualty of the whole battle, the Dornier which crashed on Victoria Station having been attacked by numerous fighters. The enemy pilot, Oberleutnant Zehbe, landed by parachute at Kennington; he was roughly handled by a civilian mob and later died from injuries received.

Some of 19 Squadron's Spitfires managed to engage the Me 109s, as had been planned; at 1210 hrs over Westerham, Flight Sergeant Unwin engaged 3/JG53's Staffelkapitän, Oberleutnant Haase, in a dogfight:

> I was Red Three with Flight Lieutenant Lawson. We sighted the enemy aircraft which were flying in vics of three. The escorts dived singly onto us and I engaged an Me 109 with a yellow nose. I gave one burst of six seconds and it burst into flames. The pilot baled out and the enemy aircraft crashed between Redhill and Westerham.

Haase was killed as his parachute failed to open. As other Me 109s dived on No 19 Squadron, Sergeant David Cox climbed and flew south. A few minutes later he found six 109s of 2/JG27 flying in the same direction. Simultaneously the Germans saw the Spitfire, and so Green One attacked from astern. Cox's target immediately half-rolled and dived away. Four of the fighters then broke off and continued south, no doubt low on fuel, but the sixth attacked Cox head-on. As his assailant reared up to pass over the fleeing Spitfire, Cox climbed and turned sharply, attacking from below. The 109 dived through cloud, pursued by the VR Spitfire pilot who, upon emerging, saw his victim's wreckage burning in a field. This was at Lodge Wood, near Uckfield, and the pilot, Unteroffizier Walburger, was captured unhurt.

611 Squadron's ORB provides a dramatic account of the action:

> 611 Squadron joined wing of Hurricanes over Duxford at 15,000 feet at 1131 hours then climbed to 27,000 feet to the left and above the wing which was at 22,000 feet. When SW of London, 50 enemy bombers and 30 Me 109s escorting above were sighted coming from south. The wing went into attack the bombers and escort turning south-east. 611 Squadron kept beside the Me 109s which were to the west and above. After the wing attack had broken up bomber formation, the Me 109s did not come down. After waiting for about seven minutes, S/Ldr McComb informed Wing Leader that he was coming down, and gave order echelon port. The Squadron proceeding at the time south-east and up sun of the enemy. The Squadron in line astern, three sections of four aircraft executed a head-on attack down onto a formation of about 10 Do 215s and Do 17s. Then flying at 18,000 feet in a south easterly direction.

S/Ldr McComb attacked Do 215 head on, hits observed, no results. Pulling up he made a beam attack on an Me 110 which turned in its back and went down. The Squadron formation then broke up. S/Ldr McComb chased an Me 109 which was in a dogfight with a Hurricane, but could not catch up with them as he was too far behind. He then proceeded to the coast in the hope of attacking homing lame ducks before returning to base. P/O Williams after making his attack with the Squadron but without any observed results, saw a Do 215 attacked by six fighters crash into a wood near BISHOPSBOURNE, KENT. Two of the crew baling out. P/O Lund dived into initial attack but enemy aircraft passed through his sights before he could fire. P/O O'Neill attacked six or seven times a Do 215 which had fallen behind the enemy formation. Four Hurricanes also attacked at same time. He chased this enemy aircraft as far as DUNGENESS where three other Spitfires carried on the attack. He then returned to base, being short of petrol and ammunition. F/Lt Leather carried out a head on attack on three Do 215s. No results observed. He then attacked a Do 215 at rear of large formation using up remainder of his ammunition. The port engine exploded and stopped. A number of other fighters also attacked this enemy aircraft and Red 2 reports seeing two crew bale out and machine crashed near BISHOPSBOURNE, KENT.

So far, Raab's Dornier had also appeared in the combat reports of two pilots from 611 Squadron; how many others it featured in is anyone's guess. The 611 Squadron report continues:

> P/O Pollard, after firing a short burst in the initial dive attack, chased, in company with one other Spitfire and a Hurricane, a Do 215. Between Rochester and Herne Bay, enemy aircraft lost height, smoke coming from port engine. Crew of two baled out and aircraft crashed on edge of a wood about four miles south of Herne Bay. He landed at Detling at 1305 hours having lost his bearings, later returned to Gl.

This was a 3/KG 76 Do 17Z which was also engaged by Pilot Officer Meaker of 249 Squadron, and both Flight Lieutenant Ken Gillies and Pilot

Officer 'Bogle' Bodie of 66 Squadron. The Dornier crashed in flames and exploded at Slurry. The very detailed 611 Squadron account continues:

> Yellow Three, P/O Brown after initial dive attack on pulling out saw no enemy aircraft. After circling for about 10 minutes he returned to home base. P/O Walker after initial dive attack on pulling out saw no enemy aircraft. He developed engine trouble and had to force land at West Malling at 1235 hours. F/Lt Stoddart fired one quick burst in initial dive attack, and then had to take evasive action in order to avoid attack from Me 109s. He circled for some time and then returned to base. F/Sgt Sadler after initial dive saw 12 Do 215s going south east so executed two frontal attacks on leader. Enemy aircraft believed hit but no results were seen. Abandoned chase at Lympne being short of ammunition and petrol. P/O Dewey fired a short burst at a Do 215 but observed no results. After circling for some time returned base. Sgt Levenson broke formation to attack an Me 109 but enemy aircraft got away. He then flew towards large formation of Do 215s flying at 18,000 feet. After sighting one Do 215 by itself at 14,000 feet he rolled over and carried out an old astern attack diving onto the enemy. Got in a long burst and both enemy aircraft motors were smoking when he broke away. Climbing again, he carried out the same attack. He broke away when both engines and both mainplanes immediately behind them were on fire.

For the overworked Luftwaffe, the presence of so many RAF fighters, which had harried them constantly from crossing the English coast to leaving it some while later, was alarming. The crushing effect that the arrival of fifty-odd 12 Group fighters had on the Germans' morale cannot be underestimated. The combined success of Fighter Command and other defences during that morning's action had resulted in few casualties and little damage being caused. Two bombs had fallen on Buckingham Palace, however, thus showing the King and Queen to be in the fight alongside humble Eastenders.

The Prime Minister, Winston Churchill, had chosen this particular morning to visit the 11 Group Operations Room at Uxbridge. As he watched squadrons being flung into battle, the Prime Minister asked Air Vice-Marshal Park what reserves he had. 'None, Sir', the commander of 11 Group replied, but to put that statement into context, he meant, of course, that all of *his* Group's squadrons were airborne. Certainly all of the Command's 'A' squadrons were committed to battle on this day, but those aircraft represented less than half of the total available.

Soon, the RDF screens indicated further formations moving out from Calais. Between 1410 and 1435 hrs, eight or more formations of German bombers and their escorts crossed the English coastline between Rye and Dover, heading for London. As Squadron Leader Brian Lane later wrote, the Duxford Wing 'ran into the whole Luftwaffe over London. Wave after wave of bombers covered by several hundred fighters.' Unfortunately, the 'whole Luftwaffe' was some 4,000ft above the wing, however, and as the Duxford fighters climbed, the 109s inevitably plunged down. Douglas reported that:

> On being attacked from behind by Me 109, I ordered 'Break up!' and pulled up and round violently. Coming off my back partially blacked out, nearly collided with Yellow 2 (Pilot Officer Crowley-Milling). Spun in his slipstream and straightened out at 5,000ft below without firing a shot. Climbed up again and saw E/A twin-engine aircraft flying westwards. Just got in range and fired a short burst (3 seconds) in a completely stalled position and then spun off again and lost more height.

Crowley-Milling was startled at so narrowly avoiding collision with his leader, but nonetheless latched on to the tail of a 109, remaining there in spite of the German's violent evasive manoeuvres; Yellow 2 fired a 'good burst', igniting his target's cockpit area before the pilot, Oberfeldwebel Hessel of 1/JG3, baled out.

Yellow 1 of 242 Squadron, Pilot Officer Stansfeld, joined two other Hurricanes attacking a II/KG53 He 111, which forced-landed on West Malling airfield – featuring in at least ten RAF fighter pilots' combat reports!

Although 310 Squadron had intended to attack the bombers, the 109s' intervention dictated otherwise; the Czechs were:

> themselves attacked by the Me 109s as the wing formation was broken up. F/Lt Jeffries ordered the squadron to climb to 24,000ft into the sun when another large formation of E/A were seen approaching from the South. The Squadron delayed the attack until they turned and when faced West, a head-on attack was launched out of the sun.

Everywhere there were twisting, turning fighters, those with RAF roundels from 10, 11 and 12 Groups. The Kommodore of JG 26, Major Adolf Galland, singled out the Hurricane of 310 Squadron's Sergeant Hubacek:

> With the Stabstaffel I attacked two Hurricanes, which were about 800 metres below us. Maintaining surprise, I closed on the wingman and opened fire from 120 metres, as he was in a gentle turn to the left. The enemy plane reeled as my rounds struck the nose from below, and pieces fell from the left wing and fuselage. The left side of the fuselage burst into flame.

Galland's Katchmarek, Oberleutnant Horten, had shot down the CO of 310 Squadron, Squadron Leader Sacha Hess: 'I had the impression that there was machine-gun fire behind me. I looked back several times but saw nothing. I re-trimmed the aircraft but at that moment I was hit – I do not know by what.'

Hess baled out, landing at Billericay 'little worse except for bruises'.

Some of 310 Squadron's pilots did manage to get through to the bombers; Sergeants Prchal and Rechka joined the queue of RAF fighters attacking the He 111 which crashed at Asplin's Head, and Sergeant Furst, together with Flying Officer B.D. Russell of 1(RCAF) Squadron from Northolt, destroyed a Stab/KG53 He 111 which crashed and exploded in the shell-filling area of Woolwich Arsenal. Pilot Officer Fejfar claimed a Do 17 which forced-landed on the Isle of Grain, the same enemy bomber appearing in the combat reports of at least three Spitfire pilots from 41 and 603 Squadrons.

Squadron Leader Satchell had climbed his 302 (Polish) Squadron hard after 242 and 310 Squadrons, but as he prepared to attack a formation of bombers, a 109 fired at his Hurricane, but overshot. Giving chase, Satchell fired, the 109-rolling inverted and diving earthwards. Some of Satchell's Poles reached the bombers, Flight Lieutenant Chlopik, leading Red Section into the attack, attacked a Do 17 which other pilots later confirmed had 'disintegrated'. In a subsequent combat, however, Chlopik was hit by another bomber's return fire and baled out – but was killed when his parachute failed. Pilot Officer Lapka was also shot down attacking a Do 17, but baled out safely; Sergeant Kowalski attacked a straggling bomber from just thirty yards, blowing its tail clean off. Later, a machine-gun panel of his Hurricane flapped open, negatively affecting his Hurricane's flying qualities, so he forced-landed in a nearby field.

The 611 Squadron ORB provides a stirring account of a Spitfire squadron engaged in this action:

611 Squadron ran into several formations of bombers before sufficient height could be reached so ignored them, attempting to get height in Westerly direction to keep Me 109s off wing. The squadron consisted of 8 aircraft in three sections flying line astern. It was not possible to out climb the Me 109s and the wing appeared to be both attacking and being attacked. When at 20,000' over West London, the Squadron Leader sighted a formation of 25 Do 17s proceeding South unmolested and being by then separated from the wing, gave the order Sections Echelon Right. The Squadron dived down on the formation, coming out of the sun. At the end of the general attack, Me 110s came down. S/Ldr McComb attacked rear E/A. Rear gunner ceased firing and smoke appeared from port engine. He then pulled up into a loop and dived again in inverted position. Guns worked perfectly in this position and E/A went down in flames. Result of attack is confirmed by Yellow Two and Yellow Leader. S/Ldr McComb then blacked out badly and came to in the clouds. After looking around and seeing nothing he returned to base. P/O Williams carried out a No 3 FC attack on an He 111. A second burst at 80 yards was given but no result observed. E/A returned machine-gun fire. He was unable then to return to Squadron which had now broken up, but observing two enemy formations, he made an astern attack on No 3 of the last section of the formation of Do 215. The formation turned north but Red 2's target fell out, losing height. He then carried out another attack finishing his ammunition. E/A descended into the clouds, one engine stopped, Red Two following. Cloud was 2,000 feet thick and on emerging no E/A was visible but two minutes later he saw enemy airman descending by parachute. Latter landed on edge of wood corner of Hawkhurst Golf Club about 15 miles North of Hastings.

F/Lt Leather followed Red Leader into attack astern and took machine next to his as his target was already aflame. He fired all ammunition and when broke away the Do 17 was in flames. He then was forced to land at Croydon at 1540 hours and later flew to Gl rejoining the Squadron.

P/O Brown had first to evade enemy fighters and then put one short burst into the Do 215 already attacked by Red Leader which had one engine out of action. Oil or glycol from E/A covered up windscreen and so he had to break away. Then he attacked one E/A which broke away from formation using deflection. E/A went into a steep spiral dive with escape hatch over pilot's seat open. No further results seen as large formation of Me 110s appeared and Yellow Two escaped into cloud.

P/O Lund attacked a Do 215 which was also being attacked by several other aircraft. He saw flashes of fire and smoke coming from E/A. While climbing back to main formation of bombers, one Me 110 came down on him so he fired one short burst before turning away and down. As the E/A passed his port side, black smoke was pouring from engine. No more E/A seen after this so he returned to base.

F/Sgt Sadler after attacking with Squadron, saw a Do 215 break away and begin losing height. He made two attacks on this E/A, his second attack being made at 50 yards. A Hurricane also attacked after him and the E/A apparently badly disabled disappeared below cloud.

P/O DH O'Neill lost touch with Blue Leader but after circling for about 6 minutes had to evade 8 Me 110s into cloud. Up again out of cloud saw Me 109s attacking one Hurricane and attacked one of these over Faversham without observing result although E/A took evasive action. After being attacked by another Me 109, he returned to base landing, however, by mistake first at Debden.

Sgt Levenson after attacking without visible result an Me 109 and a crippled Do 215 found himself at 10,000 feet over Brooklands aerodrome. He then saw about 50 Do 215s guarded by two Me 109s overhead. He climbed to 1,000' below formation and delivered a quarter frontal attack opening fire first at 100 yards, developing this into normal quarter attack at about 200 yards when all his ammunition was exhausted. He observed ammunition hitting leading E/A and the leading vie of 4 A/C broke away to port, smoke coming from engines of No 1 and No 2. No further result was seen but he assumed that No 1 was out of action. F/Lt Stoddart and P/O Dewey, owing to refuelling, took off 15 minutes after the squadron. The weather above cloud was perfect with visibility good.

Squadron Leader Brian Lane (19 Squadron):

> At approximately 1440 hrs, AA fire was sighted to the South and at the same time a formation of about thirty Do 215s was seen. I climbed up astern of the enemy aircraft to engage the fighter escort which could be seen above the bombers at about 30,000ft. Three Me 109s dived on our formation and I turned to starboard. A loose dogfight ensued with more Me 109s coming down. I could not get near to any enemy aircraft so I climbed up and engaged a formation of Me 110s without result. I then sighted 10 Me 109s just above me and attacked one of them. I got on his tail and fired several bursts of about two seconds. The enemy aircraft was taking violent evasive action and made for cloud level. I managed to get in another burst of about five seconds before it flicked over inverted and entered cloud in a shallow dive, apparently out of control. I then flew south and attacked two further formations of about thirty Do 215s from astern and head-on. The enemy aircraft did not appear to like the head on attack as they jumped about a bit as I passed through. I observed no result from these attacks. Fire from the rear of the enemy aircraft was opened at 1,000 yards. Me 110s opened fire at similar range but appeared to have no idea of deflection shooting.

Squadron Leader Lane's combat represented the only protracted dogfight between the opposing fighters on this day. Flight Sergeant Unwin was Lane's Red 3, and reported sighting 'thousands of 109s'. When the wing was attacked, at close range Red 3 fired a three second burst at a 109 which half-rolled and dived steeply into the clouds. Although the Spitfire pilot pursued his prey, he lost the 109 at 6,000ft when his windscreen froze up. Climbing back up to 25,000ft, a Rotte of 109s appeared above him, flying south. Unwin gave chase and caught both over Lydd. The first consequently burst into flames and went down vertically, and the second crashed into the sea. It is likely that these two 109s were from I/JG77: Oberleutnant Kunze, of the Geschwaderstabschwarm, was killed when his aircraft crashed at Lympne; Unteroffizier Meixner also lost his life when his 109 crashed into the sea off Dungeness at about 1455 hrs. This brought Flight Sergeant Unwin's personal total of Me 109s definitely destroyed this day to three.

As the Me 109s once more rained down on 19 Squadron, Green 1, Flying Officer Leonard 'Ace' Haines, attacked a 3/LG 2 machine flown by Unteroffizier Klick. The enemy machine's radiator was badly damaged so Klick had no option but to make a forced-landing at Shellness where he was captured. Haines went on to engage an Me 110 which he also claimed as destroyed when he saw it crash on a French beach. Green Section's other two pilots, Flight Sergeant Harry Steere and Pilot Officer Arthur Vokes, were also successful; the latter wrote in his log book:

> 'B' Flight attacked six Do 17s, one breaking away chased by F/Sgt Steere and self. One Jerry baled out. One Me 110 surprised me and bored a hole in starboard wing. After two or three turns I got on his tail and gave him everything. Dived vertically into cloud, starboard engine smoking. One probable Me 110. Hundreds of Jerries!

Sub-Lieutenant 'Admiral' Blake noted the quantity of enemy aircraft engaged as 'innumerable', but nonetheless dived to attack six Dorniers which had become detached from the main formation. He then attacked the 109s; which came down from above, firing at one particular machine twice, after which the 109 'burst into flames'. Blake next joined a queue of fighters attacking the Asplin's Head He 111, but was forced to land at Rochford because his Spitfire had been hit and was smoking badly. Pilot Officer Wallace 'Jock' Cunningham shot down a 7/JG 51 Me 109, which crashed at St Margaret's-at-Cliff, near Dover. The pilot, Leutnant Bildau, baled out and was captured. Sergeant Jack Potter, however, ill-advisedly chased the enemy far out across the Channel, being shot down off Calais by Feldwebel Luders of 6/JG 26; the British pilot was captured.

After the engagement, the Duxford Wing pilots returned individually, landing at various times from 1500 hrs onwards.

In both of these actions, the following claims were claimed for Bader's Duxford fighters:

> 19 Squadron: 12 destroyed, 2 shared, 4 probables, 1 damaged.
> 242 Squadron: 11/0/0.
> 302 Squadron: 12/1/2.

310 Squadron: 4 and 1 shared/0/0.
611 Squadron: 6 and 1 shared/4/0.

Total: 45 destroyed and 5 shared/10/1.

Owing to the volume of fighting, however, it is impossible to cross-reference the majority of claims with actual German losses.
    The Wing's casualties were as follows:

19 Squadron: 1 Spitfire destroyed, pilot POW; 2 Spitfires damaged.
242 Squadron: 1 Hurricane lost, pilot baled out wounded; 2 Hurricanes damaged.
302 Squadron: 1 Hurricanes lost, pilot killed; 1 Hurricane damaged.
310 Squadron: 2 Hurricanes lost, 1 pilot wounded.
611 Squadron: 1 Spitfire damaged.

Total: 5 fighters destroyed, 6 damaged; 1 pilot killed, 1 POW, 2 wounded.

The following day, the *Times* newspaper claimed that Fighter Command had destroyed a total of 175 German aircraft on 15 September 1940, for the loss of thirty RAF fighters and ten pilots. A day later, the British victory claim had risen to 185 (178 by fighters, seven by AA guns). In fact, the enemy had lost fifty-six machines in total, less than on 15 and 18 August 1940 (seventy-five and sixty-nine respectively). The RAF's casualties were more accurately reported, as twenty-nine aircraft and twelve pilots had actually been lost. Interestingly, the Germans claimed the destruction of seventy-nine RAF fighters, representing an over-claiming ratio approaching 3:1, which in itself, given the typically more accurate enemy combat claims, confirms how chaotic and intense the fighting was. The extent of Luftwaffe losses on this day of days convinced Hitler that Göring was incapable of achieving aerial supremacy as he had so boastfully promised. Rightly, therefore, 15 September is commemorated annually as 'Battle of Britain Day' – and Duxford's squadrons had played a big part in the day's outcome; the 310 Squadron ORB recorded that 'the day's "bag" for the Station [was] fairly conclusive proof of the efficiency of the wing formation'.
    Arguably that was not so. The Duxford Wing had been requested to patrol 11 Group airfields North of London. Instead, Squadron Leader Bader had led the wing off on another free-range fighter sweep, heading straight for the action over London, where enemy formations were already

being hacked down by 11 Group squadrons, operating in strength, thereby throwing the System in confusion.

That great day, though, Flight Lieutenant Richard Jones was flying with 19 Squadron:

> Early in September 1940, I was transferred from 64 Squadron at Kenley in 11 Group to 19 Squadron at Fowlmere in 12 Group…. My immediate impression of flying with a wing comprising five squadrons of Spitfires and Hurricanes, instead of anything between five to ten aircraft taking off from Kenley to intercept large numbers of enemy aircraft, was one of security in numbers. This gave me great confidence, looking around and seeing anything from upwards of fifty fighters keeping me company!

In this, Jones is surely right – and the arrival of the pirate-like, swashbuckling, fearless Bader over London with his five squadrons must have surely inspired and given hope to even the hardest-pressed RAF fighter pilot in action over the capital that momentous day. More importantly, was the effect that the Duxford Wing's arrival had upon the enemy's morale, which is evidenced by Cajus Bekker in *The Luftwaffe War Diaries*:

> Returning bomber crews reported resignedly: 'Over the target we were met by enemy fighter formations of up to eight aircraft…' Yesterday it was quite different. Then the bombers had only to contend with isolated Spitfire and Hurricane attacks, and London's protection had depended almost entirely on its concentrated and accurate AA fire.

According to Bekker, on 14 September 1940, the Germans had concluded that the 'British fighter defence had at last been knocked out…'

Certainly, then, a shock awaited them on the decisive 'Battle of Britain Day' – but this was not just because of the Duxford Wing's appearance over London. No, this was also because Air Vice-Marshal Park attacked in strength that day, committing all his squadrons to battle as never before. Certainly Bader's arrival was impressive, but it was not the full story – and the Luftwaffe bomber crews were already hard at it fending off large numbers of 11 Group fighters. Moreover, the Luftwaffe demonstrably suffered from poor intelligence throughout the Battle of Britain, as has previously been discussed, and failed to grasp Dowding's rotation system, or realise that there were plenty of fighters available to the defenders in northern groups. Any conclusion reached by the enemy that Fighter Command was finished, was therefore entirely erroneous – as those unfortunate bomber crews discovered, to their discomfort, on 15 September 1940. Previous accounts have tended to exclusively accredit the sudden erosion of enemy morale entirely upon the Duxford Wing's appearance – but, again, the actual facts tell a slightly different story. KG26 He 111 pilot Leutnant Roderich Cescotti remembered that he and his kameraden were 'shaken by the numbers of fighters the RAF was able to put up that day, and by the determination of the pilots'. This statement is oft-quoted evidence confirming the Duxford Wing's decisive contribution to 'Battle of Britain Day' – but Cescotti did not say that it was the sudden arrival of a large number of fighters that shook German morale, but the number engaged generally that day. The credit, therefore, is far from the Duxford Wing's alone – but all the pilots fighting over London that fateful day, from 10, 11 and 12 Groups.

Nonetheless as Bekker commented, across the Channel 'the battle was regarded as far from lost'. That may be so, but it was obvious that against such ongoing defensive strength, the German bomber force could not continue to absorb such losses indefinitely. Indeed, again as Bekker said, 'If things went on like this the Luftwaffe would bleed to death over England.'

That evening, Air Vice-Marshal Leigh-Mallory signalled all units, not just 242 Squadron at Duxford: 'Germans have made a great effort today and you have played a notable part in frustrating it. Heartiest congratulations to you all on splendid results.'

A significant day indeed.

On 17 September 1940 – the day on which Hitler postponed plans to invade southern England indefinitely – Air Vice-Marshal Leigh-Mallory reported to Fighter Command HQ on the actions fought by his Duxford-based 12 Group wing on 7, 9, 11 and 15 September 1940:

(I) During the first three wing formations, the following main difficulties were experienced:

(a) The fighters attacking the bombers were unduly interfered with by enemy fighters. This would appear due to the fact that there was not sufficient fighters both to neutralise the enemy fighters and to attack the enemy bombers successfully.

(b) It was also found that after the wing attack had been delivered, there were many enemy bombers which had become detached and were easy targets, but which could not be attacked because there were no fighters left with sufficient ammunition to carry on the engagement.

(II) As a result, the following conclusions were arrived at:
    a) For an operation of this type to be really successful, three objects have got to be achieved:
        (i) To neutralise the enemy fighters while the attack on bombers is being made;
        (ii) To break up the bomber formation;
        (iii) To shoot down the bombers after (ii) has been achieved.
    (b) From the size of enemy formations we have met up to the present, it was considered that at least two Spitfire squadrons are required to neutralise the enemy fighters.
    (c) In addition to the two squadrons required to neutralise the fighters, at least three squadrons are required to break up the enemy bomber formations and carry on the main attack on them.
    (d) It was hoped that when the bomber formations had been disintegrated, one of the two squadrons neutralising the fighters might be able to detach itself and shoot down isolated bombers.

In his report on the afternoon action fought on 15 September 1940, Leigh-Mallory stated that the Duxford Wing had been caught at a tactical disadvantage owing to not having been scrambled until 1430 hrs. This was untrue, the wing's squadrons had actually become airborne from 1405 hrs onwards. Nonetheless, on paper the wing had destroyed 105 enemy aircraft, plus forty probables and eighteen damaged, against a balance sheet of six pilots killed or missing, five wounded, and fourteen fighters destroyed. Apparently, the 12 Group Duxford Wing was performing excellently.

Air Vice-Marshal Strath Evill, Fighter Command's SASO, however, was unconvinced, writing in his covering letter to Dowding that:-

The figures of enemy losses claimed ... can, in my opinion, be regarded only as approximate.

It will be shown from these figures that the loses inflicted upon the enemy were not increased in relation to the number of fighters engaged on the later patrols when a large number of squadrons took part. Nevertheless, the losses incurred by the wing were reduced and I am, in any case, of the opinion that the AOC 12 Group is working along the right lines in organising his operations in strength.

The AOC-in-C responded:

> I am sure that L-Mallory is thinking along the right lines, but his figures do not support his theory. More aircraft per squadron were brought down by the entire strength of three squadrons (though few bombers).
>
> Little check is put on the estimate of 310 Squadron, who are exuberant in their claims.
>
> One can generally tell from reading the combat reports what degree of reliability to attach to claims – some of which are more thoughtful wishing.

It is here that Dowding undoubtedly made a grave error of judgement. Leigh-Mallory was not 'thinking along the right lines' but confounding the System by encouraging Squadron Leader Bader to fly free-booting fighter sweeps over 11 Group. If Evill should have acted upon Park's previous complaint regarding Leigh-Mallory, then Dowding should have been much more astute at this juncture, and taken his errant 12 Group AOC in hand. Indeed, he would one day say as much. It is unfair, though, that Dowding charged 310 Squadron with exuberant combat claims when 242 Squadron was by far the worst offender, so much so that this must surely have been obvious, even to a blind man, at the time.

At the Air Ministry, Air Vice-Marshal Douglas, the powerful DCAS, accepted the Big Wing's claims with question, however, and agreed with Leigh-Mallory that the defence of targets should be left to AA fire, while fighters made a concentrated attack, in strength, upon the enemy – if necessary after targets had been bombed. This, now, really was completely contrary to the System and how the battle was being, or should have been, fought.

Despite all, Fighter Command had won the Battle for London, by day at least, although much air fighting still lay ahead. While the pilots, ably supported by their groundcrews, continued to fight bravely, in the corridors of Whitehall dark political forces were starting to gather....

Chapter Ten

'It does rather take your breath away'

16 September 1940 dawned overcast and stormy, resulting in few sorties being flown by the enemy, which in any case was exhausted following its round-the-clock exertions bombing London. That morning, the usual 12 Group fighter squadrons gathered in the Duxford Sector, but there was little aerial activity and no assistance calls from 11 Group. There was, however, one wing patrol, as the 310 Squadron ORB reports:

> The Squadron, led by the CO, took off at 0740 hrs to patrol London at 27,000 feet. This again was a wing formation, the squadrons involved being the same as yesterday. They landed at 0845 hrs without having made contact with the enemy. The weather deteriorated about 1000 hrs and there was some rain and considerable mist. This provided a respite which did not come altogether amiss.

Squadron Leader Bader's log book records that he led the Duxford Wing on this patrol, in his words, of 'North Weald'. Given that enemy air activity was minimal, and 12 Group had not been requested to reinforce 11 Group, why was the Duxford Wing patrolling over 'North Weald', or, indeed, according to the Czechs, 'London'? This can only be firm evidence that the wing was suiting itself, Squadron Leader Bader confident in the support and protection of both Air Vice-Marshal Leigh-Mallory and Wing Commander Woodhall.

The following day, the weather remained overcast, with high winds and heavy rain. Only one major raid was hurled at England, a fighter sweep of southern Kent, which 11 Group largely and wisely ignored. The Duxford Wing scrambled at 1515 hrs to patrol London, but the action was further south and so the 12 Group fighters landed at 1645 hrs having seen no action. Interestingly, the 310 Squadron ORB describes the sortie as an 'offensive patrol again in wing formation'. The use of the word 'offensive' is significant, emphasising the aggressive spirit of Squadron Leader Bader's forays over 11 Group airspace – well south of his allocated patrol area.

On 18 September, the wing patrolled twice uneventfully, until the day's final attack came in – an unescorted formation of III/KG 77's Ju 88s heading for Tilbury Docks. Squadron Leader Bader's Hurricane squadrons were scrambled from Duxford at 1616 hrs; simultaneously, the two Spitfire squadrons were up from nearby Fowlmere. In spite of instructions to patrol Hornchurch at 20,000ft, the Big Wing patrolled from central London to Thameshaven at 24,000ft. Anti-aircraft fire bursting above cloud once more indicated the presence of enemy aircraft below. Leaving the Spitfires patrolling above cloud, Douglas led his Hurricanes down through it – in search of action, as described by 242 Squadron's combat report:

> 12 Group wing turned NW and sighted E/A flying in two formations close together about twenty – thirty E/A in each, unescorted, at 15 – 17,000 feet. They were approaching first bend of Thames West of Estuary, near Gravesend, and were South of Thames when attacked. Attack was launched in a dive from East to West, turning North into the enemy. Conditions were favourable to 12 Group wing which was screened from above by cloud – while E/A presented excellent target against white cloud base.
>
> Red One, Squadron Leader Bader, made a quarter attack turning astern at leading three Ju 88s, hitting the left-hand one of this section. This Ju 88 turned in left-hand dive with port engine afire and disappeared down towards North bank of Estuary West of Thameshaven.

This Ju 88, of 8/KG 77, crashed off Sheerness. It is possible that this machine had previously been damaged by Spitfires of 92 Squadron and also featured in the combat reports of both Pilot Officers Pilch and Karwowski of 302 Squadron. The 242 Squadron report continues:

> Red One lost about 3,000 feet, regained control and proceeded SE and found a lone Do 17. He closed to short range and fired short burst. E/A did not return fire; instead rear gunner baled out immediately, getting his parachute entangled in tailplane. The *Dornier* immediately fell in succession of steep dives and

two other members of crew baled out. The E/A disappeared into vertical dive into cloud at 4 – 6,000 feet and Red One considers it crashed either in estuary or South of it, near Sheerness.

Again, this raider, another 8/KG77 machine, was also attacked by various RAF fighter pilots, including Pilot Officer Hill of 92 Squadron, and Flying Officer Kowalski and Sergeant Paterek of the Duxford Wing's 302, and crashed into the sea, off the Nore. Later, Douglas recounted his impression of this combat during a Ministry of Information (MOI) radio broadcast:-

> At one time you could see planes going down on fire all over the place, and the sky seemed full of parachutes. It was sudden death that morning, because our fighters shot them to blazes. One unfortunate German rear-gunner baled out of the Do 17 I attacked, but his parachute caught on the tail. There he was, swinging helplessly, with the aircraft swooping and diving and staggering all over the sky, being pulled about by the man hanging by his parachute from the tail. That bomber went crashing into the Thames Estuary, with the swinging gunner still there.

Although Douglas's Hurricane was fitted with a cine-gun camera, he inadvertently switched on the navigation lights in error, so the combat went unrecorded.

Douglas's Red 2, Pilot Officer Willie McKnight, reported having dived on a 'Do 17' from above and behind, setting the starboard engine ablaze and watching the crew bale out, this probably being the first bomber, actually a Ju 88, attacked by his leader. McKnight then joined a Spitfire attacking a Ju 88, the crew of which also baled out, their bomber crashing North of the Thames. It is likely that this was an aircraft of 9/KG 77 also attacked by 19 Squadron's Sergeant Plzak, which crashed near Basildon.

During 242 Squadron's first diving attack, Red 3, Pilot Officer Campbell, overshot before firing at a Ju 88, which he left falling out of formation with both engines alight. He then engaged another Ju 88, at close range, which had already been attacked by a Spitfire, again watching his target erupt in flame. Red 3 then attacked a third Ju 88, but his Hurricane was hit by return fire. Breaking away, Campbell turned to assist a Spitfire which was attacking a bomber nearby, engaging the enemy aircraft which he reported seeing falling in flames. Other 242 Squadron pilots reported similarly hectic, multiple, combats.

The Hurricanes of 310 Squadron had followed Flight Lieutenant Jeffries into the attack, who shared a 'Do 17' with Pilot Officers Bergman and Fechtner, and Sergeant Prhcal (probably another 9/KG77 Ju 88, which crashed at Cooling).

On this occasion, Flight Lieutenant Wilf Clouston, commander of 'B' Flight, was leading 19 Squadron into action, who set a Ju 88's starboard engine on fire. The crew baled out, the Spitfire pilot watching their bomber crash behind a row of houses. This was the aircraft of Major Kleh, the III/KG77 Gruppenkommandeur, who was killed when his Ju 88 crashed at Eastry Mill – having also been attacked by three other 19 Squadron pilots, namely Flight Lieutenant Lawson, Pilot Officer Cunningham and Sergeant Lloyd. Flight Sergeant Steere also reported attacking a 'He 111' which had already been engaged by Green 1, Flying Officer Haines, this raider crashing on the Isle of Sheppey. Flight Sergeant Unwin shot down a Me 110, which both he and a 66 Squadron pilot confirmed crashed near Eastchurch. There were, however, no Me 110 losses that day, and so this was probably the same Ju 88 attacked by Steere. Pilot Officer Dolezal reported attacking a 'Heinkel', which he watched 'spin into the sea', this actually being one of four Ju 88s which crashed into the Thames Estuary. Sergeant Plzak also claimed a 'Heinkel', which crashed near Gillingham, this in reality being the Ju 88 down at Cooling. Flight Lieutenant Lawson, however, force-landed at Eastchurch airfield, having been hit in the glycol tank, but was unhurt and 19 Squadron was otherwise intact.

Above the clouds, at high altitude, 611 Squadron's Spitfires held off the Me 109s, 'without', according to the ORB, 'firing a shot'.

Back at Duxford there was jubilation. Such a successful interception of bombers without interference by escorting Me 109s was a gift. The Duxford Wing's claims, however, to coin Air Chief Marshal Dowding's phrase, were 'more thoughtful wishing'.

    19 Squadron: 5 destroyed and 3 shared, 1 probable.
    242 Squadron: 12 destroyed.
    302 Squadron: 7/2/1
    310 Squadron: 1 shared destroyed.
    611 Squadron: 0

    Total: 24 destroyed, 4 shared, 3 probables, 1 damaged.

In total, however, the enemy lost just eight Ju 88s in this engagement, the Duxford Wing having certainly had a hand in the destruction of six – a far cry from the twenty-four destroyed with which it was credited. In fact, the overclaiming ratio on this occasion was around 4:1. The wing itself had suffered just two aircraft damaged, the pilots safely forced-landing. In addition, the 11 Group squadrons involved lost one aircraft, the pilot of which was safe, and another damaged.

Needless to say, the inevitable congratulatory signals were sent to 242 Squadron (but none of the Big Wing's other units) by both the Secretary of State for Air and the CAS.

On 19 September 1940, high winds, heavy rain and low cloud over southern England curtailed enemy air activity, which was confined to harassing attacks by lone aircraft. Consequently, although Squadron Leader Bader took 242 Squadron down to Duxford again, the Squadron flew no patrols. Squadron Leader Blackwood led Red Section of 310 Squadron on a fruitless search for a raider in the vicinity of Duxford, but 'B' Flight of 302 Squadron intercepted and shot down a Ju 88 near Bury St Edmunds. On this day, 611 Squadron was replaced in the Duxford Wing by Squadron Leader Billy Burton's 616 Squadron. At 0653 hrs that morning, fourteen 616 Squadron Spitfires left Kirton-in-Lindsey, flying to operate from Fowlmere.

Squadron Leader Howard Frizelle Burton was also a Cranwell King's Cadet, and won the coveted Sword of Honour upon passing out in 1936. Thereafter, he flew Gauntlet biplane fighters with 46 Squadron at Digby, his logbook recording 'above average' assessments as a fighter pilot and navigator, and 'exceptional' in 'air gunnery'. In June 1939, Burton was posted to 12 Group HQ on Operations Staff Duties, so was known personally to the AOC. Three days after the declaration of war on Germany, Flight Lieutenant Burton took command of 66 Squadron's 'B' Flight, flying Spitfires. During the Fall of France, he destroyed a He 111 off the Hague, another over the French coast in addition to a Ju 88. With his Cranwell credentials, Burton was undoubtedly among 12 Group's most promising young officers. On 3 September 1940, he was promoted and given command of 616 Squadron, which had been battered at Kenley and pulled out of the line to rebuild at Kirton. Among Squadron Leader Burton's pilots were a few survivors of the earlier fighting, including Pilot Officer Hugh 'Cocky' Dundas, who had survived being shot down by Major Mölders and baled out, wounded, on 22 August 1940. Returning to the squadron on 13 September 1940, Dundas remained shaken by the experience; for this 21-year-old auxiliary pilot, flying with the fearless Douglas Bader would be an inspiration, restoring his confidence immeasurably.

There was no action for 616 Squadron on that first day operating out of Fowlmere, however, so Burton led his unit back to Kirton that evening.

By this time, many of influence were now convinced of the Big Wing's apparent superiority – among them 242 Squadron's adjutant, Flight Lieutenant Peter MacDonald MP. Without even reference to his CO, Station Commander or AOC, MacDonald had first spoken 'earnestly' with the Under Secretary of State for Air at Westminster, then exercised his right as an MP to seek an interview with the Prime Minister. Churchill was at first 'gruff', but later 'thawed', spent an hour listening to MacDonald's concern that the battle was not being properly managed by Dowding and Park, and considered his argument that attacking in strength was the way forward. Churchill was sufficiently convinced to begin 'sending for various … commanders', Wright tells us, but their identities are unknown – except to say that neither Air Chief Marshal Dowding nor Air Vice-Marshal Park were included. It is unlikely, however, that a betting man would lose money on suggesting Air Vice-Marshals Douglas and Leigh-Mallory were involved. Dowding, in fact, did not learn of this disloyal behaviour until 1968; he was stunned, remarking that 'It does rather take your breath away.'

Lord Dowding:

> Of course, so long as a squadron adjutant pays attention to his Service responsibilities, there's no harm done. Those responsibilities are clearly defined. But it is another matter when a squadron adjutant, serving under my command, starts by-passing the correct procedure and chain of command in order to get the ear of politicians. I think it was impertinent and quite extraordinary behaviour in engineering things in this way. And all done without my knowledge. No one could deny a Member of Parliament the right to attend to matters that were in his political sphere. But was it right for him to introduce this purely technical matter of the tactical use that was being made of my Command into such a political atmosphere?

The answer is simple: no. MacDonald's interference was totally inappropriate, not to mention insubordinate. Air Vice-Marshal Leigh-Mallory and his supporters, however, now enjoyed the immense benefit of prime ministerial interest – and support.

Chapter Eleven

'... the interests of the Duxford Wing'

By the end of September 1940, the German daylight bombing offensive had all but been defeated, the enemy's emphasis changing to night attacks. There was a change too in tactics for the German fighter units. Fighter sweeps, successful though they could be, had failed to draw the RAF to battle, 11 Group's controllers recognising that these incursions were no threat unless squadrons were scrambled to intercept. Having previously been frustrated by the close escort role, this was a disappointment to the German fighter pilots. To provoke a reaction from the defenders, Göring ordered that one staffel in every gruppe would become fighter-bombers – Jabos.

This affected one third of the available German fighter force, and was an unpopular decision with senior fighter leaders, who already lacked sufficient resources to achieve aerial superiority. For so long, auxiliary fuel tanks to extend range had been requested, but bombs arrived instead. The tactical thinking, however, was that if German formations included Jabos, the RAF would have to consider every sweep a threat and react to it. Some commentators have questioned the strategic merit of this tactic, arguing that fighter-bombers could achieve little overall damage. That, however, misses the point. The object of this exercise was to draw Fighter Command to battle against the Me 109s, which had the advantage of height, sun – and surprise. While this bombing had no long-term strategic impact on targets attacked, it did harass the defenders by day – at a time when nights were filled with German bombers pounding British cities. There was no rest for the defenders, and Squadron Leader Geoffrey Wellum of Biggin Hill's 92 Squadron remembered this as the most 'exhausting' phase, the high-flying Spitfire pilots flying several sorties daily, with '109s constantly in the Biggin Hill Sector, causing problems'.

The first of these raids occurred on 20 September 1940, when a sweep was ignored by Fighter Command – until suddenly bombs exploded in the City of London. Monitoring British radio frequencies, Luftwaffe intelligence reported a confusion of orders and counter-orders after the 'harmless' fighters dropped their bombs. Two Spitfire squadrons from Hornchurch were scrambled and battle joined, the RAF fighters climbing desperately while the Me 109s enjoyed all the advantages of height and sun. By close of play, four RAF pilots were dead with others wounded, while only one Me 109 was destroyed. On that day, Squadron Leader Bader had been ordered to patrol Hornchurch, obviously because 1 Group Station's Spitfire squadrons were engaged over the Maidstone area and south-east coast. In his log book, however, Douglas recorded that the patrol was actually carried out over 'London'. What would have happened, then, if another threat had been incoming, directed at the airfields north of the Thames? The 11 Group Controller had every reason to expect the Duxford Wing to be patrolling where requested – but, yet again, it was not. Fortunately there was no follow-up attack, and the wing's patrol, wherever it was, was uneventful, as was the following day's patrol between London and the Thames Estuary.

Poor weather on 22 September 1940 saw reduced enemy aerial activity, and little flying for the Duxford Wing's squadrons – but a lone raider popped out of cloud and attacked Fowlmere, destroying a 19 Squadron Spitfire on the ground before disappearing back from whence it came. The following morning, some 200 German fighters roamed over Kent and up to South London; the Duxford Wing, comprising 19, 242, 310 (on this occasion led by the Station Commander, Wing Commander Woodhall) and 616 Squadrons first patrolled base, then the Thames Estuary, but saw no action on this or the day's two subsequent patrols. On 24 September 1940, the Duxford Wing patrolled twice over the Thames Estuary without meeting the enemy. On the second patrol, the 19 Squadron ORB states that the wing 'Ran into No 11 Group wing. Almost a party.' Squadron Leader Myles Duke-Woolley DFC was leading the Kenley-based Hurricanes of 253 Squadron:

> Very often in those days, liaison between groups was not water-tight and one occasionally never knew before take-off that the 12 Group 'Balbo' would be in the area. The incident I remember ... I was leading 253 on a standing patrol over Canterbury. Normally these patrols were at 15,000ft but I seized the opportunity for practice, and was at 28,000ft in our new formation. Huns were reported to be approaching the area, but no more precise information was given regarding height, direction or numbers. We accordingly increased height to 31,000ft, and seeing nothing to the East or South I gazed

North, almost immediately seeing a black mass bearing down from the direction of London, and so handsomely below us. I recognised the aircraft soon after as the 12 Group 'Balbo' but they looked so determined that I felt they must be after some specific raid. I therefore felt that they might lead us to something interesting, and turned in behind them as a sort of voluntary top cover.

So, here we have the Duxford Wing patrolling over East Kent, not the Thames Estuary, as it should have been. The presence of the '12 Group wing' was a surprise to 253 Squadron, which was at its allotted patrol location, with a significant height advantage. Fortunately, Squadron Leader Duke-Woolley identified the rogue formation as friendly – otherwise this could have ended in a tragedy comparable to the so-called 'Battle of Barking Creek', in which 74 Squadron mistook Hurricanes of 56 Squadron for enemy fighters, shooting two of them down. Imagine how easily this kind of confusion could have been avoided if only airborne squadrons could communicate with each other. Moreover, the Duxford Wing was being controlled by the Duxford Sector Controller in 12 Group; the 11 Group sector controllers were unable to personally speak to the 12 Group squadrons operating in their air spaces. Testimony from Flight Lieutenant 'Teddy' Morten has already indicated that frequently not even Duxford knew where the wing was. This is almost incomprehensible. Moreover, having climbed over twice as high as instructed, and not reported that fact to the Sector Controller, 253 Squadron was at the altitude Me 109s frequently operated at – so it would not have been surprising if the Duxford Wing assumed the Hurricanes to be enemy fighters. This had all the makings of a shambles.

Squadron Leader Duke-Woolley continues:

> Feeling friendly disposed myself towards them, I turned in behind them, I never thought that they would mistake me for a German formation, but I forgot to realise that our formation was still unpublished, that Hurricanes just did not operate at 30,000ft, and that the 109 did look rather like a Hurricane. The 'Balbo', of course, did mistake us and thought they were about to be bounced – so they orbited. I thought they were orbiting to intercept my raid, and so orbited too. When the 'Balbo' straightened out to climb and 'engage' me, I naturally followed suit. They, equally naturally, had no intention of climbing up

on a straight course to be bounced. Thus, for some minutes, there was complete stale-mate, until the 'Balbo' started to get short of fuel and retired in good order to the South.

About a fortnight later I read a letter from 11 Group analysing in caustic terms the operation of the 'Balbo'. I remember that about eight of its trips were mentioned, the main point stressed being the comparatively short effective time on patrol. With some horror I saw one trip described under 'Remarks' in roughly these words: 'Six squadrons attempted to patrol for fifteen minutes in Canterbury area, but mistook an 11 Group squadron already on patrol for German aircraft and returned in disorder to their bases.' The story got around the Station and was received with huge delight by the ground-crew as well as aircrew. I remember feeling myself that my innocuous patrol could link me with the 11 Group report, and that if any fur was flying I was possibly going to be in the middle somewhere: the role of 'evidence' in a head-on collision between two AOCs seemed to me about as profitable as an advertisement I recalled for Cadbury's chocolate entitled 'Talking of Sandwiches' and depicting two burly giants simultaneously barging a weedy individual from opposite directions!

On at least one occasion to date, Air Vice-Marshal Park had inquired as to whether the Duxford Wing was in position, as requested, above the Hornchurch–North Weald line – only to be told that the 12 Group formation was, in fact, over Kent. From the testimony of Air Vice-Marshal Brand's 10 Group pilots it is clear that they proceeded to their patrol lines, as requested and dictated by 11 Group, remaining there until vectored towards the action. The 11 Group AOC had every right to expect that 12 Group's fighters would do likewise – and not wander off on unauthorised fighter sweeps over the 11 Group area. It would not be Air Vice-Marshal Leigh-Mallory who was under scrutiny by the Air Ministry, however – but Park.

On 24 September 1940, Air Vice-Marshal Douglas, the DCAS, informed Air Vice-Marshal Saundby, ACAS (Tactics), that a number of criticisms had been received regarding Air Vice-Marshal Park's tactics. Saundby tasked Group Captain H.G. Crowe, the Deputy Director of Air Tactics, to investigate the allegations and report back. When Saundby subsequently forwarded Crowe's report to the DCAS, he advised Air Vice-Marshal

Douglas to read both Park's response and Leigh-Mallory's on wing patrols, dated 17 September 1940; the 'Big Wing' had just gained another powerful ally at the Air Ministry.

Park's report included reference to wing formations:

> Had 11 Group delayed in engaging the enemy until its squadrons had been assembled in wings of four or five squadrons, there would have been no opposition to the first wave of bomber formations, who would have had time to escape without interception. With the available force massed into a few wings of four or five squadrons, a proportion of the second wave would have been intercepted and severely punished. The third wave of enemy bombers would, however, have had unopposed approach to the vital points of London, as the 11 Group squadrons would have been on the ground rearming and refuelling. After six months' experience of intensive fighting, I have no hesitation in saying that we would have lost the Battle of London in September if 11 Group had adopted as standard the use of wings of four or five squadrons as has been advocated in certain quarters since that critical battle was won.

Park continued regarding the high-altitude German fighter incursions currently being experienced:

> The great increase in the number of enemy fighters employed and the beginning of the autumn cloud conditions, above which the enemy fighters flew at great altitudes, increased the difficulties in obtaining accurate information. The Observer Corps found it impossible to distinguish between enemy bombers and enemy fighters. In an attempt to overcome this difficulty and to improve detailed information generally, special fighter reconnaissance patrols were introduced to patrol at high altitudes and report by R/T details of enemy formations coming in.
>
> During this phase and particularly the latter part of it, RDF warning deteriorated considerably. This, coupled with the increasing altitudes at which the enemy fighter patrols approached, made the problem of intercepting from the ground

more and more difficult. Our fighters operating from coastal aerodromes were frequently meeting enemy fighters above them, particularly when our own fighters were on the climb preparatory to being detailed to intercept raids. For this reason squadrons were being withdrawn from the forward coastal aerodromes in Kent to bases farther back, from which they were better able to climb sufficiently high before intercepting.

A series of Day Patrol Lines were introduced on 21 September between London and the Kentish coast, behind which squadrons attained their height, and assembled in pairs or wings of three squadrons. Whenever inland tracks of raids became confused, our squadrons were detailed to patrol lines and kept informed of the approach of enemy raids as far as practicable. After assembling on back patrol lines the squadrons were moved on to forward patrol lines.

Park's paragraph on the 'Method of Employing our Squadrons' makes illuminating reading:

The general plan adopted was to engage the high fighter screen with pairs of Spitfire squadrons from Hornchurch and Biggin Hill, half-way between London and the coast, and so enable Hurricane squadrons from London sectors to attack bomber formations and their close escort before they reached the line of fighter aerodromes East and South of London. The remaining squadrons from London sectors that could not be despatched in time to intercept the first wave of the attack by climbing in pairs formed a third and inner screen by patrolling along the line of aerodromes East and South of London. The fighter squadrons from Debden, Tangmere and sometimes Northolt were employed in wings of three or in pairs to form a screen south-east of London to intercept the third wave of attack coming inland, also to mop up retreating formations of the earlier waves. The Spitfire squadrons were redisposed so as to concentrate three squadrons at Hornchurch and Biggin Hill. The primary role of these squadrons was to engage and drive back the enemy high fighter screen, and so protect the Hurricane squadrons, whose task was to attack close escorts and then the bomber formations, all of which flew at a much lower altitude.

From the foregoing it is clear that Park was not averse to the use of multi-squadron formations if the circumstances demanded such a response. This was purely influenced by the enemy's changing tactics, and is clear evidence of the AOC 11 Group's flexible reaction.

Meanwhile, the battle in the air wore on. Towards midday on 27 September 1940, some 300 enemy aircraft approached southern England between Dover and Lympne, heading for Chatham. The bombers, Ju 88s of I and II/KG 77, were late at their rendezvous and were without fighter escort; 120 Spitfires and Hurricanes fell on them and eleven raiders were lost. The frantic shouts for assistance brought numerous Me 109s and 110s hurrying to the scene, a huge combat developing over 'Hellfire Corner'. At 1155 hrs, the Duxford Wing was scrambled with orders to patrol London – while 11 Group's fighters were engaged over the Kentish coast. Once more, the enemy's presence and chance of action much further south was simply too much for Douglas. According to official records, he led 19, 242, 310 and 616 Squadrons to patrol 'South of the Estuary'. Over the Dover – Canterbury area, the wing sighted a large gaggle of German fighters, just aimlessly milling around at 18–20,000ft. Douglas, however, had climbed the wing ever-higher – and had a height advantage of 3,000ft. Attacking from up-sun, this was the perfect 'bounce'. Douglas:

> I chose an Me 109 which was passing underneath me and turned behind and above him and gave a short two second burst with the immediate result that he became enveloped in thick white smoke, turned over and dived vertically. I did not follow it down, but as it was the first 109 shot down it was seen by Pilot Officer Crowley-Milling, Pilot Officer Bush and Flight Lieutenant Turner, in fact almost the whole Squadron. I also had my camera gun in action which will give further confirmation.

No one saw the 109 actually crash, however, and no likely candidate is among the enemy aircraft known to have crashed on English soil that day. Douglas also fired at several more fleeing 109s, causing 'white vapour and black smoke' to issue from one. At such close range was his attack delivered that the windscreen of Douglas's Hurricane was covered in oil from the damaged enemy fighter. This 109 was last seen over the Channel, 'gliding down quietly and apparently under full control with his engine dead'; many Luftwaffe fighters would crash-land on the occupied French coast that afternoon, this machine no doubt among them.

During what was now a fast, cut-and-thrust combat, Pilot Officer Bush of 242 Squadron fired a long burst at an Me 109 which crashed into the sea. Pilot Officer Latta shot another down into the Channel. Pilot Officer Homer, however, became a 'flamer' over Sittingbourne and was killed.

When 310 Squadron's attack was delivered, Sergeant Kaucky attacked an Me 109, upon which a Spitfire also dived and shot it down. Sergeant Komineck claimed a 109 which 'dived vertically into the sea some five miles SW of Dover', and a Do 17 probable – although the latter was undoubtedly an Me 110. Flight Lieutenant Sinclair, however, was shot down. Years later, Wing Commander Sinclair recalled:

> I was attacked by an Me 109. The first burst destroyed my ailerons, the second set my Hurricane on fire. Because my ailerons had been shot away I was unable to invert my aircraft and drop out, and as the machine entered a steep dive I had some difficulty in extricating myself from the cockpit and getting over the side. I landed by parachute in the branches of a fir tree near Callam, from which some farm hands helped me down to mother earth. My Hurricane was practically burnt out before it crashed. This was the second time I had baled out during the Battle of Britain.

616 Squadron was attacked by high-flying Me 109s; Pilot Officer Holden claimed an Me 109 destroyed, and Sergeant Copeland a probable, but the Squadron's weaver, Pilot Officer DS Smith, was shot down. Crash-landing near Faversham, he died of wounds the following day. 19 Squadron was also hit by 109s from above; Pilot Officer Burgoyne was killed and Sergeant David Cox baled out:

> Upon scramble I had jumped into the nearest Spitfire, QV-L, as mine would not start. This aircraft was nearly always flown by Sergeant Plzak, our 6'6' Czech who had dubbed me 'Little Boy'. To save time I buckled on his parachute, which was already in the cockpit – more of that later!
>
> We were top cover of the Duxford Wing but were attacked by a large number of Me 109s in the Dover area. After some hectic moments avoiding being shot down, I found myself more or less on my own between Ashford and Folkestone. I then saw towards Folkestone a Hurricane being attacked by four Me 109s. Before I could give any assistance, which was

my intention having got within a few hundred yards of the scrap, the Hurricane went down in a vertical dive inland. (The Hurricane was probably Flight Lieutenant Sinclair's, which crashed at Godmersham, a few miles north of Wye.)

The four Me 109s then turned their attentions to me. They knew their stuff as two got above me and two below. Naturally I had some hectic moments of turning this way and that as they came at me in attacks from all directions. I remember doing quite a lot of firing of my guns, but I think it was more in the hope of frightening them or raising my morale than in any real hope of shooting anything down!

All of a sudden there was a loud bang in the cockpit and for a second or two I was dazed. When I became normal again there was a lot of smoke about and my Spitfire was in a steep climb. As I lost flying speed I opened the hood, turned the aircraft over, undid my straps, and fell out, quickly pulling the ripcord of my parachute. When the canopy opened it gave me a severe jolt and several days later a lot of bruises showed on my chest and shoulders. Remember that the parachute harness was fitted for a man of 6'6' – I was lucky not to fall out of it!

As I floated down a 109 came and had a look at me and then flew off. It was then that I felt a lot of pain in my right leg and saw lots of holes in my flying boots out of which blood was oozing. Ground observers said that I took about 15 minutes to come down as I was so high up – I know that it was jolly cold up there when I came out of the aeroplane. I landed in the corner of a ploughed field near a farm. By this time I was feeling rather rough and must have looked it as the farmer handed me a bottle of whisky, from which I took a large swig. I was later taken to hospital at Walsford where a surgeon from Folkestone Hospital extracted several large pieces of cannon shell from just below my knee cap down into my ankle. I was in hospital about six weeks and off flying until December 1940.

Pilot Officer Eric Burgoyne's No 19 Squadron Spitfire was also hit by the 109s, but this pilot crashed and was killed at Coldred, just inland of Dover. Squadron Leader Lane had a lucky escape, but not at the hands of the enemy. Two days previously the squadron had begun re-equipping with Mk II Spitfires, one of which the CO was flying in this combat. After firing two short bursts, Lane's Spitfire became uncontrollable and skidded away, the pilot using all his strength to recover. This was only achieved at 3,000ft, by which time Lane was considering baling out. Back at Fowlmere the aircraft was found to have a misshapen rudder and a wrongly adjusted trim tab which prevented one elevator functioning correctly. Flight Sergeant Unwin chased an Me 109 for ten minutes; dangerously near the French coast, a 30° deflection shot sent the enemy fighter into the Channel.

This fighting was actually the heaviest for some time. The Duxford Wing's combat claims were as follows:-

19 Squadron: 7 destroyed, 1 probable, 0 damaged
242 Squadron: 4/2/1
310 Squadron: 1/0/0
616 Squadron: 1/1/0

Total: 13 destroyed, 3 probables, 1 'possible' and 1 damaged.

Only four Me 109s crashed in England, but possibly up to eight more went into the Channel, and a further seven returned home damaged – and there were at least seven 11 Group squadrons airborne, so these casualties cannot be prescribed to the Duxford Wing alone. On balance, the overclaiming ratio is likely to have been around 3:1, although it is noteworthy that 242 Squadron's claims are substantially lower than usual, doubtless for one reason: the combat was fought not against bombers but Me 109s. Douglas, however, reported that '12 Group wing as a whole did well.'

On 28 September 1940, the Big Wing twice patrolled over the Thames Estuary, although there was generally little aerial activity that day owing to poor visibility. Interestingly, although the incident went unrecorded on every document excepting Spitfire P7432's Aircraft Movement Card (Form 78), Pilot Officer Richard Jones of 19 Squadron was shot down that day:

> When patrolling the Hawkhurst area at 29,000ft, the Controller informed us that as there were apparently no enemy aircraft in the vicinity we could return to 'Pancake'. I was 'Arse-end Charlie' and relaxed slightly as we dived to 20,000ft. Suddenly about four feet of my starboard wing just peeled off – my initial thought being that this was a poor show on a new aircraft. Then a loud bang and a hole appeared above my undercarriage. I was obviously the target of an enemy fighter up-sun. Immediately

I took evasive action. Simultaneously my engine cut for good and I was suddenly in a high-speed stall and spin. My radio was unserviceable so I was unable to alert the Squadron, who returned to base blissfully aware that I had been shot down.

I recovered from the spin at about 10,000ft. The aircraft was not responding to the controls. I realised too that the hood was completely jammed. I subsequently crash-landed with a dead engine in one of only two suitable fields in a heavily wooded area just outside Hawkhurst. Unfortunately I did so among a flock of sheep and regret that several were killed. I was rescued by the army and taken to the Hawkhurst doctor who treated a flesh wound to my leg, then to their Mess prior to safely returning to Fowlmere. My Spitfire had a broken propeller and radiator, a few holes and missing parts but was otherwise undamaged.

In his log book, Jones wrote 'Shot down and crash-landed at Hawkhurst, Kent. Killed three sheep. What a bloody mess!!!' Weavers were extremely vulnerable; Jones was lucky to survive.

The weather remained poor the following day. With the threat of invasion and the Luftwaffe's heavy daylight raids on southern England thwarted, on 29 September 1940, 616 Squadron was released from further wing operations and remained at Kirton. Likewise 302 Squadron was no longer required, so the Duxford Wing reverted to its original three squadrons: 19, 242 and 310. If the aerial battle was beginning to quieten down a little, the same was not so in respect of the row about to erupt over the Big Wing.

On that day, following the failure of Dowding's SASO, Air Vice-Marshal Evill, to respond to Park's complaint concerning 12 Group and resolve matters between the two AOCs, Park now wrote directly to Dowding. Park's letter explained that when the scale of attack dictated, he had worked out a system with Air Vice-Marshal Brand for 10 Group to supply a maximum of four squadrons for reinforcement. Due to Brand's own defensive commitments, these were only requested when targets south-west of London were significantly threatened. For two months this arrangement had worked admirably, not least, Park wrote, because it was,

essential to get a small number of squadrons quickly to the point requested than to delay while his squadrons are forming up in wings, which would mean their arriving at the scene of battle after vital objectives have been bombed and the enemy

183

was retreating. The latter action undoubtedly secures a better 'bag' of enemy aircraft but does not achieve our main aim, which is to protect aircraft factories and other vital points from being bombed by day.

Arrangements with the 12 Group AOC, Park, charged, remained unsatisfactory. The Duxford Wing roaming around on sweeps, as opposed to adhering to instructions, had, Park justifiably complained, confused 11 Group's controllers and his pilots in the air. Moreover, on several occasions the Observer Corps had been confused by the wing's appearance, leading to 11 Group fighters being vectored to intercept the 12 Group fighters. Before Park's letter was handed to Dowding, however, Evill added his own observations, the SASO confirming that although Leigh-Mallory did send individual squadrons to reinforce 11 Group, it was true that he generally sent the 'Big Wing'. Evill agreed that it was 'entirely wrong' for the 12 Group wing to 'rove without control over 11 Group's sectors', and he 'presumed' that Dowding would 'wish this stopped'. Evill did, however, provide Leigh-Mallory support, stating that Park tended 'to ignore the value of utilising the large formation when time permits'. As 11 Group was nearly always outnumbered, Evill considered that by using the Big Wing approach, there were occasions when the situation could be reversed. Park should, in the SASO's opinion, have organised things so that he could have used Leigh-Mallory's strength.

Leigh-Mallory received a copy of Park's letter on 8 October 1940. In his response, Leigh-Mallory emphasised that if warning was given when the enemy was assembling over France, the Duxford Wing would have ample time to reach Hornchurch area at an appropriate height to intercept. Many years later, Lord Dowding wrote that this concept was 'contrary to the whole structure of the Command and it takes into consideration only what was in the interests of the Duxford Wing'. Leigh-Mallory's report concluded that although the wing had been in action over East Kent, this was only when drawn further south by combat or when so vectored by 11 Group. When this document arrived at Bentley Priory, Evill and Air Commodore Lawson checked but found Leigh-Mallory's final claim to be untrue. If Leigh-Mallory truly believed that was the case, it is possible that not even he was aware of the extent of Squadron Leader Bader's aerial independence.

If the Battle of Britain was waning with the changing season, the political battle was hotting up – and Dowding and Park were about to face the enemy within.

Chapter Twelve

Meeting of Infamy

On 1 October 1940, Air Vice-Marshal Park sent a comprehensive memorandum to all his sector commanders, setting out the conditions under which it was appropriate to operate three-squadron wings, and when it was not, and making clear the differences in the Dunkirk air fighting and Battle of Britain:

> There is a feeling among pilots in some squadrons that the only way to defeat the enemy raids against this country is to employ our fighter squadrons in wings of three squadrons. The object of this note is to explain why such formations have been used off and on during the past five months, yet have not been made the standard method of grouping our fighter squadrons in home defence fighting.

> 2. During the operations by 11 Group over France and Belgium, squadrons were originally employed singly. When the enemy opposition strengthened, squadrons were employed in pairs. Moreover, when squadrons could only raise three sections each, they were employed in wings of three squadrons. The conditions were that our squadrons were being operated on a pre-arranged programme and could be allotted to their tasks some hours in advance and were normally collected and despatched from forward aerodromes on the coast. This gave ample time for squadrons to be arranged into pairs of wings, under conditions which do not obtain in the defence of this country, when the enemy can and has made four heavy attacks in one day, giving only the minimum warning on each occasion.

Operations in 11 Group area of Duxford BALBOS - October 1940.

11th October & 2nd November, 1940.

Appendix B.

Time of Request.	Patrol Requested.	Time Plotted as Reached Patrol.	Time Withdrawn by No.12 Group	Time on Patrol	Interceptions Reported by 12 Group.	Remarks.
1. 11.30	Maidstone	12.15	12.20	5 mins.	n i l	Broke up and returned to base on sighting Pair of 11 Group Sqdns. above to the East.
2. offered at 11.00	Maidstone Sheerness	12.00	12.35	35 mins.	n i l	
3. Requested 11.21.	Patrol Maidstone Sheerness for 1 hour	12.15	12.40.	25 mins.	n i l	Withdrawn due to lack of oxygen. Later patrol requested, but not carried out owing to Duxford weather.
4. 16.30	Patrol in Kent	(assembled over Duxford only.)	-	-	n i l	Did not leave Duxford area owing to R/T trouble.
5. Offered at 16.30	Maidstone Line	17.20	17.25	5 mins.	n i l	
6. Requested 10.30	Maidstone then Canterbury.	11.34	11.48	14 mins.	n i l	
7. Requested at 1315 for 1400.	Gravesend Maidstone	14.17	14.55	35 mins.	n i l	
8. At 15.45 requested patrol from 16.30.	Maidstone Line	16.35	17.05	30 mins.	1 Me.109 destroyed at 17.00 nr. Lympne.	Requested when 25,000' over Hornchurch to intercept 2 raids crossing Thames near Sheppey which later bombed N. Weald. 2 11 Gp. Sqdns. intercepted.
9. Requested at 1115 for 1200.	Sheerness - Maidstone.	12.09	12.35	26 mins.	n i l	Left patrol line owing to shortage of oxygen.
10. Requested at 1345 for 1430-1530.	Sheerness - Maidstone later Canterbury - Hawkinge.	14.46	15.30	44 mins.	n i l	Offered Manston and Hawkinge to refuel as 2 raids approaching from French Coast as Wing withdrawing.

Average Time to reach Sheerness: 56 mins.   Average Patrol: 24 mins.

Air Vice-Marshal Park's analysis of 12 Group Wing operations following the 'Meeting of Infamy'.

3. In spite of the favourable conditions during the operations over France, for the employment of wings of three squadrons, the best results during the whole week of this operation were obtained by squadrons working in pairs. Whenever possible, two pairs of squadrons patrolled the same restricted area; two at high altitude to engage enemy fighter patrols, and two about 5,000 to 8,000 feet lower to engage the enemy bombers, which in those days did not normally employ close escorts as they were operating over their own territory.

4. Experience in home defence during the last two months' intensive operations has shown that there are many occasions in which the use of wings of three squadrons is quite unsuitable, because of cloud conditions and lack of time, due to short warning of approaching attack.

5. Experience over many weeks has shown that when there are two or more layers of clouds, the squadrons of a wing have great difficulty in assembling above the clouds at a rendezvous, also in maintaining touch after passing through clouds when on patrol. Instead of devoting their time to searching for the enemy, squadrons have frequently had to devote much of their attention to maintaining contact with other squadrons of than a wing of three. Unless the sky is relatively clear of clouds, pairs of squadrons have been more effective in intercepting the enemy.

6. Quite apart from cloud interference, the lack of time due to short warning of the approach of raids frequently renders it inadvisable to detail wings of three squadrons. Experience has shown that it takes much longer to despatch, assemble and climb to operating height a wing of three squadrons than one or even two pairs of squadrons. Frequently wings of three squadrons have been attacked by enemy fighters while still climbing up over their sector aerodromes. It has been found better to have even one strong squadron of our fighters over the enemy than a wing of three climbing up below them, in which attitude they are peculiarly vulnerable to attacks from above.

7. In clear weather when the enemy attack develops in two or three waves, there is often time for the squadrons or

sectors in the flank of the attack, e.g. Debden, Northolt, Tangmere, to be despatched as wings of three squadrons to meet the third incoming wave or to sweep across and mop up the retreating enemy bombers and close escort. There is rarely time for London sectors to get wing formations up to the desired height before the enemy reaches important bombing targets, e.g. factories, docks, sector aerodromes.

8. Until we have VHF in all squadrons, it is not practicable for three squadrons of a wing to work on a common R/T frequency; at least that is the considered opinion of the majority of squadron and sector commanders. Pairs of squadrons can and do work successfully on a common frequency whenever the State of Preparedness in a sector permits. Here again some squadron commanders prefer to be on a separate R/T frequency in order to have better intercommunication with their squadrons.

Conclusion

9. As a result of five months' intensive fighting in 11 Group, it is clear that wings of three squadrons are not the most suitable formations under many conditions of TIME and WEATHER. On the whole, squadrons working in pairs have obtained better results in home defence, especially as our practice since July has been to detail two or more pairs of squadrons to intercept raids in massed formation. However, when conditions are favourable, squadrons will continue to be despatched in wings of three, but the only person to decide whether wings or pairs of squadrons should be the Group Controller. He has the complete picture of the enemy's movements on a wide front from Lowestoft to Bournemouth, and must quickly decide whether the time and cloud conditions are suitable for pairs of wing formations. Squadrons must, therefore, continue to study and develop fighting tactics in wings of three squadrons, which will probably become more common in the spring of 1941.

10. Two copies of this note are to be distributed to each fighter squadron, and one copy is to be read by each sector controller.

Three copies of Park's 'note' were also sent to Bentley Priory. It is a significant document, confirming that Park was willing to use large formations when appropriate, and knew when it was not. For 11 Group, such large formations were unwieldy and took too long to gain height cohesively, and when battle was joined were split up anyway, with inter-squadron communication impossible. Interestingly, however, Park was already looking ahead to 1941, and had identified the three-squadron-strong wing as a useful offensive formation. Again, the note emphasises tactical flexibility – whereas Leigh-Mallory and Sholto Douglas argued that the three-squadron wing should be standard practice in both defence and offence.

In the air, the Duxford Wing uneventfully patrolled North Weald, such sorties becoming the norm for the 12 Group pilots, the autumn weather and enemy tactics being unsuitable for wing operations and interceptions.

On 3 October 1940, Leigh-Mallory visited 19 Squadron at Fowlmere: 'Visit from AOC discussing new tactics, principally against fighter formations and night interception. Many solutions discussed and information of the new devices and ideas being put forward and being developed for night interception.'

Flight Lieutenant 'Teddy' Morten recalled that visit:

> The AOC 12 Group and the Station Commander, Wing Commander 'Woody' Woodhall, were very close, and on the former's many visits to Duxford the pair of them would walk the Station's hangars talking 'shop'. The same loyal and close relationship existed between 'LM', 'Woody' (the 'Boss Controller'), and Douglas Bader. I know. I was there.

On 5 October 1940, Park circulated an interesting note to all fighter squadrons in 11 Group, with instructions that the memorandum also be shared with incoming units:

> The opinion has recently been expressed that a wing formation should not be led out of parachute dropping distance from land. It would appear that this attitude of mind, which is quite new, regarding flying by aircraft of Fighter Command over the sea may have been induced by the fact that during recent months we have been forced to fight a defensive battle over our own territory.

2. This is, however, quite a passing phase, during which the enemy has attempted to obtain aerial superiority over this country and to carry out mass bombing attacks by day, in the course of which he has been severely handled and has suffered very heavy losses. We must now look forward, perhaps quite soon, to such improvement in the air situation that we shall once more take the offensive in the air and put strong formations over the Channel and later over the enemy's coastal aerodromes to shoot him down as he assembles and climbs up, in the same way as he has recently done over SE England.

3. It is, therefore, most important that all squadrons and pilots should realise that their duties will occasionally take them over the sea, even though at present we do not normally pursue the enemy more than fifteen miles to sea. Moreover, the improved arrangements for the rescue of pilots who have fallen into the water should enable a much higher percentage of rescues to be made than was the case during the Dunkirk and subsequent operations – such as those over Cherbourg.

4. Finally, it is pointed out that were the practice to be followed of only flying so as to be out of parachute dropping distance of the sea, a north-westerly wind of 30 mph would prevent our aircraft at 21,000 feet from flying much further south-east than Ashford, for example; a parachutist from that height takes about seventeen minutes to descend to earth.

The note is significant because it confirms that with the crisis having passed, Park was looking ahead with an aggressive mindset, keen to take the war across the Channel to the Germans in northern France, recognising that 'strong formations' were the way forward in that respect. Again, this indicates flexibility in thought, not a complete rejection of wing tactics, of which Park has oft been accused. This is simply untrue. As already evidenced, when tactical circumstances were favourable, 11 Group was now responding with larger formations. During the time of crisis, however, these were simply impractical, owing to the number of incoming raids. During this current phase of the Battle of Britain, though, the enemy's tactics of high-altitude fighter sweeps and unpredictable fighter-bomber attacks dictated a different response. Because these fast-moving German formations meant that less warning was given by RDF, it became necessary for 11 Group to introduce standing patrols of a pair of squadrons over the Maidstone line. Immediately an incoming raid was detected, these airborne squadrons would climb to 30,000ft, there to engage the enemy's high-flying fighter screen and thereby cover additional friendly squadrons scrambling to meet the threat. This required a much higher state of daytime preparedness throughout 11 Group, the standing patrols increasing the amount of operational flying by Park's squadrons to 45–60 hours per day. While the bombing of Fighter Command airfields in August was a traumatic time, this phase would severely test the Few.

On 6 October 1940, Park issued extensive instructions to 11 Group regarding how wings were to be used:

> When the sky is mainly clear of clouds and the Group Controller receives ample warning by RDF of the forming up and approach of mass attacks over the French coast or from the South, some squadrons will be despatched in wings of three units. Moreover, this type of formation will continue to be used to bring sectors in the North and South of London in to meet the third wave of a prolonged attack or to 'mop' up raids that are retreating after having been engaged by other squadrons around London.

> 2. As a result of practical experience during the last five months by squadrons, sectors and Group Headquarters, the following brief instructions are issued. As further experience is gained by squadrons working in wing formations, fresh and more detailed instructions will be issued for the benefit of all concerned. Much of that which follows applies to squadrons working in pairs; the normal formation for reasons already stated in my letter 11G/486, dated 1 October.

Leadership

> 3. The squadron and leader of the wing must be decided by the sector commander before the beginning of daylight operations each day. After a heavy engagement it may be necessary to change the leadership, when the strongest squadron should be appointed to lead the wing.

Take-off

4. Squadrons should take-off separately and not form up in a wing on the ground.

Assembly

5. The Group Controller will order the place and height of rendezvous, according to the cloud conditions and proximity of enemy raids. The rendezvous will, whenever possible, be well inland in order to enable squadrons to join up at the height ordered before engaging the enemy. The wing leader must report immediately the wing assembles, and Sector Controller is to report to Group Controller, who will then detail wing to a raid or a patrol line above the enemy raids.

Failure to Assemble

6. If slow take-off or unexpected cloud conditions unduly delay the assembly of the wing when enemy raids are approaching targets, the Group Controller may be compelled to detail one or more squadrons of the intended wing to intercept approaching raids to break up or harass bombers before they reach the target. In this event, it will be necessary for squadrons having VHF to revert from common frequency to their own R/T channel.

Rendezvous

7. Group Controller will normally select an aerodrome or other good landmark well back from the approaching enemy raids.

R/T Frequencies

8. Until all squadrons have VHF it is not considered practical for all units in a wing to work on a common R/T frequency. This ruling is based on the experience of many squadrons in several sectors over a long period. On the introduction of VHF, squadrons will work on a common R/T frequency as soon as they assemble as a wing. If the wing becomes broken, squadrons should revert to their own R/T frequency to facilitate communication with the Sector Controller.

Formation

9. The leading squadron will normally be lower than the two following squadrons. Sectors, however, are to try out stepping down one or more of the following squadrons.

Tactics

10. Before leaving the ground it is essential that the three squadrons shall know which unit is to take on the bombers, which to attack the escort, and lastly which squadron is to act as above-guard or screen to hold off enemy high fighter screen. As the enemy close escort may be above the bombers, in rear, or on a flank or even ahead, and on other occasions may fly weaving between the bomber sub-formations, it is not always possible to lay down rigidly beforehand which squadrons in the wing will attack bombers or their escort. This makes it all the more necessary for the general tactics of the wing to be discussed and decided on the ground before a patrol.

Look-out Guards

11. Each squadron should provide its own look-out guards, especially for the period prior to assembly, and after the wing has become split up by an engagement with the enemy. The wing should normally have one squadron slightly in the rear and above, to act as cover to the whole wing against very high enemy fighters.

Pip-squeak

12. Each squadron is to provide one aircraft with pip-squeak to enable fixing at Sector Operations Room.

The Sun

13. The wing formation should whenever possible patrol across the direction of the sun. Enemy fighters attacking out of the sun will then be offered only deflection shots at our fighters.

Section Formation

14. When in wing formations, sections should normally be composed of four aircraft, consisting of two pairs of

fighters. Each squadron should, therefore, have three sections of four aircraft.

Assembly After Combat

15. It is not considered necessary or advisable for squadrons to try to reform wing after a general engagement takes place over enemy territory or over the sea, then it may be advisable to lay down beforehand the wing rendezvous.

Breaking Off from Wing

16. If squadrons are detailed to be detached from the wing formation, Sector Controller should give the order 'X Squadron break away, Vector...', and then inform the Wing Leader that X Squadron has been ordered to break away.

Clearly, 11 Group had carefully considered how best it should be used to meet the current threat. It is also noteworthy that Park had rejected the prescribed vic of three fighters as the standard section formation, replacing this with the section of four, sub-divided into two pairs – similar to the enemy's Schwarm and Rotte. Certainly, experienced squadron commanders, especially Squadron Leader A.G. 'Sailor' Malan of 74 Squadron, were experimenting with better tactical formations, Malan preferring the section of four in line astern.

Regarding the use of wings by 11 Group in practice, Park later reported having 'learned the following lessons':

a) There are relatively few days in autumn when cloud conditions are suitable for formations of wings.

b) A much longer time is required to despatch, assemble and climb wing formations.

c) The employment of wing formations considerably reduced the duration of fighter patrols.

d) Mass formations of even three squadrons are slow and cumbersome, and likely to be out-flanked, so fail to intercept the faster German fighter formations.

e) Better results can be obtained by two pairs of squadrons than by four squadrons operating in a wing.

f) The delay caused by the use of wing formations would on many occasions allow enemy fighter-bomber raids to attack vital objectives and escape without interception.

g) All squadrons must be trained to fight and fend for themselves as squadrons before attempting to work in mass formations.

With regard to the assembly of wing formations, it is often written that the 12 Group Duxford Wing lost time in forming up, and was therefore too slow and impractical for that reason alone. This, however, is not the case, as Wing Commander Douglas Blackwood, CO of Duxford's 310 Squadron, explained:

> There was never really time to get three or four squadrons off the ground and into some shape and form to attack the usual mass of enemy aircraft effectively. On one or two occasions I, as deputy senior squadron commander, was detailed by Bader and the AOC to lead the formation, so I know a little about this difficulty. Of course, Douglas Bader was at the front and so he never saw the 'Tail End Charlies' – it was chaos at the back with chaps being left behind and all sorts. Remember too that the Hurricane had not the power of a Spitfire.

With the changed tactical scenario, on 10 October 1940, Park wrote to Dowding requesting that 12 Group now take a larger share of the fighting, while emphasising that certain 12 Group squadrons would need to replace some war weary 11 Group units. The only alternative, Park suggested, was for 12 Group not to rotate its squadrons, thereby remaining at its current strength, and the 12 Group wing operate under the control of either the Biggin Hill or Kenley sector for a short period each day. In this document, Park raised a valid point: Leigh-Mallory had never sent 19, 242, 302, 310 or 611 Squadrons for a tour of duty in 11 Group, which was inconsistent with the policy of rotating squadrons.

On 13 October 1940, Air Vice-Marshal Evill sent Dowding a set of minutes regarding various aspects of the battle to date. The SASO wrote that beyond daily combat reports, Fighter Command HQ had:

> no regular source of information as to how groups are operating. We do not know whether their squadrons are sent up singly or

in twos or threes, or to what heights they are sent. We have no indication as to how squadrons in the air are disposed or whether factory areas are specifically covered. There is, in fact, no general statement of the action taken. For instance, though 12 Group's wing was called in on afternoon of 11 October, as is indicated in their Form 'Y', there is no mention in 11 Group's report that they called for this reinforcement or what they did with it.

We have, I know, received – after calling for it – a report from 11 Group on their method of operation in the first six weeks of this battle, which contains very valuable information as to methods adapted by 11 Group in that period. We have also received from Leigh-Mallory reports as to why and how he employs his wing, and reports from Park as to why he does not. Apart from these communications we do not know a great deal about the way in which they conduct operations and there is certainly no recognised routine for reports from Groups as to what they are doing.

I fully understand that you delegate the tactical conduct of operations to the groups, and that we must neither bother them with demands for a lot of written information, nor show a lack of confidence in their conduct of operations, which would, indeed, be entirely unjustified in view of the results which they have achieved.

Evill's comments regarding Park's reports are somewhat puzzling, given that the latter's are comprehensive and do not explain 'why he does not' use wings. Evill had missed the point, so far as the wing scenario went. Park *was* using wings, when appropriate, as his reports confirmed. Park's tactics were clearly defined and flexible – but unbeknown to him, behind closed doors at the Air Ministry, a critique of his handling of the battle over south-east England was being prepared.

On 14 October 1940, Air Vice-Marshal Stevenson, the Deputy Director of Home Operations, produced an 'Air Staff Note on the Operation of Fighter Wings' for the DCAS, Air Vice-Marshal Douglas, this document being based solely upon Leigh-Mallory's report dated 17 September 1940. In due course, Stevenson's memorandum was shown to Park, whose responses are shown below in italics:

It has become apparent that on some occasions our fighters have been meeting the enemy on unequal terms both as regards numbers and height. In order to overcome or reduce this disadvantage, fighters must be operated in tactical units large enough to deal effectively with enemy formations and these units must be so controlled that they encounter the enemy without tactical disadvantage.

2. It is the purpose of this note to examine the circumstances in which fighter units of more than single squadrons should be operated and to evolve general principles for their employment.

3. It would be well first to summarise the disadvantages under which our own fighters have in some instances operated. These are briefly as follows:

    (i) Numerical Inferiority: Squadrons have been sent up singly or in pairs to meet large formations of bombers escorted by still larger formations of enemy fighters. The operations of three squadrons have not been effectively coordinated with the operations of other squadrons in the same group, and adjacent groups, with the result that fighters have operated independently and effectively.

    Pairs of Spitfire squadrons engage high fighter screen. Pairs of Hurricane squadrons to each raid and escort. Wing formations from Tangmere, Northolt, Debden, North Weald. Not 'adjacent Groups': only 12 Group.

    (ii) There have been few opportunities for fighter formation leaders to discuss or concert operations with leaders of other fighter formations.

    Group and Sector conferences are frequent.

    (iii) Fighters are frequently told to patrol at a height which puts them at the mercy of high-flying fighters.

    See Instruction to Controllers No 25.

    (iv) Fighters are vectored towards enemy formations in such a way that by the time they reach the plan position of the enemy, they are below him.

For many units assemble at height over base or on their patrol line.

(v) The limitations of High Frequency Radio Telephony preclude the possibility of operating a number of squadrons on the same frequency.

4. Examination of the disadvantages leads us to recommend the adoption of the following principles for operating fighter formations larger than squadrons.

Is an aim to engage bombers before they reach target?

Fighter Wing

5. The minimum fighter unit to meet large enemy formations should be a wing of three squadrons.

Depends on time available and clouds. Impossible for London sectors!

'Balbo'

6. When necessary, to secure superiority in numbers or to reduce inferiority as far as possible, a force of two fighter wings should be operated as a tactical unit. This tactical unit of two wings will be referred to in this paper as a 'balbo'.

Too clumsy and rigid for Home Defence fighting

Composition of a Wing

7. A wing should be of three squadrons of the same type and if possible mark of aircraft.

Yes.

8. All squadrons of a wing should operate from the same aerodrome, or failing this, from aerodromes within two or three miles of each other.

No. Dispersment reduces vulnerability.

Composition of a Balbo

9. A balbo should be of two wings. One wing may be of one type of aircraft and the other wing may be of another. Wings composing a balbo should be so disposed that the wing having the aircraft of higher performance is further back from the zone of operations.

Control of a Wing

10. In order to ensure sympathetic and effective control of the wing, one of the squadron commanders from the squadrons composing the wing should supervise the controlling wing from the Sector Operations Room.

Continuous Watch in daylight?

Control of a Balbo

11. The wings composing a balbo will come from different sectors. The control of each wing will be supervised by a squadron commander from the wing, but the Group Headquarters should detail one of the sectors to coordinate the operations of the two wings of the balbo. The Direction Fixing positions of both wings should be shown in the Operations Room of the controlling sector.

Variations in Control Neccessitated by VHF or HF R/T

12. VHF facilitates the control of balbos, but if squadrons are fitted with HF it is considered that difficulties in inter-communications are outweighed by the advantages in meeting large enemy formations with large fighter formations.

Control of Balbos With VHF R/T

13. All the squadrons in each wing should operate on sector frequency (Button 'B') and would have to be controlled on this frequency. Inter-communication between wings in a balbo would be by means of the Command frequency through aircraft on watch on this frequency.

Yes.

Control of Balbos with HF R/T

14. Squadrons should operate on their squadron frequency; inter-communication between squadrons by R/T is impracticable except through ground stations. It will frequently happen when using HF that balbos will pass out of R/T range of their sectors. When this happens it may be confidently expected that weather will be such that large enemy formations will be clearly visible from a distance, and vectoring, therefore, will be unnecessary.

    Yes.

15. The control of balbos operating at a distance from their controlling sectors even with VHF is complicated by the sectors not having operations tables big enough to show the whole area over which balbos may have to fight. It is recommended that smaller scale 'balbo tables' should be provided to show the tracks of enemy formations of more than, say, fifty aircraft. These tables should be small-scale replicas of the Fighter Command table (say ten miles to one inch). Consideration would have to be given to the method by which this information might be passed to sectors.

    One group must <u>control all</u> squadrons in its sectors.

Unity of Wings

16. 'Espirit de Wing' and consequent operational efficiency would be fostered by regarding wings as units and moving them complete from one station to another when rest or reinforcement is necessary, but this is obviously impractical at present. It would be difficult to engender in a balbo the same spirit of unity which should inform a wing, but much could be done to promote good cooperation by encouraging personal contact between the pilots and particularly the leaders of the squadrons concerned.

Location of Wings

17. Wings should be located at stations from which they can gain advantage in height over the enemy before they meet him, without having to turn. This may be impracticable except in special cases.

Group Combined Tactical Plan

18. The tactical plan on which the primary group should work ought to be based on the principle that although the aim is to destroy enemy bombers, the enemy fighters must be contained to enable the bombers to be destroyed.

Need to protect vitals of area?

Role of Wings

19. The wing with higher performance aircraft should take on enemy fighters. The wing with the lower performance aircraft should take on bombers, if any.

Yes.

Clearly, Park had all the answers to every detail in Stevenson's note – hardly surprising given that by now he was the most experienced fighter leader in the service. That being so, it is incomprehensible that such a memorandum was compiled and circulated by the Air Ministry without consultation with Dowding or Park. Stevenson's fifth point makes abundantly clear the thinking at the Air Ministry, and traction achieved by 'Big Wing' supporters: 'The minimum fighter unit to meet large enemy formations should be a wing of three squadrons.' The Air Staff Note was circulated, notifying the AOCs of 10, 11 and 12 groups that the CAS was holding a conference on 17 October 1940 to discuss day-fighter formation tactics and hear a report from Dowding regarding the progress of nocturnal defences. Stevenson's note was to 'form the basis for discussion'. The agenda for this forthcoming meeting was circulated; again, Park's comments are italicised:

Is it agreed that the maximum fighter unit to meet large enemy formations should be a wing of three squadrons?

To meet enemy bomber formations only.

Is it agreed that a larger fighter formation than a wing should operate as a tactical unit? If so, is it agreed that this unit should consist of two wings?

Not over UK but on offensive sweeps.

By what name should such a unit (referred to in this agenda as a 'Balbo') be known?

Are any insurmountable obstacles foreseen in operating all the squadrons of a wing from the same aerodrome?

No, but congestion, take-off delay and all being bombed on the ground together should be considered.

Is it agreed that the wing and 'Balbo' should be controlled by a squadron commander from one of the squadrons composing the formation?

No, by Ground Sector Controller.

Are there likely to be any difficulties in coordinating the operations of the two wings or 'balbo'?

Yes, limitation of R/T and clouds.

In weather conditions which enable the enemy to operate in mass formation, it is likely that the fighter leader may be able to dispense with sector control. Is it agreed that in these conditions he should inform the sector controller and take over control of the wing or 'balbo', being informed by the Controller of the location, size, speed, course and height of the enemy mass?

These conditions are best suited for Sector Controller, as he gets good information from Observer Corps, recce aircraft, AA units and Group HQ.

Has the Conference any comments on the method of R/T control of 'balbos' described in 12–15 of the attached Air Staff Note?

VHF as common frequency.

Can wings be regarded as permanent units and moved complete when necessary, from one station to another?

No, unless squadrons are added.

Is it agreed that wings should be deployed at stations from which they can gain advantage in height over the enemy without having to turn?

No, depends on length of warning.

Short report by C-in-C Fighter Commander on present position regarding night interception.

On 15 October 1940, Park sent a memorandum to his sector commanders, the following being the relevant extract for our purposes:

Use of Wing Formations Against Present Enemy Tactics
The use of wings of two or three squadrons is effective against enemy bombers with close fighter escorts for the following reasons:
  (a) Much more warning from RDF plots is received while the enemy bomber and fighter formations are assembling over the French coast; this gives the Group Controller plenty of time to order squadrons up to operational height, in some cases well before the enemy raids commenced to approach our coast;
  (b) The bomber formations fly mostly between heights of 15,000–20,000 feet;
  (c) Formations of enemy bombers and escorting fighters can be sent over to this country only in good weather conditions which are suitable for interception by wings.
2. Against the present enemy tactics, very high fighter patrols or raids, the use of wing formations has been found to have serious disadvantages for the following reasons:
  (a) The warning received from RDF plots is insufficient to place squadrons at the required height in time to intercept the <u>first</u> wave of enemy fighters;
  (b) The heights of enemy aircraft are much greater, thus requiring more time to intercept from above;
  (c) The present enemy tactics are generally confined to days when considerable cloud is present.
3. Results have shown that wings or pairs of squadrons have only been successful in intercepting when there is a second

or third wave of enemy fighters, and this can be only done if the squadrons take off and climb to operational height and then effect a rendezvous. When two or three squadrons take off and climb together, the rate of ascent is found to be slower, thereby wasting valuable minutes during which time one or two squadrons, operating singly, could attain position above the enemy fighter formations.

4. The first wave of enemy fighter aircraft has usually been intercepted only by the Spitfire squadron carrying out Standing Readiness Patrol, and sometimes by one or two Spitfire squadrons from 'Stand-by'.

5. Rigid squadron formations and wing formations have been found to be ineffective against very high fighter raids for the following reasons:-

   (a) They can't be broken up easily by attacks from above by small formations of enemy aircraft. Instances have occurred of even one or two enemy fighters having broken up a pair of squadrons.

   (b) If enemy fighter aircraft happen to be below they can usually see a large formation of our fighters, and on account of their superior speed at high altitude they are able to withdraw before we can engage.

The first paragraph 'a' of the foregoing memorandum is significant, and relates exclusively to 11 Group. Supporters of the 12 Group 'Big Wing', however, argued that Duxford's squadrons should be scrambled immediately RDF indicated an enemy formation assembling over Calais, so that the wing could be at height in time to intercept the incoming enemy over Canterbury. As previously explained, however, the reality of this theory in practice was impractical, because the technical limitations of RDF meant that it was unable to differentiate between assembling raids and the constant heavy enemy air traffic over the Pas-de-Calais. The earliest warning of a raid, therefore, was when one began moving out over the Channel, towards the English coast – just seven minutes flying time away. In this scenario, time, distance and height are the key factors, so the following must be borne in mind:

1. From the time a plot appeared on the RDF screen, it took around five minutes before the first RAF fighters were scrambled.

2. The distance between Duxford and Canterbury is some seventy miles.

3. Pilot's Notes indicate that the Spitfire Mk II's average climbing speed was 180 mph. Thus it would take twenty-three minutes to travel from Duxford to Canterbury, longer for a number of aircraft in formation. Moreover, not all the aircraft were new Spitfire Mk IIs – most were inferior Hurricanes. Then, the time between the first indication of an incoming raid and squadrons being scrambled has to be added, and all this time German aircraft are approaching Britain. Arguably, then, it would potentially take over thirty minutes from the raid's first detection by RDF to the Duxford Wing arriving over Canterbury.

4. A German bomber formation incoming at three miles per minute, it would take approximately fourteen minutes to fly from Calais to Canterbury, assuming a direct course – half the time it would take Duxford's squadrons to be in position.

While the foregoing mathematics indicate the impossibility of the Duxford Wing scrambling and intercepting an incoming raid over Kent, the wing could certainly be in position to attack the retiring enemy – after the target had been bombed. This, though, was unacceptable to Park – the defender of London – who referred to the matter in his robust response to Stevenson's Air Staff Note. On the same day Park wrote his report on the use of wing formations, he replied to Stevenson, enclosing copies of his instructions to 11 Group sectors of 1 and 5 October 1940, suggesting that these should be circulated prior to the conference, 'in order to save a great deal of valuable time'; unsurprisingly, it was caustic in places, and indicates how one-sided Stevenson's communication had been:

> Your Air Staff Note is, apparently, based on the experience of 12 Group on the five occasions in which they have reinforced my Group. We in 11 Group used wings of three squadrons in May, June, July, August, September, and are still using them when conditions of time, space and weather make them effective.
>
> During the last big attack by the German long-range bomber force, the squadrons in 11 Group, operating in pairs of

squadrons destroyed 115, plus 28 probably destroyed, plus 41 shot down damaged, for a cost of 15 pilots. 12 Group employed their large wing formation on that date ... they destroyed 13 enemy aircraft, plus 6 probably destroyed, plus 3 damaged, for a cost of 2 pilots. As you have included in the papers for the conference detailed results by 12 Group wings, I think you should include the attached statement, showing the results by 10 and 11 Groups on the last big battle with bombers over England. We were both using mainly pairs of fighter squadrons as our geographical situation does not afford the time to despatch, assemble and engage with wing formations BEFORE THE BOMBER RAIDS HAVE REACHED VITAL OBJECTIVES. I may be wrong in imagining that our primary task is to protect London, aircraft factories, sector aerodromes, against enemy bombers, and not merely to secure a maximum bag of enemy aircraft after they have done their fiendish damage.

You must appreciate, of course, that *conditions of time and space do not permit squadrons in 12 Group to engage incoming raids*, but mainly outgoing raids after they have been attacked by pairs of Spitfire and Hurricane squadrons located around London and have had their close escort and themselves pretty badly shaken by AA fire.

It beggars belief that Park even had to write the foregoing. If the proposed conference was genuinely to review tactics to date and consider what, if any, improvements could be going forward, surely the AOC 11 Group, as now the most experienced group commander, would have been the first consulted? Moreover, that Stevenson's critical memorandum only included data from 12 Group speaks volumes.

Park also made out his own 'Points for Air Ministry Conference', reiterating the content of his previous reports concerning the use of wings, making several noteworthy comments:

Our AIM has been to engage bombers BEFORE they reach vital objectives, using maximum force in time given – wings or pairs, or single squadron, or even Station Commanders.

FLANK SECTORS, North and South, have been used in wings of three frequently, but can only engage out-going bomb raids with good results because:

206

i)   Raids coming in being engaged by pairs of Spitfire and/or Hurricanes and so lost their escorts.
ii) have been subjected to heavy AA fire.
iii) have expended much of their ammunition.

DUXFORD WINGS, 4/5 squadrons, like the Debden and Tangmere wings have arrived to intercept *out-going* bomb raids.

DANGER TO MORALE of squadrons being taught by northern groups that it is not safe to enter the south-east area except in wings of 4/5 squadrons. 616, 266, 66 Squadrons from 12 Group possibly imbued with Big Wing idea not fought so well as 13 Group squadrons trained to fight singly…

DEBDEN squadrons found to be TOO FAR NORTH, so moved one squadron to North Weald.

DUXFORD ROVING WINGS caused considerable confusion to London defences and prolonged Air Raid Warnings through wandering uninvited and unannounced over East Kent after retreat of enemy.

REINFORCEMENTS from 10 Group; arrangement entirely satisfactory because:
a) They proceed to the place and height requested.
b) They do not delay to form up wings of 4/5, so arrive after Brooklands, Kingston, Kenley etc have been bombed.
c) They remain under the direction of 11 Group, so avoid confusing Observer Corps, 11 Group squadrons and ARW system.

Although Park was wrong about the Duxford Wing wasting time forming up, it is impossible to argue with what he says.

On 15 October 1940, the 242 Squadron ORB recorded that 'Squadron Leader Bader proceeded on four days leave.' This was significant.

Two days later, the following RAF officers assembled in the Air Ministry's Air Council Room:

AVM W.S. Douglas	DCAS
ACM Sir H.C.T. Dowding	AOC-in-C Fighter Command
AM Sir Charles Portal	AM(P)

AM Sir Phillip P.B. Joubert de la Ferte	ACAS (R)
AVM K.R. Park	AOC 11 Group
AVM Sir C.J. Quintin Brand	AOC 10 Group
AVM T.L. Leigh-Mallory	AOC 12 Group
AC J.C. Slessor	D of P
AC D.F. Stevenson	DHO
AC O.G.W.C. Lywood	PDD of Signals
GC H.G. Crowe	ADAT
WC T.N. McEvoy & Mr J.S. Orme	Secretaries
SL D.R.S. Bader	CO 242 Squadron

The presence of a mere squadron leader at this high-level meeting of senior officers is astonishing – especially without the knowledge and consent of his Commander-in-Chief. According to Brickhill, Dowding looked at Bader 'severely'; as Lord Dowding later commented, 'I should think I would have been.' Later, the Parliamentary Secretary-of-State for Air, Harold Balfour, contested this view:

> Maybe it was against service discipline and custom for such a junior officer to be present at this high-level conference but even today I can see no real objection. Here were a lot of middle-aged experts meeting to resolve differing views on fighting strategy and tactics. Here among them was one of the men actually doing the daily job and I think it must have brought a refreshing breath of reality that Bader was there to give his views.

Were this an open and genuine analysis of tactics, however, to agree best practice for the future, surely Park and Brand would have been invited to bring along one of their squadron commanders, so as to afford a fair hearing to all perspectives, enabling the most informed decision to be made? Squadron Leader 'Sailor' Malan, the CO of 74 Squadron, immediately comes to mind, a highly experienced fighter pilot and leader who had flown extensively in 11 Group and with the Duxford Wing, while resting in 12 Group. Likewise, Brand had no shortage of experienced squadron commanders to choose from, not least Squadron Leaders Harry Fenton (238 Squadron) or George Darley (609 Squadron), whose squadrons had frequently reinforced 11 Group. Clearly, whatever Balfour's perspective, the whole thing was undoubtedly a fait accompli, and Dowding and Park realised – too late – that the meeting's purpose was purely to push forward the adoption of wings – period.

Of Bader's involvement, Park later wrote that 'he was used to make room for Leigh-Mallory.' Dowding, who was unaware of Flight Lieutenant Peter MacDonald MP's disloyalty at the time, commented that 'Leigh-Mallory had quite enough incentive of his own, without bringing Douglas Bader in'; the AOC-in-C was not to learn of Leigh-Mallory's statement to Park that he would 'move heaven and earth' to get Dowding sacked until 1968 – after which, things must have become very much clearer.

Lord Dowding:

> I do not think Bader would ever have allowed himself consciously to become embroiled in such a move. It would probably have come as a shock to him to hear that Leigh-Mallory ever entertained such an idea. It was one thing to disagree with my views, and to express criticisms forcibly, but it was another altogether to intrigue against his own Commander-in-Chief, which is why I think the latter was out of the question.

While 'out of the question' so far as Douglas Bader's involvement went, that was clearly not the case where both Leigh-Mallory and MacDonald were concerned. Mutiny may be too strong a word – but arguably that is what was happening.

So that there can be no ambiguity about this infamous meeting, the minutes, which are lengthy, are herewith reproduced verbatim:

> DCAS explained that he was presiding at the meeting as CAS was unable to be present owing to indisposition.
>
> 2. There were three propositions that he would like the meeting to consider:
>   (i) We wish to outnumber the enemy formations when we meet them.
>   (i) We want our superior numbers to go into the attack with a coordinated plan of action so that the protecting fighters are engaged by one part of our force, leaving the bombers to the remainder.
>   (iii) If possible, we want the top layer of our fighter formation to have the advantage of height over the top layer of the enemy formation.

3. This was the ideal, but it was obviously not always possible of attainment. For instance, the time factor might not allow us to do what we wanted. It might be necessary to engage before he reached some vital objective, and in such cases, there might not be time either to collect a superior force or to obtain superior height. DCAS then invited comments on the propositions he had outlined.

4. AOC of 11 Group said that with factors of time, distance and cloud that were often involved in the operations of 11 Group it should not be laid down as a general principle that the wing of fighters was the right formation to oppose attacks, even those made in mass. He felt that the satisfactory use of the wing by 12 Group related to ideal conditions when enemy bombers were in retreat, separated from their escort. 11 Group, using formations of one or two squadrons had, on the other hand, quite recently obtained results against bombers on their way in which compared not unfavourably with those of the wing sorties from 12 Group.

5. The AOC outlined to the meeting the principle that applied in 11 Group for operations against enemy bombers with a fighter screen; this involved the use of squadrons in pairs at different heights to engage separately the top fighter screen, the close escort and the bombers.

6. AOC-in-C Fighter Command said that the great problem was to obtain early knowledge as to which of perhaps many raids was a major one. The Observer Corps did good work but were often baffled by the extreme height of enemy formations. He therefore attached great importance to the development of GL and LC organisation; Kent and Sussex would be covered by the end of November. This beam control had, of course, the disadvantage that the plot of only one formation at a time could be brought through into a Sector Operations Room, but it would be a big help when a big raid was known to be coming in.

7. AOC 11 Group referred to experiments he had been making with reconnaissance Spitfires, which, in favourable conditions, were useful for obtaining early reports of big formations. The general installation of VHF would give better results from this reconnaissance work.

8. Incidentally there has been two recent occurrences of extremely experienced pilots on reconnaissance being shot down over 25,000 feet by raids of which RDF had given no indication.

9. Experience showed that this reconnaissance work was not suitable for young pilots, whose commendable keenness led them to engage, rather than shadow, the enemy.

10. Reverting to the general question of fighter tactics the AOC said that to meet the present 'Tip-and-run' raids he felt that the only safe system was that now employed in 11 Group. The reconnaissance Spitfire section was always backed by a strong Spitfire squadron patrolling on the Maidstone patrol line at 15,000 feet, as soon as the first RDF warning was received this squadron went up to 30,000 feet and then to 35,000 feet, so as to cover the ascent of other squadrons; one of these was always at instant readiness and, generally, the present situation demanded an exceptionally high degree of readiness throughout the Group.

11. AOC 12 Group said that he would welcome more opportunities of using the wing formation, operating, say, from Duxford and coming down to help 11 Group. We could get a wing of five squadrons into the air in six minutes and it could be over Hornchurch at 20,000 feet in 25 minutes. If this type of counter-attack intercepted a big formation only once in ten times the effort would have been worth it. On two recent occasions good results had again been obtained, once against fighters alone.

12. ACAS(R) drew attention to the shortness of some of the warnings that groups had recently received.

13. AOC-in-C Fighter Command said that he had recently given written orders that an 'Arrow' should go down on the operations table on receipt of the first 'Counter'. It must be realised that the enemy's approach at great height presented a difficult problem.

14. AOC 11 Group said that he could face the problem when it was a large bomber raid that was coming in. Could it not be accepted that if his group had, say, 20 squadrons at readiness, that was generally sufficient to meet any enemy formation?

15. Discussions followed on this question and it was generally agreed that additional fighter support would often be advantageous, since the more we could outnumber the enemy the more we should shoot down. The AOC-in-C said that he could, with his group commanders, resolve any difficulties of control in sending such support. The other main difficulties to be met, it was agreed, were those involving the time factor, though in this connection it was mentioned that the Me 109s carrying bombs had not, so far, been found over 22,000 feet.

16. Squadron Leader Bader said that from his practical experience time was the essence of the problem; if enough warning could be given to bring a large number of fighters into position there was no doubt they could get most effective results.

17. Air Marshal Portal inquired how such a local concentration might affect the responsibility of a group commander for the defence of all the area of his group. AOC 12 Group said that satisfactory plans were prepared to meet the possibility of other attacks coming in: he was satisfied that the concentration of a wing was not incompatible with his general responsibilities as Group Commander.

18. This raised the question of whether some of 12 Group's squadrons might be moved to 10 Group, which was, the C-in-C agreed, at present somewhat weak should any concentrated attack develop in the West. On the other hand, the protection of the Midlands and of the East coast convoys was a big commitment for 12 Group. Though it was a serious limitation he had, as C-in-C, to keep in mind the necessity of meeting every threat with some force.

19. Further discussion followed in which the importance of a long warning from the RDF was stressed. ACAS(R) said that everything was being done to get the south-east coast RDF stations back to full efficiency following the damage suffered from enemy attacks. He mentioned the recent example when a 25 minute, steady, RDF warning had not been received without delay in 11 Group. It was decided that 11 Group should have the services of a

certain member of the Stanmore Research Station, who had previously been of assistance to them.

20. DCAS said that he thought the views of the meeting could be summarised as follows:

The employment of a large mass of fighters had great advantages, though it was not necessarily the complete solution to the problem of interception. In 11 Group, where the enemy was very close at hand, both methods described by AOC 11 Group and those of AOC 12 Group could, on occasion, be used with forces from the two groups cooperating.

21. The AOC-in-C said that it would be arranged for 12 Group wings to participate freely in suitable operations over the 11 Group area. He would be able to resolve any complications of control. In reply to DHO, the C-in-C said that cooperation of this kind, in the present circumstances, hardly be employed generally throughout the Command, as similar conditions seldom arose elsewhere.

22. With reference to the formal agenda prepared for this meeting, the following observations were made:

Items 1 and 2

Items 1 and 2 formed the basis for the general discussion as shown above. It was agreed that when conditions were suitable, wings of three squadrons should be employed against large enemy formations, and that where further forces could be made available without detriment to other commitments, larger fighter formations than wings should operate as tactical units. It was agreed that it would, on occasion, be convenient to operate two wings together as a unit and that, for want of a better name, such a unit should be provisionally known as a 'Balbo'.

Item 3

It was agreed that it would not always be practicable to operate the combined squadrons of a wing from the same aerodrome, particularly in winter when aircraft might be confined to the runways. It was, however, agreed that all squadrons of a wing should operate from the same sector.

Item 4

It was agreed that, as was now the practice, the wing or 'Balbo' should be controlled by the sector commander. It was considered undesirable for a squadron commander from one of the squadrons to control such a formation.

Item 5

No major difficulty was foreseen in coordinating the operations of the two wings of a Balbo; it was agreed that one sector commander should control the two wings, and that when possible the two wings of a Balbo could work on a common frequency.

Item 6

It was agreed that, in the conditions which enable the enemy to operate in mass formation, the fighter leader could dispense with sector control and that if he was given information about enemy movements he should be responsible for leading his formation to the battle.

Item 7

It was agreed that all squadrons of a Balbo could operate effectively on the same frequency with HF R/T and that by using VHF a theoretical maximum of seven Balbos could be operated.

Item 8

It was not thought that wings could be regarded as permanent units to [be] moved complete, but that whenever possible the same squadrons should operate together as a wing.

Item 9

It was agreed that where practicable, wings should be deployed at stations from which they could gain advantage in height over the enemy without having to turn.

Item 10

23. AOC-in-C Fighter Command, in amplification of his earlier reports, gave the meeting an interim account of the

development of the Airborne Interception Beaufighter. As yet, troubles with the Mk VI AI Beaufighter, and its engines, were causing much unserviceability, but he was satisfied that the system was sound in principle.

24. The method of using searchlights in clumps promised good results and was about to be developed in the South.

25. DCAS and DHO referred to the grave problem of maintaining civil morale in London, in the face of continued attack, over the two or three months that might be expected to pass before the system outlined by the C-in-C was practically efficient. To bridge the gap during the intervening period it was suggested that a temporary wing of two Defiant and two Hurricane squadrons should be formed to specialise in night-fighting on a 1914–1918 basis. C-in-C Fighter Command said that continual experiments had been made on these lines, many of them by AOC 10 Group who had, since the last war, been a specialist in night interception, but with the height and speed of modern night raids the old methods had not so far proved effective. He felt certain that now the only sound method would be a combination of AI and GL (or LC); his Defiant squadrons were, however, now being normally employed on night interception. While it was his considered opinion that the diversion of Hurricanes to night interception was a dangerous and unsound policy, with our present strength of fighter squadrons he had nevertheless agreed with reluctance to implement the Air Staff decision to do so. These aircraft, he felt, might show reasonable results in clear weather when the controlled clumps of searchlights began to work round London towards the end of November, but a real solution to the problem would only be found through the logical development of a system based on the two new radio aids to interception.

26. AOC-in-C said that he would be prepared to experiment with a 'Fighter Night' over London, but this was not a course he could recommend. As people heard the fighters over London they would imagine that the noise represented so many more enemy aircraft, and the experiment would be justified only if it succeeded.

27. A preliminary draft of the scheme which the DCAS and DHO had explained to the meeting was handed to the C-in-C Fighter Command, who undertook to examine it.

Copies of the minutes were sent to Dowding, the three group commanders present, and Squadron Leader Bader.

Dowding had typically placed little importance on the meeting prior to attending, his feeling being that the Germans' tactics had changed so much that any thought of using massed fighter formations from a defensive perspective was 'out of the question'. To Dowding, the Air Staff were not looking ahead, as the meeting claimed, but to the past. His error of judgement rapidly dawned on Dowding in the Air Council Room when he realised that this was actually a post-mortem of Fighter Command tactics – and both he and Park were being called to account. At that point, Dowding acknowledged that he had 'possibly made a mistake in allowing my group commanders so much liberty in running their groups their own way'. Of the two AOCs involved, Dowding said that:

> I was entirely on Park's side without, up to that time, having to say much. There was no need for me to say it. He was carrying out his assigned task and there was no need for any comment from me. But I had come by then to realise that Leigh-Mallory was not conducting the affairs of his group in the way I expected of him. I did not want to say you mustn't do this and you mustn't do that. I expected more of my group commanders. And that was why, by mid-October, I had come to realise I would have to do something about what was going on and get rid of Leigh-Mallory.

Dowding's style of command was one of trusting his group commanders to operate in accordance with his broad strategic wishes, deploying tactics consistent with that aim and within the parameters of the System. It was now clear that where Leigh-Mallory was concerned, that trust had been betrayed. Equally, Dowding's failure to heed warnings also came into sharp focus. Although Dowding later argued that because of his 'hands off', trusting, management style, Leigh-Mallory had been able to connive behind the scenes, the AOC-in-C himself largely unaware of 'what was going on', Park had, as we have seen, expressed his concerns about 12 Group in writing to Dowding on 29 September 1940. No action, however, was taken, and Evill, Dowding's SASO, had failed to deal with Park's previous complaint.

In his memoir *Years of Command* (see bibliography), Air Vice-Marshal Douglas, the DCAS, referred to a 'clash of personalities' between Park and Leigh-Mallory culminating in 'an unnecessarily heated argument' between them 'one afternoon at the Air Ministry'. The DCAS claimed that from this point on, he was personally,

> drawn into the argument, and just as Dowding's name has since become linked with Park's, so mine has become associated with Leigh-Mallory's... It has since become clear that Dowding, also, was not as deeply involved in what has come to be called the 'Wings Controversy' as many writers and historians would have us believe.

Dowding disagreed: 'I don't see how it would be possible for me to have become more deeply involved.'

When later reporting on the meeting, Air Vice-Marshal Douglas wrote that:

> At this meeting it was confirmed that wings of three or more squadrons were the proper weapon to oppose large enemy formations when conditions are suitable ... It was my view that the best way of defending an objective was not so much as to interpose a screen of fighter squadrons between that objective and the enemy, as to shoot down a high proportion of the enemy force sent to attack it, irrespective of whether the objective was bombed on a particular occasion or not.

It is doubtful that Britain's civilian population would have agreed.

Dowding, Brand and Park objected to the meeting's minutes, and prepared to write to the DCAS accordingly. Concurrently, on 20 October 1940, Park continued to try and find a way forward in terms of cooperation with 12 Group, writing to Leigh-Mallory that he would be 'delighted' to have the Duxford Wing's assistance *provided* that it patrolled where requested until engaged. Park emphasised that the wing's position would also have to be communicated to the 11 Group Controller, to avoid throwing the Observer Corps and AA units into confusion, as had Bader's previously unauthorised fighter sweeps over 11 Group. Leigh-Mallory refused, arguing that he could maintain R/T control from Duxford and fix the wing's position

South of the Thames using Direction Finding. Park's exasperation can only be imagined, but Leigh-Mallory had his sights firmly set on a greater aim than cooperating with 11 Group: he was determined to replace Park.

On 21 October 1940, Park issued a lengthy statement to the Air Ministry concerning the meeting's minutes:

> The AOC 11 Group pointed out that the Air Staff Note and proposals attached to the Agenda were based on the experience of 12 Group using wing formations only on five occasions, whereas 11 Group had accumulated five and a half months' experience in using wings of three squadrons when the conditions were suitable. The first essential is adequate time to despatch, assemble, climb and move across country the wing formation. The short warning given to squadrons situated around London seldom gave sufficient time for the employment of wing formations. To be effective, wing formations required sky mainly clear of cloud layers. Lastly, the possibility of employing squadrons in wing formations was dependent on the State of Preparedness of squadrons at each sector, and this was directed by the intensity of enemy activity.

> 2. The primary aim of 11 Group has been to engage the enemy bomber formations BEFORE they reached vital objectives, such as aircraft factories, ammunition factories, London and sector aerodromes. When conditions were suitable, squadrons were employed in wings, otherwise in pairs, and in emergency in single squadrons, if necessary to save an important factory from being bombed. On several occasions, single aircraft flown by station commanders have saved sector aerodromes by means of head-on attacks which broke up the enemy bomber formation when about to attack. The AOC 11 Group emphasised that if he had delayed engaging enemy bomb raids until after his squadrons had been put to operating height in wing formations, they would seldom have intercepted before vital objectives had been effectively bombed, and that to have adopted this policy would probably have led to the German long-range bomber force achieving decisive results in their heavy scale attacks on the south-east of England during August and September.

The DCAS, C-in-C Fighter Command and Air Marshal Portal agreed that AOC 11 Group had followed the correct policy, and must continue this against future mass attacks by bombers.

3. The AOC 11 Group described how sectors on the North and South flanks of London had frequently despatched their squadrons in wings of three into Kent, in order to intercept bomb raids, but owing to inevitable delay in forming up and manoeuvring in wing formation, these squadrons arrived in time to intercept the outgoing bomb raids. These outgoing raids had been fairly easy to deal with, because during their inward journey they had already been attacked by pairs of Spitfire squadrons and Hurricane squadrons which had effectively dealt with the high fighter screen and close escorting fighters, and frequently broken up bomber formations which were retreating, having expended much of their ammunition. The AOC 11 Group pointed out that the Duxford Wing operated under these favourable conditions, and therefore it was not sound to compare their results in air combat with squadrons stationed around London, which were forced to engage the incoming bomb raids, fighter screen and close escorts. In spite of the difficult conditions under which 11 Group squadrons fought, mainly using pairs of squadrons, the results obtained on the last two occasions when the enemy employed his long-range bomber force compared very favourably with the results obtained by the Duxford Wings. For example, on 27 September, 11 Group squadrons destroyed 102, plus 28 probably destroyed for a loss of 15 pilots, and on 30 September destroyed 31, plus 20 probably destroyed for a loss of only 2 pilots.

4. The AOC 11 Group mentioned the danger to the high morale of squadrons in being taught by 12 Group that it is not safe to enter the south-eastern area except in wings of four or five squadrons, and that he had to issue special instructions to squadrons recently trained in 12 Group and now in 11 Group emphasising the entirely different conditions under which squadrons located around London must operate, because of the close proximity of the German Air Force.

5. The AOC 11 Group stated that the arrangements in the last two months for obtaining quick reinforcement from 10 Group had been entirely satisfactory, and had on a number of occasions resulted in saving from heavy bombing the aircraft factories at Brooklands, Kingston and Langley, as well as sector aerodromes to the west and south-west of London. The reasons for this were that 10 Group squadrons had always proceeded immediately to the place and height requested by 11 Group, and had placed themselves under 11 Group's direction, so avoiding confusion to the Observer Corps, Air Raid Warning system and 11 Group squadrons. Moreover, 10 Group squadrons did not delay in forming wings which would have prevented their arriving in time to engage the enemy before he had bombed the vital factories.

6. The AOC 11 Group then proceeded to describe the confusion that had been caused to the fighter defences, the ground defences and the ARW system in the south-east through his Group not being informed when Duxford Wings had been unable to patrol the area requested, but had proceeded unknown to 11 Group, to the Kentish coast between 20,000–25,000 feet, thus causing new raids to be originated by the Observer Corps and AA units. This had not only prolonged the air raid warnings, but had necessitated the despatch of 11 Group squadrons to intercept friendly formations which had reported as fresh raids, indicating a third or fourth wave of attack.

7. The AOC 11 Group explained that he had not made a practice of calling for reinforcements from 10 and 12 Groups if he had adequate squadrons to meet the enemy bomber attacks, because he understood that the other groups had only sufficient squadrons to meet daylight attacks in their areas. As 12 Group stated they could always spare four of five squadrons from their area, he agreed, however, to call of them for a wing, whenever it was reported to be available in time to make effective interception, provided it would go where requested and 11 Group could be constantly informed of the position of the reinforcing wing.

Air Vice-Marshal Douglas, however, refused to allow Park's comments to be added to the minutes – nor did he consider the AOC 11 Group's remarks concerning the Duxford Wing's failure to comply with instructions to be 'appropriate' to the document.

Dowding objected to a statement in which it was said he agreed with a particular point of view: 'Please do not say that I agree, reluctantly or otherwise. I am carrying out orders which I believe to be dangerous and unsound with our present strength of fighter squadrons.' Dowding's comment was ignored, and no correction made.

Brand also suggested amendments, which were likewise ignored.

The only possible conclusion is that the meeting's outcome was a foregone conclusion before the first word of the offending minutes was recorded, and the ultimate document arising is neither a fair nor accurate record of what was said that day in the Air Council Room. The results would soon be plain to see.

The war in the air, however, was still being fought. On 21 October 1940, Park issued a memorandum to all 11 Group sectors concerning '11 Group offensive sweeps':

> When weather conditions are suitable and enemy activities justify their use, the Group may order offensive sweeps to be made.
>
> 2. At present, during daylight, there is almost continuous enemy air activity about the French coast and within the area Calais – Cap Griz Nez – Dungeness – Dover. This activity may develop into a mass attack by enemy bombers under cover of fighters. The enemy cannot, however, assemble and launch mass raids from north-west France later than about one-and-a-half hours before sunset and land back in daylight. It is proposed, therefore, to make use of this period whenever possible to surprise the enemy by making a sweep in strength through the Dover Straits.
> 3. For this purpose a wing of three squadrons, from North Weald or Northolt, may be ordered to provide sweeps. The executive order for the despatch of these sweeps will be issued by the Group Controller on the authority of the AOC.
> 4. Wings are to assemble, squadrons in company, in the vicinity of their bases and proceed to the area of sweep at a height of 25,000 feet.
> 5. Dispositions within the wing, the direction and method of approach to the sweep are to be decided by the Wing Leader in the light of the weather conditions prevailing.

6. Units comprising a sweep are not to remain in the vicinity of hostile territory, but are to make their sweep from SW–NE, engage any hostile aircraft encountered, and are to return immediately to their bases unless otherwise ordered by the Group Controller.

7. Fighter cover for the withdrawal of a sweep will be arranged on each occasion by the Group Controller as follows:-

   (i) Two Spitfire squadrons, on common R/T frequency, patrolling one squadron at 30,000 feet, one at 25,000 feet, on the Canterbury patrol line during the sweep. The Group Controller is to withdraw these squadrons to the Maidstone patrol line as soon as the sweep has withdrawn inland over Kent.

   (ii) Two Hurricane or Spitfire squadrons on Readiness Patrol at 15,000 feet on the Maidstone patrol line to counter any late raids by the enemy.

8. In case of additional cover for London area being required during the course of, or withdrawal of, a sweep, squadrons at the disengaged sectors will be brought to a specially high state of Preparedness.

These instructions are further evidence that Park was not simply thinking in defensive terms, and inflexibly using small formations. On the contrary, the AOC 11 Group was very much looking to go on the offensive, using whatever formation size was appropriate, and balancing this with the need to concurrently defend the Group area.

On 25 October 1940, Leigh-Mallory requested 11 Group's permission to send the Duxford Wing on a patrol over Kent. Park agreed, and asked that the wing patrol the Sheerness – Maidstone line at 25,000ft. Once the 12 Group formation passed south of the Thames, however, 11 Group received no reports on its progress or position. This was clearly impractical and inappropriate, and so Leigh-Mallory at last agreed to the sensible operating procedure Park had suggested five days previously. With the Battle of Britain almost over, it can only be regretted, with the benefit of hindsight, that this agreement was not reached three months before.

The following day, Sir Archibald Sinclair, Secretary of State for Air, visited Duxford and Fowlmere to discuss the wing situation with its pilots. A subsequent visitor was Harold Balfour, the Under Secretary of State for Air:

Sinclair asked me to go to Duxford fighter station and listen to what Douglas Bader and other formation leaders felt. Churchill had visited 12 Group units at Duxford and also the Secretary of State just the week before he asked me to pay my visit. Sinclair had come away feeling that there was a conflict of operational views between the two groups which was felt acutely by units at Duxford. So up to Duxford I flew. I had my talk with Douglas Bader and others. To my chief, in compliance with his request, I wrote for him a true account of what I found. This was the famous 'Duxford Memorandum'.

So here we have politicians interfering in service matters, and only visiting 12 Group.

The row over tactics and the merits, or otherwise, of the 'Big Wing' generated a controversy involving Churchill himself. In this telling photograph, the Secretary of State for Air, Sir Archibald Sinclair, listens to Bader expounding his theories. The Under-Secretary, Harold Balfour, was subsequently despatched to Duxford and instructed to prepare a paper on the matter, leading to a conference at the Air Ministry on 17 October 1940. As a result of this, ultimately wings were adopted as standard practice (quite wrongly), and many believe that it was as a result of this insubordination and political interference that Dowding was replaced by Sholto Douglas, and Park soon afterwards by Leigh-Mallory.

On the same day, 242 Squadron moved permanently from Coltishall to Duxford. Leigh-Mallory visited the squadron two days later, congratulating the unit which, he said, 'was equal if not superior to any squadron in the RAF'. It is doubtful that squadrons which had, unlike 242 Squadron, taken in turn in the frontline with 11 Group, would have agreed.

On 29 October 1940, the Duxford Wing patrolled the Sheerness–Maidstone line twice without event, then, on the day's third patrol, at 1615 hrs, the wing was, according to the 19 Squadron ORB, 'unable to set favourably' because 'Squadron Leader Bader's radio was unserviceable'. In such a circumstance it is difficult to understand why Douglas did not return home and hand control over to one of his flight commanders. Nonetheless, the 11 Group report on the afternoon's action provides essential information concerning both RDF and the Duxford Wing's involvement:

Area of Attack

1. About 200 E/A were engaged in the attack, which was made in three waves.

   In the first wave about 30 E/A crossed the North Foreland at 1624 hrs, followed by a second formation of 20 which flew across the Estuary to the river Crouch. Some of these reached North Weald, which was dive-bombed at about 1700 hrs.

   The second wave followed almost immediately in two formations of 30 and 20 E/A, but did not penetrate further than the Dover–Deal area.

   At 1646 hrs, the third wave of three formations crossed the coast and headed towards Biggin Hill. In this attack, several Italian aircraft were reported. This is the first occasion on which the Axis Partner's Air Force has been recorded as taking part in daylight raids on this country.

RDF Information

2. The first plot of Raid 50, 15 + at 6,000 feet, appeared over Cap Gris Nez at 1601 hrs. The raid reached North Weald about 1700 hrs.

   The first plot of Raid 4, 12 + (no height), appeared over Dunkerque at 1606 hrs. At 1617 hrs the strength was increased to 50 +. This raid was in the Chelmsford area at 1648 hrs.

   The first plot of Raid 3 appeared 10 miles NE of Dunkerque as 12 + (no height), at 1607 hrs. This raid was lost over Margate at 1628 hrs.

The first plot of Raid 9 (bombers), 20 + (no height), appeared near Arras at 1625 hrs and reached Dover area at 1633 hrs.

The first plot of Raid 12 appeared as 4 + (no height), at Cap Gris Nez. No RDF warning was received of Raids 60, 61 and 62, which were picked up by the Observer Corps and plotted in the Tonbridge – Dungeness area.

Observer Corps Information

3. Observer Corps picked up the enemy formations and plotted them accurately. The tracks of Raids 4 and 50 were lost in the North Weald area.

They reported two enemy formations which crossed the coast near Dungeness, and a third, Raid 60, which appeared inland in the same area. Those three raids totalled approximately 60 aircraft. Raid 61 appeared at 1646 hrs and Raid 62 at 1647 hrs.

Weather

4. Clouds 3/10ths at 3-4,000 feet, thin layer at 27,000 feet. Visibility good below low cloud.

Action by Group Controller

5. At 1607 hrs, Nos 17 and 46 Squadrons were ordered to patrol North Weald at 15,000 feet and at 1619 hrs to proceed to Maidstone patrol line at 25,000 feet.

At 1615 hrs, Nos 501 and 253 Squadrons were ordered to patrol Brooklands at 15,000 feet and at 1630 hrs to patrol Biggin Hill patrol line on Readiness Patrol.

At 1621 hrs, Nos 222 and 92 Squadrons from Hornchurch and Biggin Hill respectively were ordered to patrol Hornchurch at 15,000 feet.

At 1626 hrs, No 74 Squadron was ordered to patrol Biggin Hill for aerodrome protection.

At 1711 hrs, Nos 41 and 603 Squadrons were ordered to patrol Rochford at 20,000 feet.

In addition, the 12 Group wing took off from Duxford at 1608 hrs. They originally were asked for by 11 Group to patrol Maidstone–Sheerness, then to intercept two raids that were crossing the Thames Estuary heading for Essex before attacking North Weald. Later, 12 Group wing was asked to make a sweep through North Kent.

Action by Fighter Squadrons

6. At 1630 hrs, 12 Group wing was reported to be over Hornchurch at 25,000 feet, proceeding towards Sheerness. Immediately, two raids that had been approaching Sheerness turned northwards across the Thames Estuary; 12 Group was requested to intercept these raids between North Weald and the coast, as it was feared that the enemy was about to attack fighter aerodromes in Essex. As the Duxford Wing continued, however, to proceed towards Sheerness, Hornchurch was requested to try and inform it by R/T of the new patrol line, but was unable to communicate with the wing because of continuous R/T traffic between the wing and Duxford. Immediately it was evident that the Duxford Wing might fail to intercept the raids, a pair of 11 Group squadrons were ordered from East Kent to try and overtake, but unfortunately the enemy reached North Weald first and bombed the aerodrome, causing some casualties and damage. The enemy, however, was intercepted by 11 Group squadrons immediately after completing his bombing and heavy casualties were inflicted.

Clearly the significant point in the foregoing is 11 Group's inability to provide the Duxford Wing instructions – due to the 'continuous R/T traffic between the wing and Duxford'. Air Marshal Sir Denis Crowley-Milling once enthused regarding 'DB's constant chatter on the R/T' being 'totally inspiring'. Unfortunately over another group area, the downside to this was the inability for the sector controller through whose airspace the wing was travelling to get a word in edgeways and issue instructions – with fatal consequences in this instance. Ironically, had 12 Group simply patrolled the airfields North of the Thames, as the System had originally envisioned, it would have been perfectly situated to protect North Weald.

The 11 Group report continued:

Immediately it was seen that the Duxford Wing was not going to intercept the raids, 12 Group was requested to make a sweep through North Kent to intercept two more raids heading towards Biggin Hill aerodrome, but the AOC 12 Group recalled the Duxford Wing because of a report that the weather was no longer fine at Duxford and he was afraid of difficulty in landing so many squadrons at one aerodrome. The Duxford Wing, therefore, missed an interception with these two raids, which fortunately did not proceed far inland, probably because they saw additional 11 Group squadrons climbing from Biggin Hill area.

The day's combat statistics were reported as follows:

Enemy casualties were 16 destroyed, 6 probably destroyed and 5 damaged, for the loss of 1 RAF pilot, who was killed.

In fact, eight Me 109s were lost over England that day, so overclaiming was an acceptable 2:1. The 11 Group pilot killed was the unfortunate Sergeant Girdwood of 257 Squadron, whose Hurricane had been hit by a bomb while scrambling during I/LG2's low-level fighter-bomber attack – which the Hornchurch Sector Controller had been unable to vector the Duxford Wing to intercept, owing to the incessant radio chatter between its leader and Duxford. Pilot Officer Franek Surma, also of 257 Squadron, was also shot down minutes after getting airborne, but fortunately baled out and survived. The Duxford Wing itself, however, had not fared well. Shortly after take-off, only a mile from Duxford, Pilot Officer Emil Fechtner and Flight Lieutenant Jaroslav Maly of 310 Squadron collided; the former was killed, having been awarded the DFC only the previous day. Over Essex, 19 Squadron reported seven Me 109s stalking them above, and were missing a pilot upon returning to Fowlmere: the popular Sub-Lieutenant G.A. 'Admiral' Blake, a FAA pilot serving with the Squadron. Weaving behind Squadron Leader Lane's Spitfires, Blake had been ambushed and picked off by an unseen enemy fighter and was killed – the last pilot lost by the Duxford Wing during the Battle of Britain.

Justifiably, Leigh-Mallory was criticised by Fighter Command HQ for his handling of the Duxford Wing on 29 October 1940. In addition to the wing's avoidable inability to protect North Weald, while the wing was over Kent, airfields in its own Group area, in East Anglia, had been bombed. The rebuke arising read simply 'Leigh-Mallory must not forget his own responsibilities in future.'

Sub-Lieutenant G.A. 'Admiral' Blake, a popular Fleet Air Arm pilot flying Spitfires with 19 Squadron – and who became the Duxford Wing's final casualty on 29 October 1940.

Of this final phase of battle, Park later reported:

Use of Mass Formations – Big Wings and 'Balbos'

The Air Ministry held a conference ... to examine a proposal that wings should be adopted as standard formation for air fighting, and that was whenever possible. 'Balbos' – mass formations of six squadrons – should be employed against enemy raids on this country. These proposals arose as a result of remarkable results against fighters as well as bombers.

As a result of the Air Ministry conference, the Duxford Wing was invited to operate in 11 Group area on every possible occasion during the last half of October. In view of the results obtained in 11 Group when employing mass formations, the operations of the Duxford Wing have been watched with close interest. The attached table of patrols by the Duxford Wing shows that in ten sorties, it effected one interception and destroyed one enemy aircraft. On only a few days was the weather considered fit for the Duxford Wing to operate. On several days that were unfit for these large formations, the squadrons in 11 Group were operating at high pressure, in pairs.

The intensity of the air fighting over 11 Group territory during the second half of October can be gauged by the fact that its squadrons accounted for 83 enemy aircraft destroyed, plus 62 probably destroyed, plus 66 damaged; a total of 211 aircraft accounted for in the period covered by the attached

228

table, Appendix 'B' (author's note: see Fig. 1). Moreover, during this short period, the squadrons in 11 Group, by successful interception, prevented scores of enemy raids from proceeding inland and bombing vital objectives. On numerous occasions the enemy turned about and retreated at speed before our fighters could come within effective range.

From watching the operations of the Duxford Wing of four squadrons during the second half of October, confirmation was obtained of the lessons previously learned in 11 Group in the employment of smaller wing formations. Other lessons appear to have been brought out as under:

1) Mass formations require the assistance of good sector controllers if they are to effect interceptions of enemy fighter formations;
2) Large wings of four or five squadrons suffer serious difficulties in R/T communications;
3) Increasing the number of squadrons in a wing does not appear to increase the chances of interceptions or the area of search effectively covered;
4) It is inadvisable to concentrate four or five squadrons on an aerodrome in the autumn, because all are likely to be weather-bound together.
5) The maximum size of a wing should be three squadrons, not four or five as previously practised in the North.

Park concluded by saying that:

I wish to pay high tribute to the fine offensive spirit of pilots in all squadrons during the past two months of difficult fighting. During the second phase of operations, the morale of our pilots has been severely tested, because the enemy has had a great advantage in superior performance at high altitude in the Fighter versus Fighter battle. When well-led, however, our pilots have out-fought the enemy at all heights. With few exceptions, Squadron commanders and flight commanders have quickly adapted themselves to the changing tactics of the enemy.

The enemy's superior numbers enable him to throw our fighter forces on the defensive, resulting in the majority of the fighting in the past three months taking place either over British territory or close to our shores. Our constant aim, however, has been to intercept the enemy as far forward as possible and make him shed his bombs harmlessly in open country or in the sea. The aim of all squadrons in the Group now is to inflict such heavy punishment that the enemy will find it too hot to send his fighter patrols or daylight raids inland over home territory, and our pilots will not be satisfied until the air over the Homeland is again free of the German Air Force.

According to the Air Ministry, when later deciding the qualifying period for award of the Battle of Britain Clasp to the 1939–45 Star, the Battle of Britain ended on 31 October 1940. Dowding himself, however, considered the Battle won when Hitler indefinitely postponed his plans for a seaborne invasion, on account of the Luftwaffe failing to achieve the necessary aerial superiority, which was on 17 September 1940. By night, though, the bombing of British cities continued, leading German historians to conclude that the Battle did not conclude until the last big night raid on London, on the night of 10/11 May 1941, after which many Luftwaffe units were sent east ready for the invasion of Russia the following month. Whatever, the fact is that the Germans failed to destroy Fighter Command and control British skies, which is what prevented their proposed Operation Seelöwe from going ahead. That being so, assisted by the English Channel and changing seasons,

"IF YOU DON'T BELIEVE ME, HERE ARE THEIR PROPELLORS"

by holding out, Fighter Command had achieved a great victory – the architects of which were Dowding and Park. Unfortunately, and still unbeknown to them, the political battle at Whitehall was lost – and the final curtain of the Big Wing Controversy was about to fall.

Although the 'Big Wings' claims were accepted at the time, providing an impression of great execution, we now know that on occasions the Wing over-claimed by up to 7:1, and that the claims of 11 Group, fighting in smaller formations, were far more accurate.

Chapter Thirteen

Cast Aside

Although the Battle of Britain was officially over, at least so far as the Air Ministry was later concerned, there was no sudden end to the day fighting's final phase, in fact the two fighter forces continued to clash over south-east England and the Channel until the weather finally turned in early 1941. Throughout this time, the Duxford Wing continued patrolling, uneventfully.

On 3 November 1940, Air Vice-Marshal Douglas wrote to Air Chief Marshal Dowding, enclosing Balfour's 'Duxford Memorandum', in which the Under Secretary stated that there was 'a conflict of operational views between 12 Group and 11 Group', which had 'passed from being confined to operational questions and has, in the minds of those concerned, become a personal issue with the pilots, who feel resentful against 11 Group and its AOC, as well as the Air Ministry'. Balfour clearly sympathised with 12 Group's perspective, writing that this was because they were at 11 Group's 'disposal' but were 'never called to function, according to their new practised tactics of wing formation, until too late', denying Duxford's pilots 'opportunities to shoot down Germans'. Balfour alleged that 11 Group objected to 12 Group 'poaching' over its area and 'are jealous of the wing formation being likely to shoot down 11 Group Germans'. Balfour went on to criticise the System, when he clearly misunderstood its technical limitations and modus operandi, and alleged that the morale of 11 Group pilots was 'unnecessarily shaken' owing to 'having to meet enemy forces in superior numbers', and were 'not succeeding in repelling the enemy in a way that a large formation can do'.

The DCAS's covering letter included a postscript: 'The US of S asks me to say that he hopes Bader will not get into trouble for having been so outspoken.'

Dowding was shocked:

> The only natural conclusion that I could come to was that the political branch of the Air Ministry was now concerning itself

with the details of the running of my Command…. It was becoming a political issue…. No matter how strongly I might feel about the Parliamentary Under-Secretary making enquiries in the way he did, and my disagreement with the facts provided, it was still my duty to reply to the Air Ministry letter…. It was my job, even if it was such a waste of everybody's time, to set them right.

Having tasked Air Vice-Marshal Evill with assembling the required facts and data, Dowding replied on 6 November 1940: 'I agree that this operation is causing so much friction and ill-feeling that I must withdraw the control of combined operations between numbers 11 and 12 Groups from the Group Commanders themselves and issue the orders through my own Operations Room.'

This step overturned the intended System and Dowding's policy of entrusting his group commanders with tactical control. That it was necessary can only be considered, whichever way the matter is approached, as a failure in Command, which Dowding himself later acknowledged. Regarding Balfour, Dowding wrote that 'the story which Balfour has collected by his direct methods is wrong in its conclusions and in the facts on which these conclusions are based.'

Balfour's 'Duxford Memorandum' had also claimed that 12 Group was not being provided all available RDF information. Dowding contested this, confirming that in reality 12 Group received all RDF information covering southern Kent and Cap Gris Nez direct from Bentley Priory. Balfour also alleged that 12 Group was denied Observer Corps reports, which Dowding similarly quashed; the problem was 12 Group's use of a locally arranged but unauthorised system which had been stopped by the Southern Area Observer Corps Commandant. Regarding the charge that 12 Group was being called too late, he wrote that 'My criticism is that the recent conference and all the fuss that has been made has resulted in 11 Group calling for assistance from 12 Group too early, but without the slightest excuse.' Dowding also emphasised that the continual use of certain squadrons in the Duxford Wing,

diverts them from the normal tasks of 12 Group, which are the defence of its own area, including some highly important industrial districts … I am inclined to the conclusion that for the moment in this present phase, the use of the Duxford Wing is a misemployment of a valuable element of very limited strength … Leigh-Mallory has many commitments of his own … and should 'keep his eye on the boat.'

With regard to politicians and officials from outside Fighter Command being provided critical information regarding internal matters, Dowding considered that 'improper', adding:-

There remains the question of the Under-Secretary of State listening to the accusations of a junior officer against the Air Officer Commanding Group, and putting them on paper with the pious hope that that officer will not get into trouble… Balfour has been in the service and ought to know better.

Indeed, Dowding blamed Squadron Leader Douglas Bader for much of the trouble: 'a good deal of the ill-feeling which has been engendered in this controversy has been directly due to young Bader, who, whatever his other merits, suffers from an over development of the critical faculty.' Dowding added that while he had enormous regard for Bader's courage, that had nothing to do with the matter in hand: 'This might give an opportunity of moving young Bader to another station where he would be kept in better control. His amazing gallantry will protect him from disciplinary action if it can possibly be avoided.' Clearly, too late, Dowding realised that the Leigh-Mallory–Woodhall–Bader alliance needed breaking.

In Dowding's response, his acute displeasure was plain, provoking the wrath of the Air Staff and politicians alike. Having sent his letter, however, Dowding got on with the job in hand; the night Blitz, of course, was a much more important battle to fight.

On the same day Dowding responded to the DCAS, 6 November 1940, the Duxford Wing was patrolling between Dover and Deal when Me 109s of II and III/JG 26 swept westwards over the Channel on a *freie jagd*. Battle was joined but although claims were made, no enemy fighters crashed in England. Between 1427 and 1620 hrs, forty-two more JG 26 Me 109s intruded. Over Canterbury, 310 Squadron was bounced: five Hurricanes were hit; two pilots baled out, while the others crash-landed. Such was the ferocity of this attack that only Flight Lieutenant Willie McKnight of 242 Squadron brought his guns to bear, shooting down Feldwebel Schedit of I/JG 26, this enemy machine also being attacked by 19 Squadron's Flying Officer Haines. However, 242 Squadron's Sub-Lieutenant Gardner forced-landed his shot-up Hurricane, and Pilot Officer Hart was killed by Oberleutnant Johannes Seifert, Staffelkapitän of 3/JG 26. 19 Squadron's Flight Lieutenant 'Farmer' Lawson, flying a new cannon-armed Spitfire, claimed a 109 which 'literally fell to bits'. Hauptmann Rolf Pingel, Gruppenkommandeur of I/JG 26, shot down Pilot Officer Hradil of 19 Squadron, who crashed in flames off Southend's pier. Flight Sergeant 'Grumpy' Unwin claimed a German fighter but in turn his Spitfire was severely damaged, possibly by Hauptmann Gerhard Schöpfel, Gruppenkommandeur of III/JG 26. The Duxford Wing had not fared well in this engagement; two pilots had been killed, a further five aircraft destroyed with another damaged.

On 8 November 1940, the Duxford Wing was patrolling over Canterbury. Squadron Leader Brian Lane:

> Sighted Me 109s over Canterbury and turned to give chase. Hurricane squadron chased <u>us</u> and their leader put a burst into my engine!! Apparently CO of one of the North Weald squadrons. Blacked out, then minus oxygen forced-landed at Eastchurch OK. Jennings escorted me down and refused to leave me. Damn good of him.

The speed and confusion inherent in aerial combat frequently and understandably led to both aircraft misidentification and such incidents of so-called 'friendly fire'; this was a far from uncommon experience as, in the heat of the highly charged moment, speed deceived the human eye. The offending Hurricane pilot was Squadron Leader Lionel Gaunce DFC, CO of 46 Squadron. Flying Officer Pat Wells was flying Hurricanes with 249 Squadron, which shared North Weald with 46:

> After this incident Squadron Leader Bader arrived from Duxford. He first approached the 249 Squadron dispersal but we told him that we knew nothing about it. He then taxied over to 46 Squadron. While he did so we telephoned to let them know that Bader was coming. I dread to think what happened when he got over there as he was fuming!

If Douglas had previously considered 242 Squadron to be his own fiefdom, he clearly now considered that to apply to all squadrons in the Duxford Wing. Indeed, this fitted perfectly with what the Air Ministry described as Espirit d'Wing.

After the Battle of Britain, there were decorations aplenty for the Duxford Wing.

Squadron Leader Bader and his beloved 242 Squadron pictured at Coltishall after the Battle of Britain.

The day-fighting at this time, however, was a sideshow to the main event: the night Blitz on British cities. Britain's nocturnal defences, however, remained inadequate – a huge concern for Dowding. Airborne interception radar remained in its infancy and the Bristol Beaufighter – which had greater speed and firepower than the Bristol Blenheim Mk IF currently pressed into service as a night-fighter – was only just becoming operational. Consequently, both Spitfires and Hurricanes were used as night-fighters – although neither had been designed as such. With two rows of exhausts glowing either side of their Merlin engines, situated in front the pilot, and small canopies, visibility was not good. Moreover, with a narrow track undercarriage, the Spitfire could be tricky to land at night – as Douglas Bader had already discovered. Nonetheless desperate measures were called for. 'Fighter Nights' were therefore launched that dreadful winter, during which Spitfires and Hurricanes patrolled above British cities. Guided by searchlights and anti-aircraft fire, the fighters sought out German bombers – but more often than not landed without having espied a raider. On the night of 14/15 November 1940, the Luftwaffe, guided by radio beams, decimated the heart of Coventry. Only three of 242 Squadron's pilots were night operational: Bader, Turner and Ball. That night they patrolled above the burning city but, typically, saw not one German bomber.

The Coventry attack and apparent lack of progress in combating the night raiders has been suggested as a factor in the Air Ministry's attitude to Dowding towards the end of the Battle of Britain and immediately afterwards, and contributed to what happened next. Dowding wrote that on 16 November 1940 he received a telephone call from Sinclair, of whom he had been critical in his robust response to the DCAS ten days earlier, as Robert Wright related in *Dowding and the Battle of Britain*:

> He told me that I was to relinquish my command immediately. I asked what was meant by 'immediately' and was told that it would take effect within the next day or so. Since that was tantamount to being given 24 hours' notice, and verbally at that, I pointed out that it was perfectly absurd that I should be relieved of my Command in this way unless it was thought that I had committed some major crime or whatever. But all I could get in reply was that the decision had been reached, and that was that, with no explanation for such a precipitate step being taken.

Sinclair also told Dowding that he was to take no disciplinary action over Bader, and advised him that his successor was to be … Air Vice-Marshal Sholto Douglas.

In his memoir *Wings Over Westminster*, however, Balfour argues that Wright:

> portrays Dowding in retirement as an embittered, disillusioned, double-crossed, intrigued against and betrayed by his Air Ministry associates and political masters. The truth is that Dowding was shamefully served by successive Chiefs of the Air Staff over his personal career. Promised the future appointment as CAS in 1937, this was repudiated. Between this and his final retirement his service was extended for short terms no less than four times and the requests conveyed in cold, discourteous, terms. He was never, as he should have been, promoted to Marshal of the RAF. In all this, Dowding had grounds for complaint.

Balfour is absolutely right when mentioning Dowding's 'one great failure in the Battle of Britain', that being not having intervened in the dispute between 11 and 12 Group early on, which 'contributed to the regrettable circumstances of his departure'. Balfour is wrong, though, when continuing, 'But for this failure no one can tell what the effect might be upon the duration of the battle and the cost in lives.' Clearly, Balfour is implying that had big wing tactics been adopted throughout, the Battle could well have been shortened and lives saved. The evidence and facts presented in this book conclusively proves otherwise: the Duxford Wing was nowhere near as effective as certain influential men were so keen to believe at the time, and lives were, in fact, lost because of it.

Balfour also claimed that 'there was no political intrigue against Dowding', and that he himself had done his 'duty in a proper manner in accordance with the wishes of the Secretary of State', contesting Dowding's description of how his Command was so abruptly terminated:

> It just doesn't stand up. Of course, his relinquishment had been discussed with the Secretary of State, and A.J.P. Taylor endorses this in his letter to *The Times*, dated 22 January 1970, when he reveals notes of a conversation between the Secretary of State and Dowding at the Air Ministry on

17 November 1940. Sinclair's notes of this discussion show clearly that arrangements for a change in command had already been under discussion and had been decided upon. I can confirm this meeting was held. Each morning I received a copy of the Secretary of State's engagements for that day and he received a similar slip giving mine. On Sinclair's slip was marked 'Meeting with Dowding'. Any subsequent telephone conversation was not to convey notification of a decision but to agree a date and details for implementation of a decision already known to both parties. One final comment: Dowding says that Churchill told him that he had known nothing of the change in command until he read it in the papers. This is pure nonsense and someone's memory must seriously be at fault. Churchill was Prime Minister and also Minister of Defence. Any Service Secretary of State would not have made a vital change in command without reference to, and prior agreement with, the Minister of Defence.... Whether Dowding's memory was at fault or Churchill's accuracy of statement, I shall never know, but I would wager any sum that Churchill knew and had approved the change, and also the name of Dowding's successor.

By the time Balfour's book was published in 1973, though, Lord Dowding was dead and unable to respond, having passed away in 1970 at the age of 87. Wright's book was published in 1969, but whether Dowding's memory was affected by the passage of time, as Balfour argued it was, is impossible to say.

Some argue that Dowding's dismissal was more a matter of natural retirement, having just fought and won a demanding, critical, battle. In August 1940, however, the Air Ministry had extended Dowding's period of service 'indefinitely', so with the daylight battle won, 'Stuffy' had turned his technical mind to resolving the night bombing. Others argue that his failure to address this sooner was actually Dowding's downfall, especially as his old enemy Viscount Trenchard was consequently calling for his dismissal. There can be absolutely no doubt, though, that Dowding's 'one great failure' in the Battle of Britain, and the 'Big Wing Controversy' arising, was a primary factor in his dismissal. As Dowding himself acknowledged, he should have known what was going on, because 'it is the Commander's job to know', and acted decisively. Had his SASO, Air Vice-Marshal Douglas

Evill, brought before him Park's letter of complaint dated 27 August 1940, however, the Commander-in-Chief *would* have known. But Evill did not – and does appear to be 'the one that got away', apparently escaping criticism and responsibility for so failing Air Chief Marshal Dowding.

Still, though, the politics rumbled on.

On 17 November 1940, Dowding received a letter from the CAS:

> With reference to your recent correspondences with Douglas (DCAS) about a report made by Balfour after conversation with Woodhall and Bader, the Secretary of State has directed that no reproof should be offered to either of the two officers on account of the conversations referred to.

On the same day, Leigh-Mallory reported to Bentley Priory regarding the Duxford Wing's operations, therein refuting 11 Group's allegations that the wing only intercepted bomber formations after 11 Group fighters, which had also broken up the escorting fighters. Although the AOC 12 Group claimed that the wing had actually intercepted raids before 11 Group on all but one occasion, the evidence presented in this book proves otherwise.

On 25 November 1940, Dowding was replaced as Commander-in-Chief by Air Marshal Sholto Douglas. Before leaving his office at Bentley Priory for the last time, 'Stuffy' Dowding sent one last signal to Fighter Command:

> In sending you this, my last message, I wish I could say all this is in my heart.
>
> I cannot hope to surpass the simple eloquence of the Prime Minister's words 'Never before has so much been owed by so many to so Few.' That debt remains and will increase.
>
> In saying goodbye to you I want you to know how continually you have been in my thoughts, and that, though our direct connection may be severed, I may yet be able to help you in your gallant fight.
>
> Goodbye to you and God bless you all.

A month later, when the church bells rang out across England to celebrate Christmas Day, the primary architect of victory in the Battle of Britain, Air Chief Marshal Sir Hugh C.T. Dowding, was well out of earshot, having been packed off out of the way to America, on a public relations trip to which he was completely unsuited.

Inevitably, Park was also replaced. On 27 December 1940, the victor of the Battle for London left 11 Group to take over 23 Group, Flying Training Command, at South Cerney, Gloucestershire. His successor was none other than Leigh-Mallory.

An eye-witness to Leigh-Mallory's take-over at 11 Group HQ was one of Park's former Group Controllers, Group Captain Thomas Long:

> I well remember Leigh-Mallory and his 12 Group 'followers' dashing in and out of the Ops Room shortly after they arrived and discussing the type of weather boards which should be displayed for the Controller and adjacent staff to note. Time and again they had to change the deep blue to 'duck egg' blue etc etc until we thought that they would never finish their caperings. All the staff on the Floor looked on with supressed amusement.
>
> I remember that after LM assumed command of 11 Group he issued several directives on the policy of his Balbos. In this paper, he said that the Wing Leader was fully responsible for <u>all</u> enemy formations in the sky. The Wing Leader had to intercept each formation with adequate resources etc. History does not relate would have happened, as for our good fortune the Luftwaffe never attempted a raid on England again during my time at Group. I ask you: how on earth could a wing leader see a picture spread out over miles in each direction, and possibly a depth of activity of 10,000ft?
>
> Shortly after LM became AOC, he said he would like to try a 'real battle' as we fought them in 1940. So one was selected at random, and on 29 January 1941, he said that he would take it on. He asked me to be the Umpire, as I had been in the Group at the time of this raid, which was made against Kenley and Biggin Hill on 6 September 1940 (in fact I was the last of the 'Old Brigade' left, the others having 'seen the light' and left as hurriedly as they could...). Now, we were in the depths of winter so the actual readiness state at each station was one squadron at Readiness, one at fifteen minutes Available, and the third or more at thirty minutes Available. That was the state as displayed for this exercise. Before we started the plotting, I asked LM if he was satisfied with this state, and he replied that he was 'Ready to go!' – so we went!

Now this actual raid was a very rapid one in that the main attack came in without much weaving around over the Pas-de-Calais, in fact within ten minutes it was on its way over the coast of Gris Nez and flying fast towards London over the Kent and Sussex counties.

LM's first order shook the entire Floor – as the WAAF and RAF plotters knew what we had to cope with during the actual battles. His order was, as far as I can remember, to either Biggin Hill or Hornchurch, 'Wing patrol Maidstone at 30,000ft' (you will recall the readiness state as not exactly being on alert at any station). I sent up a message to the Ops Officer adjacent to LM to say that it would take fifteen minutes or more for that wing to get airborne (stations 'played' this battle on the ground but did not take-off as it was thick fog everywhere that day. But for the exercise we had a perfect summer's day!) Believe it or not, the same wing order went out to Kenley and North Weald, and finally Northolt! So we on the Floor, where I had taken up my perch on a plotting desk, watched the outcome, as NO squadron had time to take-off except the first wing from Biggin Hill or Hornchurch. By this time the raids had crossed into Kent and were heading for the airfields around London, to the South. The plots eventually showed Kenley and Biggin Hill 'bombed' with their fighters still not airborne!

Naturally that ended the 'battle', so I went upstairs to the Controller's Room, and LM asked me how it had gone. I had to reply that Kenley and Biggin Hill had both been bombed with aircraft still grounded etc. Having heard me patiently, he said that next time he would do better! BUT the impression left with the WAAF and RAF plotters was one of amazement that he made so many errors with his 'abominable wings'. One plotter said to me, 'Thank God you never did that when controlling', which sums up the feeling.

It was hardly an auspicious start for the new AOC 11 Group.

In March 1941, the official Air Ministry account of the Battle of Britain was published, failing to mention the names of either Dowding or Park; even Churchill was surprised, complaining strongly to Sinclair on 12 April 1941, likening the scenario to Nelson's name being omitted from a pamphlet on Trafalgar, adding that 'This is not a good story.... The jealousies and cliquism which have led to the committing of this offence are a discredit to the Air Ministry.'

Consequently, in June 1941, Dowding was invited by the Air Ministry to provide a despatch on the Battle of Britain which, he considered in a private letter to his friend Lord Beaverbrook on 1 July 1941, to be 'an odd request, after this lapse of time, and after they have already issued an official account, but I will do my best to provide a document of some historical interest'. Dowding's Despatch was published in the *London Gazette* on 20 August 1941. Two years later, in recognition of his great service, Dowding received a hereditary peerage and became the first Baron of Bentley Priory.

Park remained embittered to his dying day at how Dowding and himself had been treated and remained very clear as to why. In private correspondence, on 18 May 1960, he wrote:

> The reason why Dowding was cast aside was because he had strenuously fought the Air Ministry, and there were one or two air marshals who were ambitious to get his job. Dowding was too friendly with Churchill for a frontal attack, and so Air Staff attacked him through his principal tactical commander of 11 Group, and fostered a controversy about the tactics of AOC 11 Group, and Leigh-Mallory of 12 Group.
>
> The tasks and locations of the above two groups were quite dissimilar, so that comparison of their tactics – after the Battle was well and truly won – were quite specious. For example, 11 Group was charged with the defence of London, munitions factories, Portsmouth, and other vital points; whereas 12 Group was responsible for the defence of a northern area. Moreover, 11 Group aerodromes were in the frontline and under heavy bombing attacks, which frequently put some temporarily out of action. In order to continue the Battle, it was therefore vital for 11 Group to intercept and disrupt bombing attacks before they reached their aerodromes, otherwise they would have lost the Battle of Britain.
>
> 12 Group was outside the Battle area and its aerodromes were not under attack, so, if it chose, it could devote additional time to scramble and assemble massive wings of 4/5 squadrons. On numerous occasions, when 11 Group had called for 12 Group for a pair of squadrons to cover a vital aerodrome quickly, it delayed to form up its Big Wing which arrived too

late to prevent Hornchurch, and another time North Weald, from being severely damaged by enemy bombing. I reported this verbally and in writing to Dowding, but as far as I know he took no action against Leigh-Mallory, who was a personal friend of the Air Secretary and the DCAS.

10 Group, on my right rear, never delayed when asked to send one or two squadrons to reinforce and cover Portsmouth, Southampton etc, when all my squadrons were fully engaged elsewhere. Incidentally, AOC 10 Group used exactly the same tactics as 11 Group by employing pairs of squadrons, as opposed to Big Wings favoured by 12 Group, and yet Brand (AOC 10 Group) was not arraigned before the assembled Air Council as I was in October 1940, to explain why I did not copy 12 Group's tactics which were supported by the DCAS, who later displaced Dowding at Fighter Command.

To show how personal was this attack on me at Air Ministry, I was given no warning of the Air Council meeting, nor was I told beforehand even the object of the meeting, whereas AOC 12 Group had prepared his brief and was permitted to bring along the principal protagonist of the Big Wing (Bader), who made extravagant claims of his successes to the full Air Council.

During October and November, 11 Group kept accurate records of the times they called on 12 Group for reinforcement, and on the majority of occasions the Big Wing led by Bader arrived too late to intercept raids on London, even after they had dropped their bombs. This was reported in writing to Dowding and to Air Ministry – who no doubt mislaid the document.

On several occasions, when the 12 Group wing had claimed abnormally big victories in the south-east of England, I told my staff to check with the ground defences in the area for confirmation of enemy shot down. To our surprise and disgust, I remember two occasions in late August when we could get no confirmation of 12 Group claims from Observer Corps, Searchlights or Gun Stations. It may possibly be that 12 Group squadrons shot the enemy down over the English Channel and not over land as reported, but my staff were unconvinced!

BADER'S BIG WING CONTROVERSY

> … If I were not so busy earning my living, I would write a book and disclose the intrigue that caused Dowding and myself to be cast aside after defeating the Luftwaffe in 1940, and so making easy the task of air commanders from then onwards.

After his exile to Training Command, Park was appointed AOC Egypt, and on 14 July 1942, took over as AOC Malta – arriving on the besieged Mediterranean island during an air raid. This certainly concerned the enemy, an intelligence report stating that Park's arrival was likely to 'make the air forces in the eastern Mediterranean more active'. Again, in private correspondence, in 1960 Park recalled that when he took command of Malta – where he would encounter Wing Commander 'Woody' Woodhall once more:

> my airfields were being bombed three or four times daily with consequent loss of aircraft and personnel on the ground. The tactics in vogue were to despatch our fighters to the rear of Malta while they assembled and climbed in big formation, and then to come in and attack after the bombs had been dropped and the enemy was diving away in full retreat under the cover of its fighter escort. These tactics were being employed by the Commander of the Fighters, who had been the Station Commander at Duxford in 12 Group which had originated the Big Wings led by Bader in 1940. I immediately sent this officer back to England, and changed the tactics to what I called a

Later in the war, having first been relegated to Training Command, Air Vice-Marshal Park was posted to command Malta's air defences. There he found that the Controller was none other than Wing Commander Woodhall, who was employing similar tactics to 12 Group's in 1940. Park sent Woodhall home and took over himself, intercepting with smaller formations which suffered no more or less casualties but effected greater execution on the enemy.

244

forward interception plan used in 11 Group. I sent the fighter squadrons forward, climbing to meet the enemy bombers head on, and to intercept them well before they reached Malta, when the bombers were in tight formation, heavily laden and unable to take evading action. The result was that within two weeks, with exactly the same number of squadrons, I stopped the daylight raids on Malta, and our casualties to our fighters were no greater than previously. Incidentally, this enabled the Navy, Army and civil authorities to clear up the bomb damage and bring back our submarines to operate against enemy convoys that were feeding Rommel in North Africa. According to German accounts... Rommel was defeated through lack of petrol and other supplies, due to the losses caused by aircraft and submarines from Malta.

Yet again, Park's tactical skill saved the day – and lives.

In January 1944, Park became AOC-in-C Middle East, and a year later Allied Air C-in-C of the South East Asia Command (SEAC). In 1946, Air Chief Marshal Sir Keith Park retired from the service and returned home to Auckland. There, in 1968, the victor of the battles of London and Malta became most anxious regarding the making of the film *Battle of Britain*, concerned about how Dowding and himself would be portrayed. According to Reuter's, the ageing Park charged the film-makers with covering up 'a dirty little wartime intrigue, which led to the sacking of Lord Dowding, Chief of the RAF Fighter Command then'. It had, coincidentally, been arranged for Lord Dowding to visit Pinewood Studios, near London, to meet the actor playing him – Laurence Olivier. Trevor Howard was to play Park, to whom Dowding also spoke, sharing with him Park's concerns. Dowding watched the scene being filmed showing a meeting between 'Park', 'Leigh-Mallory', played by Patrick Wymark, and Olivier as 'Dowding', at Bentley Priory, in which the two AOCs' differences in opinion over the Big Wing were briefly discussed. In reality, this is the meeting that never happened – but should have, Dowding's one, fatal, 'failure of command'. Afterwards, Dowding said nothing – but was sufficiently satisfied to write to Park the following day, 8 July 1968, reassuring him that the treatment of them both would be 'actively sympathetic'. Ultimately, Park thought the film 'entertaining', although pointing out that the meeting as described never took place, and that the confrontation in the Air Council Room, which was infinitely more dramatic, was not mentioned, presumably, he opined, to save the face of

Dowding was never made a Marshal of the RAF, as many believe he should have been, but was given a hereditary peerage and made Baron of Bentley Priory. The names of Dowding and Park, however, were omitted from the Air Ministry's published account of the Battle of Britain – which surprised and angered even Churchill.

certain RAF officers and politicians. To be fair, Trevor Howard played a good part in the film, which was most certainly 'actively sympathetic', so for once Park really had nothing to complain about.

On 15 February 1970, Lord Dowding died, aged 87. When visiting Pinewood, it was none other than Group Captain Sir Douglas Bader who insisted on pushing the 'old man' around in his wheelchair, and now said:

> Lord Dowding is probably unknown to most of the younger generations. Yet it was because of him as much as any other man that they have been brought up in the English way of life, speaking the English language. They might have been speaking German. Without his vision, his planning, his singleness of purpose, and his complete disregard for personal aggrandisement, Fighter Command might have been unable to win the Battle of Britain in the summer of 1940. What rankled most with the fighter pilots of 1940 was that he was never made a Marshal of the RAF. Seldom in our history has a man deserved so much of his fellow countrymen but wanted and received so little. He surely earned his place alongside Nelson and Wellington and other great military names in our history.

Lord Dowding's ashes were buried in Westminster Abbey, where a tablet commemorates that 'He Led The Few in the Battle of Britain.'

Air Chief Marshal Park died on 12 September 1975. A memorial service was subsequently held at St Clement Danes, in which the Lesson was read by

During the making of the epic Battle of Britain film in 1969, Lord Dowding and Air Vice-Marshal Park were understandably concerned at how they would be portrayed. Dowding therefore attended the set, where none other than Group Captain Sir Douglas Bader insisted upon pushing the old man's wheelchair; Lord Dowding was happy with the film, which actually concealed his one command failure: not getting Park and Leigh-Mallory together to resolve their differences. Dowding died in 1970, Park, who remained embittered, in 1975.

Lord Dowding's simple marker in Westminster Abbey.

247

Air Commodore A.R.D. MacDonell, the Laird of Glengarry and Chairman of the Battle of Britain Fighter Association. Perhaps surprisingly, the Address was read by Group Captain Bader at the Association's unanimous invitation:

> The awesome responsibility for this country's survival rested squarely on Keith Park's shoulders. Had he failed, Stuffy Dowding's foresight, determination and achievement would have counted for nought. This is no sad occasion. Rather it is a time during which we can let our memories drift back to those halcyon days of 1940 when we fought together in English skies under the determined leadership of that great New Zealander we are remembering now. Keith Park was one of us. We all shared the great experience. That is what we remember today. British military history of this country has been enriched with the names of great fighting men from New Zealand, of all ranks and in every one of our services. Keith Park's name is carved into that history alongside those of his peers.

Whether the Group Captain's words at the passing of both architects of victory in the Battle of Britain healed any rifts from beyond the grave, we will never know.

Chapter Fourteen

'... so called controversy?'

What, though, after the event, did Group Captain Sir Douglas Bader think of the Big Wing? Despite the various books written about the Battle of Britain, referring to the tactical controversy, only one author, the late Dr Alfred Price, interviewed Sir Douglas about the matter, before the legless hero's death on 5 September 1982; that conversation is reproduced below:-

AP: *I am very interested in the Big Wing, and how one got it to work...*

DB: You are the first author who has ever come to see me about it. Despite everything published about my wing you are the only one who has ever bothered to come and talk to me about it, and after all I am the only chap left alive who can tell you. All, however, played on this so-called controversy between Leigh-Mallory and Park, and of course Dowding being sacked.

AP: *You say 'so-called controversy'?*

DB: Yes. I was only an acting squadron leader at the time, but I got fairly close to Leigh-Mallory. He was one of those warm people, he was a tremendously good commander and everybody who served with him was very fond of him. He would come over and say 'Well done' and all that sort of thing. What happened was that on 30 August 1940 we got off a squadron, just twelve of us, and we had everything in our favour; height, I knew where they were, and we had the sun. We shot down a few without any problems whatsoever. When we were writing out our combat reports afterwards, Leigh-Mallory rang me up and said 'Congratulations, Bader, on the Squadron's fine performance today', and so I said 'Thank you very much, Sir, but if we'd had more aeroplanes then we would have shot down a whole lot more.' He asked what I meant and I explained that with more fighters our results would have been even better. He said 'Look, I'd like to talk to you about this', and so I flew over to Hucknall and told him what I thought. He agreed and created the Duxford Wing, under my leadership and comprising 242, 310 (Czech) and 19 Squadrons. Leigh-Mallory said to try the idea and see what we could do with three squadrons. There was actually no problem at all. We usually got off the ground in four minutes, at worst five.

AP: *And this five minutes is from scramble to last aircraft wheels off?*

DB: Yes. Now other people, who were ignorant and didn't bother to come and see me, assumed, and therefore stated in print, that the wing took a long time to get off the ground. Not so. As the two Hurricane squadrons got off from Duxford, the Spitfires from Fowlmere, there was no forming up as such. I just set course and kept going and everyone else just formated on my lead.

AP: *Would the second squadrons have taken off behind you, or in any direction regardless of wind?*

DB: You would have three, then they'd go off together.

AP: *So it was always in threes and line abreast?*

DB: Oh yes, and as soon as the first three were getting towards the far hedge then the next three would be taxiing into position.

AP: *On 15 September 1940, you did it with five squadrons?*

DB: That's right, 242, 310, 302, 611 and 19, the latter two being at Fowlmere.

AP: *So once off ground you would go into an orbit?*

DB: No, I used to get off the ground and get absolutely right on course. The chaps then joined me, and the Spitfire squadrons stayed above us.

AP: *As I understand it, the Hurricane climbed more steeply than the Spitfire?*

DB: Yes, but not as fast, you see. I usually set the pace to climb at about 240 mph. We reckoned to be at the Estuary at about 20,000ft, and I think that was forty-eight miles away.

AP: *So would the Spitfires throttle back to stay with you?*

DB: Yes, but they would be 5,000ft above us. The Germans always came in at 17,000ft, every bloody time. Our Controller, 'Woody', would ring me up and say that they were building up over the Pas-de-Calais, and I remember saying, 'Well why the hell don't we get off now and get the buggers forming up?' You see the bombers would come from their bases in France and orbit the Pas-de-Calais, that area around Calais and Boulogne, and the fighters would then take off from their airfields within that area, such as at Wissant and St Omer. Of course the fighters had very short range, not more than forty-five minutes. They would climb up and join the bombers and then the whole armada would set course over the Channel. If our Duxford Wing had got off when they were building up, we'd have got about seventy miles South of base, probably down to Canterbury area, and we'd have got 'em there, on the way in. We would have been at the right height and would therefore have controlled the battle. Our 60, or 36, fighters would have got 'em, absolutely bang on. The problem was, of course, that those controllers down South only had a map showing the 11 Group Sector and the north of France. You couldn't blame the controllers as none of 'em had been doing it for long, but you couldn't expect him to call on 12 Group, he'd say 'Where the hell is 12 Group?!' There was an order from Park saying that they were not to engage over the sea, so what happened was that 'Sailor' Malan, Al Deere, and all the chaps who had been at Dunkirk and were therefore a little more knowledgeable, after having been clobbered a few times due to being too low, they would climb North, away from the Germans, get height and then come back.

AP: *This idea to meet the incoming raids near Canterbury was never accepted, then?*

DB: The thing was you see, Leigh-Mallory was totally loyal. I used to go on at him about why we couldn't go off early and be down there, but he said 'Look, we can't go until Air Vice-Marshal Park requests us. Do please remember, Bader, that they've got plenty of problems down there without us adding to them.' You see, he was very, very loyal. He never once said anything disparaging to me about either Park or Dowding.

AP: *So it would have been totally unethical for Leigh-Mallory to put his fighters into Park's area without the latter's authorisation?*

DB: Quite right. The thing was that the battle should have been controlled from Fighter Command HQ, where they had a map of the whole country and knew the state of each squadron, instead of just the 11 Group control centre which focused entirely on their area. The other point is that we never suggested that 11 Group should use wings, they couldn't, they were far too near the Germans. It was right for Park to use his squadrons as he did, and even if the battle had been controlled from Fighter Command HQ then I would not say that they should have been used any differently.

AP: *But Park tended not to call you in until his squadrons were committed?*

DB: Yes. But what a sight the wing must have been to those hard-pressed 11 Group boys.

AP: *Yes, I was talking to Group Captain Bobby Oxspring and he said that on 15 September 1940, he and another 66 Squadron pilot were weaving above their Squadron, feeling very lonely, when suddenly the wing hove into view with sixty fighters!*

DB: Absolutely. My point now is that all of these books have been written about the so-called controversy, but history has to be put right before it is too late. The point is that we should have been called for in good time, when the enemy was building up.

AP: *So you are saying that time was lost not because of the wing taking off and forming up, but because you were not requested early enough by 11 Group?*

DB: Yes. There was no time lost through us getting off. Once we were off we were off, there was no milling about, all this was done on the climb and en route. No time was lost.

AP: *Could a wing climb as fast as a squadron?*

DB: No. The leader is the fellow who sets the pace, to give the blokes at the back time to settle down and so on, and obviously a squadron in a hurry is faster than a wing because the leader has less blokes to worry about.

AP: *So with your wing off the ground, with the Spitfires as Top Cover, you did not therefore need weavers?*

DB: No, we never had weavers.

AP: *So what sort of formation would you be in?*

DB: Each squadron in threes, we always climbed in line astern.

AP: *So four lots of three in line astern?*

DB: Yes.

AP: *And the Spitfires 5,000ft higher, also in threes?*

DB: Yes, always in threes, the 'Finger Four' came later.

AP: *And were you all on the same radio frequency?*

DB: No, only the squadron commanders were on the same frequency. We had four buttons on the VHF in those days, which we had just received before the Battle of Britain. It was ridiculous anyway, trying to tune this thing with someone shooting up your backside! Anyway, the other pilots each had their own squadron frequency. The Controller would talk to me in my frequency. To talk to the chaps I would have to keep changing frequency from squadron to squadron. Later, of course, we got it so that we were all on the same frequency. When we were above the enemy I would say 'Diving, diving now, attacking now', and my section of three would go down, followed by everyone else. As soon as we made one pass, the formation was broken up.

AP: *So would you personally attempt to control the wing once you had attacked the enemy?*

DB: No. My objective was to get the wing into the right position, and then say 'Attacking now', after which it was entirely up to them.

AP: *Did they await your order?*

DB: Oh yes.

AP: *But once you engaged, each man knew what he had to do?*

DB: Yes.

AP: *When 611 Squadron joined the wing, they were actually stationed at Digby. Presumably they flew down to Fowlmere and joined you there, or did they meet you in the air.*

DB: Oh no, not in the air, not possible, really. We were actually based at Coltishall, so we would fly to Duxford in the morning, joining 310, who were based there, 19 Squadron, of course, being at Fowlmere, and 611 likewise would arrive at Fowlmere from Digby. We would then wait there and operate from there in the event of a scramble.

AP: *And it would have been impossible to operate all squadrons from the same airfield?*

DB: Yes, it would have taken much longer. Duxford and Fowlmere were perfect as they were only three miles apart.

AP: *After an engagement, what happened?*

DB: We landed back separately, you see, you might collect an odd bloke with you, but essentially you landed separately. It was actually very difficult, as all of these pilots would be calling up on the R/T for a Homing bearing. It wouldn't be dark, although sometimes hazy, and you had to find a field among many fields. It could be very difficult. You must also remember that a lot of these chaps were very young and actually had little experience. The Battle of Britain was won not by Malan, Stanford-Tuck and myself, who got all the accolades, it was won by kids of 19 or 20, who maybe shot down either nothing, or just one or two before being killed themselves. They were the blokes who won the Battle of Britain. Make no mistake there.

AP: *If they shot nothing down, how did they contribute?*

DB: Well, by being determined, by going off to fight and being prepared to die if necessary, that's the point. The Battle of Britain was not won by one pilot, it was won by the whole nation. The Navy also had colossal losses bringing convoys into this beleaguered island, the people on the ground who took the bombing, those are the people who won. It was a united national effort, no doubt about that. Churchill, of course, called us the 'Few', and we loved him for it, but if we hadn't got planes and ammunition and gasoline, which was all brought in, we could never have fought in the first place. And let's not forget the nurses, doctors, and emergency services, they were even building Spitfires under bridges in Southampton! So don't think that it was Bader and Tuck who won the Battle of Britain, don't make any mistake on that point, it has to be said, don't just dismiss it, remember that if nothing else.

AP: *On 'Battle of Britain Day', did it occur to you that it was a special day, a turning point?*

DB: Nothing like that ever occurred to us, we were just thinking in terms of our own engagement, not the overall scenario. Of course we saw 11 Group fighters in the air and thought 'Bloody good show, there they are', but my only vision was confined to my wing getting at the enemy, not what the rest of Fighter Command was doing. Certain individual things stick in your mind, like a Spitfire diving vertically and colliding with a Dornier; Sinclair and Boulton colliding, and so on – I couldn't warn them because I was on a different frequency. Gordon baled out, but Boulton went down like a falling leaf and was killed.

AP: *To conclude, earlier you referred to the 'alleged controversy'. Are you saying that you never detected any controversy between the two commanders supposedly concerned?*

DB: No. Leigh-Mallory was absolutely, rigidly, loyal, and I got to know him pretty well. It got beyond the stage of 'Bader', it was 'Douglas', and so on.

AP: *Surely, though, an Air Vice-Marshal would feel that whatever he did at a higher level was not for discussion with a Squadron Leader?*

DB: Agreed, but why didn't we all know what was happening? There have been some appalling books written on the subject which malign me tremendously, saying that I had done my best to torpedo Park and Dowding. It is absurd to suggest that a mere Acting Squadron Leader would have such power. Some of the authors concerned should have known better. No one but you has ever bothered to come and see me about it, as I have said.

AP: *But I have heard from a former controller that Leigh-Mallory was reluctant to provide squadrons to cover 11 Group airfields.*

DB: No, and let's get this absolutely right. There were actually two wings. I had the first at Duxford and Harry Broadhurst the other at Wittering, and they also went down South into action. Leigh-Mallory would not release squadrons to 11 Group but said that we would stay in 12 Group as the Duxford and Wittering Wings.

AP: *A case of either you have a wing or nothing?*

DB: Yes. In other words, I am not sending these squadrons down to relieve 11 Group squadrons and therefore lose them completely to 12 Group. It was simply because he wanted to keep our wings together, which was good sense.

AP: *But it has been said that 12 Group was reluctant to send squadrons as top cover for 11 Group airfields.*

DB: No, the problem was that they always asked for us too late.

AP: *So Leigh-Mallory would assist whenever he was asked?*

DB: Oh Christ yes! He was longing to be asked, so was I!

AP: *Sir Douglas Bader, thank you.*

It is unfortunate that when Price interviewed Sir Douglas, comparatively little factual information was available about the operation of the Duxford Wing and especially, the friction between 11 and 12 Group – which is a pity, because this was a unique opportunity to ask some probing questions. Nonetheless, some interesting points arise.

Sir Douglas's denial of any controversy is implausible. He was, after all, at the centre of it all and present in the Air Council Room on 17 October 1940, when what Lord Sholto Douglas later described as 'an unnecessarily heated argument' between Leigh-Mallory and Park took place – and Acting Squadron Leader Bader would certainly have been fully aware of the meeting's gravitas. That said, Lord Dowding remained convinced that Bader, a junior officer, was not directly involved in any complicity against him personally – but in being so outspoken to politicians, it is hardly surprising that Dowding blamed 'young Bader' for much of the trouble, who, instead of seeking the 'Bubble Reputation', should have simply done his job as a squadron commander. Equally, it is difficult to see with what justification Sir Douglas can claim that Leigh-Mallory was 'loyal' to Dowding, when the evidence is clearly contradictory. It is fair comment, however, that authors of books commenting on the Big Wing Controversy, in the interests of fairness, should have approached Sir Douglas for his side of the story, and that can only be considered a questionable omission on those writers' parts. Had they done so, I feel sure that the outcome of any investigation would conclude that Acting Squadron Leader Bader was determined to get into action and do his 'bit' at any cost – but in the wider political 'intrigue' he was simply a naïve and unwitting tool of those with ulterior motives.

Also of interest is Sir Douglas's reference to Group Captain Bobby Oxspring's impression of the Duxford Wing's arrival over London. In his memoir, *Spitfire Command*, Group Captain Oxspring wrote that as the main German bomber stream continued to advance on London,

> at that moment we witnessed the glorious sight of five squadrons from the Duxford Wing ... come sailing into the raid. The impact of a further sixty Hurricanes and Spitfires charging in on the already sorely harassed bomber fleet was too much. Bombs were jettisoned indiscriminately on south-east London, and the raiders fled for home.

While this may have been the impression, it was not the case that the raiders 'fled', and certainly not just because of the Duxford Wing's appearance. The Do 17s of II and III/KG 76 were only lightly escorted and suffered accordingly – but reached their target: London, albeit with heavy losses. In total, six bombers were destroyed and two more were damaged. As Price wrote in *Battle of Britain Day*, KG 76

> had taken a fearful mauling. But given the lack of escorts and the overwhelming concentration of fighters engaging the formation over London, it is surprising that any Dornier survived. That three-quarters of the German force did so is testimony to the leadership of Major Alois Lindmayr, and the discipline and flying skill of his crews. Despite the intensive attacks by RAF fighters, the majority of the bomber crews held their place in formation and traded blows with their assailants. The formation was still intact when its 'Seventh Cavalry', the Messerschmitts of the withdrawal covering force, linked

up with it. By any yardstick, Lindmayr had conducted a remarkably successful fighting withdrawal.

Oxspring also wrote that some 'twenty-five squadrons got to grips with the enemy that day', totalling '300 aggressive Hurries and Spits'.

This is all further evidence that the Duxford Wing's arrival was certainly impressive, bolstering further still the confidence and morale of 10 and 11 Group pilots already in action, which is not to say that their morale was in any way deficient before the wing's arrival – but the wing's intervention was not as decisive as previous accounts have claimed, and, as we have seen, little evidence exists to confirm the popular narrative that the enemy's morale was devastated by Bader's arrival over London.

What is interesting is that Sir Douglas mentions the existence of a 'Wittering Wing', led by Wing Commander Harry Broadhurst. 'Broady' was five years older than Douglas Bader and a transferee into the RAF from the Royal Artillery in 1926; eleven years later he was an experienced peacetime fighter pilot awarded the AFC, following this up with a DFC for the destruction of a lone raider in bad weather conditions during early 1940. By 28 May 1940, Wing Commander Broadhurst had 2,599.50 flying hours in his log book and was the sector commander at Wittering. Unlike Wing Commander Woodhall at Duxford, Broadhurst did not double as the Sector Controller but flew on a virtually daily basis. On 30 June 1940, for example, he recorded having led '229 Squadron in wing formation'. On 15 September 1940, Broadhurst's log records a 'wing patrol over the Estuary', and on 24 September, 'wing patrol over Duxford'. The ORBs of the squadrons concerned in the former sortie, however, record that the patrol was over Duxford, protecting that Sector while the Duxford Wing was reinforcing 11 Group. If Broadhurst was leading a formation over the Thames Estuary, then this could be evidence of Wittering squadrons also straying from their specified patrol line and making an unauthorised sweep over the 11 Group area. On 25 October 1940, Broadhurst wrote, 'wing patrol Duxford – North Weald'. On that day, eleven Spitfires of Wittering's 266 Squadron proceeded to Duxford, flying one patrol with the Duxford Wing; 'Broady', therefore flew in a formation led by Squadron Leader Bader. Indeed, throughout the plethora of documents covering the period, reference is repeatedly made to 'the 12 Group wing', and that to mean the Duxford – not Wittering – squadrons. It is also implausible, then, to suggest that Wittering was operating a formation led by Broadhurst on a similar scale to that led by Bader at Duxford. While Wittering's squadrons on occasion flew together, this was by no means comparable to what was happening at Duxford.

Also significant in the interview is Douglas's insistence that RAF fighters during Battle of Britain should have been controlled by one central operations room, at Bentley Priory, rather than individual groups. There may have been some merit in such an alternate system, but the System was established – and worked. Had the Cranwell 'Old Boys' network not assisted Douglas's return to the RAF and specifically to his old friend Stephenson's 19 Squadron at Duxford in 12 Group, and had he instead been posted to one of Park's 11 Group squadrons, it would be interesting to know whether this perspective would have even arisen – because then there would have been more than enough action even for 'young Bader'. The 'close relationship' with his 12 Group AOC, Leigh-Mallory, and Station Commander, Woodhall, would not then have arisen, and arguably neither would the 'Big Wing'.

Interestingly, in his memoir *Soldier, Sailor, and Airman Too*, Group Captain Alfred 'Woody' Woodhall made no mention of any friction with 11 Group or controversy around the Duxford Wing. As previously shared, in his autobiography, *Years of Command*, Lord Douglas, who succeeded Dowding in command, sought to distance himself from any involvement in the 'Wing Controversy'. The one man we have never heard from on the subject, and never will, is Air Chief Marshal Sir Trafford Leigh-Mallory, who was killed, together with his wife, in a flying accident on 14 November 1944, while en route to take command of SEAC's air component. The Leigh-Mallorys were passengers in an Avro York which crashed into the French Alps, killing all aboard, the subsequent Court of Inquiry concluding that the tragedy, a consequence of bad weather, might have been avoided had Leigh-Mallory not ignored his aircrew's advice by insisting that the flight pressed on.

People may wonder why, all these years later, this tactical and political controversy still matters. Writing in his autobiography *Wings Over Westminster*, Harold Balfour, the Under-Secretary of State for Air, summarised the reason succinctly: 'for it is history, and all history is important'.

Chapter Fifteen

'Twelve Legions of Angels'

So what did the Few themselves think of all this, of the 'Big Wing' and appended controversy?

Over the years I was able to pose that question to a number of pilots and other personnel from 11 and 12 Group.

Wing Commander Douglas Blackwood, CO 310 Squadron, Duxford Wing

I suppose I would not be speaking unreasonably by saying that the wing was eventually a failure in so much as there was never really time to get three or four squadrons off the ground and into some shape and form to attack the usual mass of enemy aircraft effectively. On one or two occasions I was detailed by Bader and the AOC to lead the formation, so I know something of the difficulty. But when we did attack a formation of enemy bombers, the wing was extremely successful. I would say that the main reason for any loss of effectiveness was primarily due to a sort of jealousy between the AOCs of both 11 and 12 Groups. 11 Group felt that it was their responsibility to protect London without 12 Group interfering.

Squadron Leader James Thomson, Hurricane pilot, 302 (Polish) Squadron, Duxford Wing

The Big Wing was a wonderful operation to take part in as we felt that we were answering numbers with numbers. However, subsequent study suggested that Air Vice-Marshal Park's strategy may have been the sounder. He used smaller numbers to break up the attacking formations, so disrupting their concentration of force over the target area and the effectiveness of their attack. It also enabled him to retain some aircraft for the defence of their bases during that most vulnerable operation: refuelling and rearming. Furthermore, the Big Wing took some time to form up and reach the area under attack; occasionally it missed the boat.

The relative merits of the two methods were argued openly by the circulation of correspondence on the subject between the two Groups. Many of us felt that this was a diversion of mental effort from the main aim of defeating the Luftwaffe and was not entirely becoming of the authorities concerned.

Squadron Leader Waclaw 'Vic' Bergman, Hurricane pilot, 310 (Czech) Squadron, Duxford Wing

In those heady days I was a mere pilot officer who loved flying, loved the Hurricane, and was able to point my guns at a German target. But my English was limited. I have always had the impression that the initial interception of the enemy was left to No 11 Group. We were then to follow the raiders and damage or destroy as many as possible on their return journey. More than once, the wing was released for lunch when Douglas Bader pegged into the dining room and called 'Come on boys, we are wanted!' That was followed by the clatter of cutlery on the unfinished plates – rush for the door, transport to dispersals, and in fifteen–twenty minutes all twelve Hurricanes of 242 Squadron took off in formation on the grass airfield, immediately followed by ours of 310, and 19 Squadron's Spitfires from Fowlmere soon appeared overhead, their job being to protect us from the enemy fighters while we Hurricanes went for the bombers. It did not always work out like that, though. In mid-September our squadron was meeting a formation of Do 17s when we were jumped by a swarm of Me 109s: I was shot down.

Warrant Officer Anton Markiewicz, Hurricane pilot, 302 (Polish) Squadron, Duxford Wing

While flying with the Big Wing in 1940 I was in favour of it. Destroying German aircraft before they reached the target,

Warrant Officer Antoni Markiewicz was a Pole who flew Hurricanes in the 'Big Wing' with 302 Squadron, and remembers how displeased Squadron Leader Bader was whenever the wing failed to get into action.

or forcing them to drop their bombs just anywhere would be a great achievement. But to use a large force to do that left the industrial Midlands without adequate protection. It was rather risky. No doubt Fighter Command knew that, and did not want to take any chances. One thing I do remember is that if we missed the Germans Bader was very displeased, and let us know in simple language!

Squadron Leader Sir Kenneth Stoddart, 611 Squadron, Spitfire pilot, Duxford Wing

We of 611 Squadron were stationed at Digby and for a period of time flew down to Fowlmere on a daily basis, returning home at dusk. The only views I may have had about Big Wings or anything else in those days would have been made in ignorance; apart from Dunkirk, they were the first days that the squadron was truly involved in a big action.

Wing Commander George 'Grumpy' Unwin, 19 Squadron, Spitfire pilot, Duxford Wing

It didn't take Douglas Bader long to realise that sending a squadron of fighters to take on huge bomber raids was not the answer, especially as these raids were usually escorted by fighters. As he put it – if only we had three times the number

Wing Commander George Unwin of 19 Squadron, who believed in the 'Big Wing' concept.

of fighters as a unit we could shoot down three times the number of enemy aircraft. In my opinion there was a further factor that was behind his argument for the Big Wing: for the first five months of his return to the RAF he had been flying Spitfires; with 242 Squadron he was on Hurricanes, and no matter what the loyal Hurricane pilots may say, it was no match for the 109. Agreed, it could out-turn the Hun, but obviously this is far outweighed if the target is leaving you by 30 mph. On the other hand, the Hurricane had it over the Spitfire as a gun platform, both from the steadiness of that platform and concentration of fire. In my opinion the Hurricane was capable of shooting down bombers more effectively, provided it was not interfered with by the 109s. The Hurricane casualties at this time support this argument. Once we had the Big Wing operating it was very obviously the answer in that the Hurricane casualties dropped appreciably, while the number of German aircraft destroyed increased. The wing started operating in the first week of September 1940, and was in action until November. In my opinion it was an unqualified success.

As for the argument as to the value of flying sixty fighters together, there really was no basis for this disagreement between the two AOCs, for the simple reason that it would not have been feasible to assemble such a large number of fighters from the aerodromes in No 11 Group in time to intercept an incoming raid. We at Duxford and Fowlmere had a full fifteen minutes of flying to arrive at the battle area (north of the Thames) and with our two aerodromes only a couple of miles apart we could easily assemble the wing en route to London. I am convinced that the real trouble was caused by Keith Park steadfastly refusing to use the strength of Duxford to anywhere near its capabilities. Day after day we would sit at readiness without being called on to help out. When we were called out, quite often it was merely to patrol the No 11 Group aerodromes while their squadrons were rearming and refuelling. On other days we were too late on the scene. The most glaring example of this was when we were scrambled as a wing and vectored to London area. After about seven minutes our Controller, using plain language, said 'They are bombing North Weald, go there quickly!' This was the day that North Weald was very heavily damaged. When we arrived it was all over, we were too late, I suggest that sixty fighters could have considerably lessened that damage. The total flying time from Duxford to North Weald is six–seven minutes.

One other very important factor was the effect the Big Wing had on the German aircrews. They had been told that the RAF was just about finished and that all would soon be over. This was to boost their morale which by the time was pretty low – imagine their feelings when instead of being met by a depleted squadron, no less than sixty descended on them!

Flying Officer Ken Wilkinson, 19 Squadron, Spitfire pilot, Duxford Wing

Fighter Command's strategy of aerodrome locations was successful in that there were very few attempts in daylight of mass bombing raids over the east coast of England and Scotland, but the possibility always remained. The squadrons resting at Wittering, Kirton, Newcastle, Drem,

Montrose, etc maintained the defence of the east coast. Most critics seem to forget that we had a lot to defend – this aspect may have had some bearing on the infrequent calls upon the Duxford Wing. If one can be satisfied that there was little or no likelihood of a major bomber offensive from the east, then the Duxford Wing was right. Seeing these large numbers of bombers and fighter escorts, and realising that 11 Group was continually taking a pasting, there had to be some help we could give; if sixty additional RAF fighters arrived from the north in time, chances were that the Luftwaffe could have been deterred earlier. Being the lowest of the low (i.e. a brand new RAFVR sergeant pilot), I had no idea about the arguments that we are now told were taking place regarding tactics, but my personal experience tells me that Fighter Command was dedicated to protecting our country and so I am loathe to believe that <u>one</u> Group AOC was pursuing selfish interests contrary to the common objective of defeating (or negating) the Luftwaffe.

Flight Lieutenant Richard Jones, 19 Squadron, Spitfire pilot, Duxford Wing

Early in September 1940 I was transferred from No 64 Squadron at Kenley in No 11 Group to No 19 Squadron at Fowlmere, a part of No 12 Group. By then, the latter was a

Flight Lieutenant Richard Jones flew in both 11 and 12 Groups, and was comforted by the security of numbers while operating with the wing.

part of Douglas Bader's Big Wing. My immediate impression was the experience of flying with a wing comprising five squadrons of both Spitfires and Hurricanes, instead of anything between 5–10 aircraft taking off from Kenley to intercept large numbers of enemy aircraft. To me this experience gave enormous confidence, looking around and seeing anything from fifty upwards of fighters keeping me company! The Big Wing must have had a great effect on the lowering of enemy morale, who, for the first time, encountered such a formidable opponent.

Wing Commander Frank Brinsden, 19 Squadron, Spitfire pilot, Duxford Wing

The constraints of Bader's ponderous formation was a disaster in my opinion, a retrograde step. Nothing was achieved by arriving en masse because the wing disintegrated almost immediately battle was joined. In fact time, and therefore advantage, was lost during assembly and this compounded the effect of scramble orders. These observations on tactics are, of course, in retrospect, but I do recall at the time feeling some unease or dissatisfaction at No 19 Squadron's inability to do better.

Wing Commander Frank Brinsden of 19 Squadron felt that the 'Big Wing' was a retrogressive step'.

Wing Commander David Cox, 19 Squadron, Spitfire pilot, Duxford Wing

When the wing went into action, the Spitfire squadrons, or squadron, was left to their own devices to combat the 109 escorts.

I think five squadrons was too many. I remember going round and round for some fifteen to twenty minutes waiting for the wing to form up and get going. This resulted in the wing often arriving late at the patrol line given by the 11 Group Controller.

There is no doubt that some of the 11 Group squadrons blamed the Big Wing's late arrival for their airfields being bombed. This caused some bad feeling between the pilots. Even as late as the 1960s, an ex-pilot of 11 Group's 41 Squadron in a pub in Grimsby nearly gave me a punch on the nose, as during discussion on the war he found out I had been in 19 Squadron and part of the Big Wing!

Wing Commander David Cox, right, flew with 19 Squadron in 1940 and felt that the Squadron was called into action too late. He is pictured here later in the war while serving in North Africa, with Group Captain Bobby Oxspring, an 11 Group pilot who was inspired by the Big Wing's impressive arrival over London on 'Battle of Britain Day'.

I think a wing of three squadrons would have made better time. Why not the other two Spitfire squadrons operating as a further wing? They would have made the patrol line quicker and with the advantage of height. However, I do think that at times the wing could have been called for earlier by 11 Group.

Was the Big Wing a success? I doubt it. Its best effect was on the afternoon of 15 September 1940 when I remember the words of Bobby Oxspring, a flight commander in 66 Squadron, saying what a wonderful sight it was to see some sixty fighters suddenly appear. No doubt it was a bit of a shock to the Luftwaffe!

Regarding Bader, I was only a sergeant pilot and he was a snob, so wouldn't deign to converse with the likes of me at that time. He wasn't a man you could like, I would say, but he was an inspiration. His voice over the radio when we were in the air gave us confidence.

Wing Commander Bernard 'Jimmy' Jennings, 19 Squadron, Spitfire pilot, Duxford Wing

As I recall, the pilots had two views on the Big Wing. Firstly that it was rather cumbersome, even when led by Brian Lane, a wonderful pilot.

Wing Commander Bernard Jennings of 19 Squadron flew extensively with the 'Big Wing' and believed it 'too cumbersome'.

Secondly, if you were in one of the rear squadrons, those in front would get the first attack and we would have to go down and help them out at our best advantage. Or if we were the front squadron, then we had plenty of cover and help available.

Air Marshal Sir Denis Crowley-Milling, Hurricane pilot, 242 Squadron

No leader has ever equalled Douglas Bader, in my experience, and I flew with him in both the Duxford and later Tangmere wings. He never ceased encouraging we young, inexperienced, pilots and helped us conquer our fears. We were captivated by his charisma and indomitable fighting spirit. In the air, over the radio, he kept up this constant flow of talk, cracked jokes and made us all feel ten times the men we were. I was lucky to have been under his guidance during the Battle of Britain. Naturally, Douglas wanted to get we of 242 Squadron into the action. He used to say 'Why don't they get us airborne when the Germans are building up over the Pas-de-Calais?' He felt that we could then proceed south and meet the enemy formation on the way in. We agreed, because it was impossible to accept sitting comparatively idle while our friends in the South were getting all the action.

Flight Lieutenant H.E. 'Teddy' Morten, Ops 'B' Controller, Duxford

Squadron Leader Bader would frequently telephone Ops 'B' at Duxford to get the form. At mess parties he would discuss tactics, the 'Hun in the sun' and all that, demanding to know why the wing wasn't scrambled sooner by 11 Group. Alternatively he would insist on speaking to 'Woody' to get scrambles effected. It did seem that 11 Group were a law unto themselves.

Squadron Leader Peter Brown, 611 Squadron, Spitfire pilot, Duxford Wing

I served in 12 Group for a year as a regular pilot with 611 Squadron. My experience included convoy patrols, Dunkirk, North Sea 'X' Raids and wing operations from Duxford. I flew

Squadron Leader Peter Brown was convinced that the Big Wing Controversy was why Dowding and Park were apparently so badly treated after the Battle of Britain was won.

several times with the five squadron Duxford Wing, including on 15 September 1940. We had all been aware in 611 Squadron that a tremendous battle was being fought by 10 and 11 Groups, and wanted to play our part in it. Nothing of any real significance, however, was happening in the 12 Group Sector. I did not, however, agree with the wing, and am convinced that the Controversy was why Dowding and Park – the real victors – were so badly treated afterwards. In October 1940, I was posted to 41 Squadron, at Hornchurch in 11 Group. By then I considered myself an experienced pilot – but the dramatic change in the tempo of operations and combat, owing to the presence of Me 109s, was traumatic.

Wing Commander H.R. 'Dizzy' Allen, 66 Squadron, Spitfire pilot, 11 Group

Had Bader served in 11 Group he might have realised that his 'Big Wing' idea was balderdash, for the frontline anyway – and that was the line that mattered.

Group Captain Tom Gleave, 253 Squadron, Hurricane pilot, 11 Group

Douglas Bader was completely wrong about tactics. He had been out of the service for ten years and lagged far behind on modern concepts. All he was thinking of was the old First World War 'flying circuses' – which were irrelevant to the Battle of Britain, which was fought by modern aircraft and technology.

Group Captain Thomas Long, 11 Group Controller

All very well for LM and his 'yes' men to say that the Balbo would have won the Battle of Britain, I think he would have lost it with his policy had he been (which thank heaven he was not!) AOC during August and September 1940.

Air Commodore Peter Brothers, Hurricane pilot, 32 and 257 Squadrons, 11 Group

I was surprised by Peter Townsend's suggestion in *Duel of Eagles* that Air Vice-Marshal Park formed an 11 Group wing to avoid criticism. He was far too strong a character to do that, and in fact exercised flexible tactics, alternating to whichever was appropriate at the time. My log book shows that the most operational sorties I flew in 257 Squadron between 28 September and 8 October 1940 were in a wing with 73 and 17 Squadrons from Castle Camps, we being based at Martlesham Heath, all in the Debden Sector and so nearly as far North of the Thames as Duxford. We then moved to North Weald and between 9–27 October, operated together with 46 and 249 Squadrons. All sorties are recorded as 'Defensive Wing Patrols', a total of sixteen.

Apart from one occasion which I have not recorded but vividly remember, our wings saw little action. We were just below cloud when two Me 109s swept past to the left and below us, shooting down two Hurricanes of 17 Squadron, which was leading, then pulled up and vanished into cloud. All far too quick for our great lumbering formation to react.

Air Commodore Peter Brothers, an 11 Group Hurricane pilot, who was clear that Douglas Bader 'got it wrong'.

By October 1940, the period of intensive activity was drawing to a close and so we could afford wasteful standing patrols – the 'Maidstone Line at 20,000 feet' being the usual one. We were far enough inland to form up into a wing when enemy activity was brewing. All this was so different to my days at Biggin Hill, Manston or Hawkinge, when we were scrambled late to ensure that the raid was the real thing and not a 'spoof' to get us airborne, then catch us on the ground refuelling.

Douglas Bader, a close and dear friend, based further North at Duxford, allowed his fretful anxiety to be in the forefront of the activity to cloud his judgement. Dowding's SASO, Air Vice-Marshal Douglas Evill, was right when he said, 'It was quite useless to argue whether wing formations are or are not desirable, both statements are equally true under different

272

conditions.' Those conditions were to come later to us in 11 Group.

Leigh-Mallory, unlike Park, lacked experience in the fighter world and was also very ambitious. You have, correctly in my view, indicated that because Douglas Bader was a pushy, newsworthy, character, 'LM' used him and his operational experience to draw attention to himself and conceal his ignorance.

In the confusion of battle, it was inevitable that claims made later proved to be duplicated or worse. Apart from the few would-be aces, one of whom fired and claimed me as an Me 109 destroyed without even hitting me, I believe everyone reported what they honestly thought had happened. Douglas Bader put the whole thing into context after the war, though, when he said 'What does it matter? We won, didn't we?'

Flight Lieutenant Wallace 'Jock' Cunningham, 19 Squadron, Spitfire pilot, Duxford Wing

> Lord Dowding's is the big success story here – a strong man who had resisted political pressure to throw away a lot more fighters in France for a battle already lost. He was preserving Fighter Command for the battle to come. Again, a success story in the Battle of Britain. Clearly, his was the credit for the strategy. He

Flight Lieutenant Wallace Cunningham was another 19 Squadron pilot to whom, beyond doubt, Dowding was the real hero, to be revered and not 'sold short'.

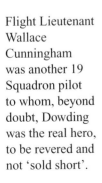

listened, said little but acted decisively. I had direct experience of his quick and clear thinking when our 20 mm cannons were performing badly; he visited the Squadron, heard what we had to say, and within hours we were re-equipping with machine-gun Spitfires. So, treasure the memory of 'Stuffy' Dowding – do not sell him short. His was the victory in directing and sustaining his 'Twelve Legions of Angels'.

Epilogue

On 20 December 1940, two Spitfires of 66 Squadron strafed a French coastal airfield, believed to have been Le Touquet. 9 January 1941 saw five RAF squadrons sweeping over France as a wing, the German controller sensibly not reacting. The following day, however, saw eleven RAF fighter squadrons escort six Blenheim bombers to Forêt de Guines, the theory being that the enemy fighters could not ignore such an attack. Codenamed 'Circus 1', all but one of the RAF fighter squadrons involved belonged to 11 Group, now commanded by Air Vice-Marshal Leigh-Mallory. It will come as no surprise to the reader that the only squadron supplied by 12 Group was Squadron Leader Douglas Bader's 242 Squadron. During Circus 1, however, the RAF fighters came off second-best, losing two aircraft, while the enemy suffered no losses. Such operations, however, were to be a common feature of Fighter Command – now led by Air Marshal Sholto Douglas – 'reaching out', going on the offensive, taking the war to the Germans in north-west France and adopting an aggressive posture. In these complex operations, often involving hundreds of aircraft, wings, naturally, were the standard formation flown by the RAF fighters – the way for this having been paved by the operations and background politics of the 'Big Wing' in 1940.

In the spring of 1941, Fighter Command was reorganised with each sector station accommodating a wing of three fighter squadrons, the Spitfire having replaced the Hurricane as the RAF's frontline day fighter by this time. That March, the new post of Wing Commander (Flying) was created, which was every fighter pilot's dream job: freed of administrative responsibilities, the Wing Leader's job was to coordinate his wing's operations and lead these in the air. Such a Wing Leader was appointed to every sector station. Needless to say, Douglas Bader was promoted to Acting Wing Commander and was among the first Wing Leaders appointed. Indeed, he was even given the choice of wings: Wing Commander Bader chose Tangmere, on the South coast, near Chichester, considering it far enough from London that the capital would not be a distraction for his pilots.

So it was that on 18 March 1941, Wing Commander Bader arrived at Tangmere to take up his new appointment. The events of that far-off summer may have faded from living memory, but remains no less dramatic. Fortunately, when researching the Tangmere Wing twenty-five years ago, many survivors remained alive, enabling the collation of a rich source of unique first-hand accounts of that 'season', which saw the true effect and consequence of the 'Big Wing' argument.

All of that, however, is another story, which we will investigate in *Bader's Spitfire Wing: Tangmere, 1941*.

Acknowledgements

The majority of this book was researched in the mid-1990s, since when many of those kind people who contributed to my research have passed away, including all of my old friends among the Few. Other survivors quoted in this book, all now sadly deceased, have my enduring gratitude for providing me their memories and views.

Regarding my specific research into the life and times of Group Captain Sir Douglas Bader, I will always similarly remain grateful to the late Lady Bader and Dr Alfred Price.

Odette, The Hon. Lady Dowding, daughter-in-law of the late Lord Dowding, provided access to unique family photographs and records, as did Mr Keith Park, nephew of the late Air Chief Marshal Park, and Martin Woodhall, son of the late Group Captain A.B. Woodhall. Lady Broadhurst kindly provided access to her late husband's flying log book.

More recently, fellow author Ian Sayer kindly provided access to his private archive, which included revealing private correspondence from Air Chief Marshal Park and Group Captain Long.

As always, my publisher Martin Mace and the Pen & Sword team were a pleasure to work with.

Bibliography

General

The Bader Papers, The Douglas Bader Foundation
Taped interview of Group Captain Sir Douglas Bader by Dr Alfred Price (undated)
Air Vice-Marshal J.E. Johnson Papers
Air Marshal Sir Denis Crowley-Milling Papers
Sayer Archive
Dilip Sarkar Archive, correspondence and interviews
Woodhall, Grp Capt A.B., Soldier, Sailor and Airman Too, unpublished memoir.

Flying Log Books

Air Marshal Sir Denis Crowley-Milling
Air Vice-Marshal Sir Harry Broadhurst
Air Vice-Marshal J.E. Johnson
Group Captain Sir Douglas Bader (RAF Museum, Hendon)
Group Captain H.F. Burton
Wing Commander B. Jennings
Wing Commander G.C. Unwin
Squadron Leader B.J.E. Lane (TNA, AIR 4/58)
Squadron Leader W.J. Lawson (TNA, AIR4/6)
Flight Lieutenant R.L. Jones

The National Archives

AIR 43/27   Court of Inquiry report into flying accident, Pilot Officer
                 D.R.S. Bader

AIR 16/956	11 Group Combat Report (CR), 30 August 1940
	242 Squadron CR, 30 August 1940
AIR 16/281	Report on Fighter Tactics, Squadron Leader D.R.S. Bader,
	2 September 1940
AIR 16/635	Report on German Attacks on England, 11 September –
	2 November 1940, Air Vice-Marshal K. Park
AIR 16/957	12 Group CR, 7 September 1940
AIR 16/957	310 Squadron CR, 7 September 1940
AIR 27/1	1 Squadron Operations Record Book (ORB)
AIR 27/252	19 Squadron ORB
AIR27/528	56 Squadron ORB
AIR 27/601	66 Squadron ORB
AIR 27/1371	222 Squadron ORB
AIR 27/1471	242 Squadron ORB
AIR 27/1661	302 Squadron ORB
AIR 27/1680	310 Squadron ORB
AIR 27/1949	501 Squadron ORB
AIR 27/2109	611 Squadron ORB
AIR 27/2126	616 Squadron ORB
AIR 50/92	Douglas Bader's CRs
AIR 50/10	19 Squadron CRs
AIR 50/18	41 Squadron CRs
AIR 50/62	145 Squadron CRs
AIR 50/116	302 Squadron CRs
AIR 50/122	310 Squadron CRs
AIR 50/155	452 Squadron CRs
AIR 50/162	501 Squadron CRs
AIR 50/172	610 Squadron CRs
AIR 50/173	611 Squadron CRs
AIR 50/176	616 Squadron CRs

Films and Programmes

Reach for the Sky, Directed by Lewis Gilbert, Rank Organisation, Pinewood
  Studios, London, 1956

This Is Your Life: Group Captain Sir Douglas Bader, Presented by Eamonn
  Andews, Thames Television, 1982

Secret Life of Douglas Bader, Directed by Simon Berthon, Twenty Twenty
  Television, 1996

Websites

www.douglasbaderfoundation.com: Website of the charity founded in Sir Douglas Bader's name to promote his example to inspire and assist amputees.

www.dilipsarkarauthor.com

Published sources

'AHE', 'Cranwell and its Traditions', *Journal of the Royal Air Force College*, 1930, pp. 12 – 15

Anon, *The Battle of Britain*, Air Ministry Pamphlet 156, Crown Copyright, 1943

Anon, *The Rise and Fall of the German Air Force 1939–1945*, Air Ministry Pamphlet 248, Crown Copyright, 1948

Bader, Douglas *Fight for the Sky: The Story of the Spitfire and Hurricane*, Sidgwick & Jackson Ltd., London, 1973

Balfour, H., *Wings Over Westminster*, Hutchinson, London, 1973

Bekker, C., *The Luftwaffe War Diaries*, MacDonald & Co Ltd, London, 1967

Bialer, U., *The Shadow of the Bomber: The Fear of Air Attack and British Politics, 1932–1939*, Royal Historical Society, London, 1980

Branson, N., and Heinemann, M., *Britain in the 1930s*, Weidenfeld & Nicholson, London, 1971

Brickhill, P., *Reach for the Sky: The Story of Douglas Bader DSO DFC*, Collins, London, 1954

Burns, M.G., *Bader: The Man and His Men*, Cassell & Co., London, 1998

Caldwell, D., *The JG 26 War Diary, Volume One: 1939-1942*, Grubb Street, London, 1996

Campion, G., *The Good Fight: Battle of Britain Propaganda and the Few*, Palgrave MacMillan, London, 2010

Cox, S., and Probert, H. (eds), *The Battle Re-Thought: A Symposium on the Battle of Britain, 25 June 1990*, Royal Air Force Historical Society, 1990

Dean, Sir Maurice, *The Royal Air Force in Two World Wars*, first edition, Cassell Ltd., London, 1979

Douglas, Sholto, with Wright, R., *Years of Command*, Collins, London, 1963

Dunn, B.N., *Big Wing: The Biography of ACM Sir T Leigh-Mallory*, Airlife, Shrewsbury, 1992

Fenton, Air Cdre H.A., *The Man Who Holds the Watering Pot*, privately published, 1995

Flint. P., *Dowding and Headquarters Fighter Command*, Airlife, Shrewsbury, 1998

Foreman, J., *RAF Fighter Command Victory Claims of World War Two, Part One: 1939-1940*, first edition, Red Kite, Walton-on-Thames, 2003

Hall, Flt Lt R.M.D., *Clouds of Fear*, Bailey Brothers and Swinfen Ltd, London, 1969

James, T.C.G., *The Battle of Britain*, first edition, Frank Cass Publishers, London, 2000

Johnson, AVM J.E., *Wing Leader*, first edition, Chatto and Windus, London, 1956

Lucas, P.B., *Flying Colours: The Story of Douglas Bader, World War II's Most Renowned Hero of the Air*, Granada Publishing Ltd., London, 1985

Mackenzie, S.P., *Bader's War: 'Have a Go at Everything'*, Spellmount, Stroud, 2008

Mason, F.K., *Battle Over Britain*, Aston Publications, Bourne End, 1990

Mosley, L., *Battle of Britain: The Story of a Film*, first edition, Pan Books, London, 1968

Newton Dunn, B., *Big Wing: The Biography of Air Chief Marshal Sir Trafford Leigh-Mallory*, Airlife, Shrewsbury, 1992

Orange, V., *Park: The Biography of Air Chief Marshal Sir Keith Park*, Grub Street, London, 2001

Orange, V., *Dowding of Fighter Command: Victor of the Battle of Britain*, Grub Street, London, 2008

Oxspring, Grp Capt R.W.O., *Spitfire Command*, William Kimber Ltd, London 1984

Price, A., *Battle of Britain Day: 15 September 1940*, Sidgwick & Jackson, London, 1990

Probert, Air Cdre H., *High Commanders of the Royal Air Force*, HMSO, London, 1991

Ramsey, W. (ed.), *The Blitz Then and Now, Volume One*, After the Battle, London, 1987

Ramsey, W. (ed.), *The Blitz Then and Now, Volume Two*, After the Battle, London, 1988

Ray, J., *The Battle of Britain: Dowding and the First Victory, 1940*, Casell, London, 2009

Townsend, P., *Duel of Eagles*, Fontana, London, 1972

Turner, J.F., *Douglas Bader: A Biography of the Legendary World War II Fighter Pilot*, Airlife, Shrewsbury, 1995

Turner, J.F., *The Bader Tapes*, The Kensal Press, Bourne End, 1986

Turner, J.F., *The Bader Wing*, Airlife, Shrewsbury, 1990

Wright, R., *Dowding and the Battle of Britain*, Corgi, London, 1970

Wynn, K., *Men of the Battle of Britain*, Frontline Books, Barnsley, 2015

Other books by Dilip Sarkar

(in order of publication)

Spitfire Squadron: No 19 Squadron at War, 1939–41
The Invisible Thread: A Spitfire's Tale
Through Peril to the Stars: RAF Fighter Pilots Who Failed to Return, 1939–45
Angriff Westland: Three Battle of Britain Air Raids Through the Looking Glass
A Few of the Many: Air War 1939–45, A Kaleidoscope of Memories
Bader's Tangmere Spitfires: The Untold Story, 1941
Bader's Duxford Fighters: The Big Wing Controversy
Missing in Action: Resting in Peace?
Guards VC: Blitzkrieg 1940
Battle of Britain: The Photographic Kaleidoscope, Volumes I-IV
Fighter Pilot: The Photographic Kaleidoscope
Group Captain Sir Douglas Bader: An Inspiration in Photographs
Johnnie Johnson: Spitfire Top Gun, Part I
Johnnie Johnson: Spitfire Top Gun, Part II
Battle of Britain: Last Look Back
Spitfire! Courage & Sacrifice
Spitfire Voices: Heroes Remember
The Battle of Powick Bridge: Ambush a Fore-thought
Duxford 1940: A Battle of Britain Base at War
The Few: The Battle of Britain in the Words of the Pilots
Spitfire Manual 1940
The Sinking of HMS Royal Oak In the Words of the Survivors (re-print of Hearts of Oak)
The Last of the Few: Eighteen Battle of Britain Pilots Tell Their Extraordinary Stories
Hearts of Oak: The Human Tragedy of HMS Royal Oak
Spitfire Voices: Life as a Spitfire Pilot in the Words of the Veterans

How the Spitfire Won the Battle of Britain

Spitfire Ace of Aces: The True Wartime Story of Johnnie Johnson

Douglas Bader

Fighter Ace: The Extraordinary Life of Douglas Bader, Battle of Britain Hero (re-print of above)

Spitfire: The Photographic Biography

Hurricane Manual 1940

River Pike

The Final Few: The Last Surviving Pilots of the Battle of Britain Tell Their Stories

Arnhem 1944: The Human Tragedy of the Bridge Too Far

Spitfire! The Full Story of a Unique Battle of Britain Fighter Squadron

Battle of Britain 1940: The Finest Hour's Human Cost

Letters From The Few: Unique Memories of the Battle of Britain

Johnnie Johnson's 1942 Diary: The War Diary of the Spitfire Ace of Aces

Johnnie Johnson's Great Adventure: The Spitfire Ace of Ace's Last Look Back

Spitfire Ace of Aces – The Album: The Photographs of Johnnie Johnson

Sailor Malan – Freedom Fighter: The Inspirational Story of a Spitfire Ace

The 'Real' Spitfire Pilot

Index

285